HAWKER HURRICANE
DEFENDER OF THE SKIES

STEVE PHILPOTT

Published by

MELROSE BOOKS

An Imprint of Melrose Press Limited
St Thomas Place, Ely
Cambridgeshire
CB7 4GG, UK
www.melrosebooks.co.uk

FIRST EDITION

Copyright © Steve Philpott 2018

The Author asserts his moral right to
be identified as the author of this work

Artwork by Anna Platts

ISBN 978-1-912026-45-6

All rights reserved. No part of this publication may be reproduced, stored in a retrieval system, or transmitted, in any form or by any means electronic, mechanical, photocopying, recording or otherwise, without the prior permission of the publishers.

This book is sold subject to the condition that it shall not, by way of trade or otherwise, be lent, re-sold, hired out or otherwise circulated without the publisher's prior consent in any form of binding or cover other than that in which it is published and without a similar condition including this condition being imposed on the subsequent purchaser.

Printed and bound in Great Britain by:
Ashford Colour Press Ltd
Unit 600
Fareham Reach
Fareham Road
Gosport
PO13 0FW

Contents

Introduction		v
1	Hurricane Design and Development	1
2	Hurricane Production	20
3	The Phoney War – United Kingdom	28
4	Phoney War – France	32
5	Battle of France	37
6	The Desert Air Campaign 1940–1942	52
7	East Africa	68
8	Dunkirk	77
9	Battle of Norway	85
10	Battle of Britain	90
11	Malta	101
12	Channel Front – Post Battle of Britain	140
13	Battle of Greece	149
14	Crete	157
15	Iraqi Campaign	166
16	Syrian Campaign	169
17	Cyprus	175
18	West African Campaign	176
19	Iranian Campaign	178
20	Russia	180
21	Singapore	182
22	First Burma Campaign	189
23	Sumatra	195
24	Java	198
25	Ceylon	202
26	Second Burma Campaign	206
27	Torch and Tunisia	223
28	Italy	232
29	Yugoslavia	235
30	Sea Hurricane	237

31	Belgian Hurricane	246
32	Finnish Hurricanes	250
33	Romanian Hurricanes	252
34	Yugoslav Hurricanes	254
35	Soviet Hurricanes	259

Conclusion	281
Appendix A	284
Bibliography	285
Acknowledgements	286

INTRODUCTION

This book is dedicated to the men who flew, fought and in many cases died, in Hurricanes and Spitfires during World War II. No part of this book is in any way intended to denigrate their courage or achievements. The purpose of this book is to redress a general misconception of history regarding those aeroplanes. To be strictly accurate, there are two widespread misconceptions about the Hurricane and Spitfire; firstly, that the Spitfire won the Battle of Britain and secondly, that the Spitfire was the most important British fighter of the war. This book attempts to explain why these misconceptions persist, even over seventy years after the end of the war, and asserts that the Hurricane was not only more important to this country during the Battle of Britain, but also of greater significance during World War II as a whole.

I believe that the history of this country would have been significantly different, had not the brave and clever men of the Hawker Aeroplane company made some inspired decisions regarding the design and production of the Hurricane in the early 1930s.

There are several reasons for the misconceptions regarding the Hurricane and Spitfire. Firstly, the Spitfire is one of the most aesthetically beautiful aeroplanes ever built. When combined with the sound of its magnificent Merlin engine (which also powered the Hurricane, of course), the Spitfire is a truly memorable flying machine, which delights those who see it fly. In the dark days of World War II, it was hardly surprising that the British Public were (rightly) inspired by this aeroplane.

Secondly, the Spitfire was built in greater numbers than any other British military aircraft and served in the Royal Air Force well after the end of World War II. The Hurricane had less development potential than the Spitfire and although it served right through to the end of the war, it was superceded by Spitfires in the pure fighter role, in all theatres, by 1944.

However, the Hurricane not only destroyed more enemy aircraft than the Spitfire in the crucial Battle of Britain (in fact, more than all other

British defences combined), as is well known, but also, when real combat kills are compared, rather than claims, the Hurricane comes out ahead, if the respective periods each aeroplane served in 'fighter roles' are analysed. In addition, the Hurricane was far more effective in ground attack roles than the Spitfire.

Chapter One

Hurricane Design and Development

The Hurricane was, by the standards of the time, an advanced technology fighter on the edge of aeronautical achievement. The design team that achieved this innovation leap was less than one hundred in number. They were led by Sydney Camm, who had been Chief Designer at Hawker Aircraft Ltd since 1925.

The Hurricane was a huge leap forward from the company's previous biplane designs. It pioneered such innovative features as a monoplane cantilever wing, housing multiple guns outside the propeller disc; a retractable undercarriage and wide-span trailing edge flaps, none of which had been previously incorporated into an RAF fighter.

The final design was known as the Interceptor Monoplane and was only possible due to the simultaneous development by Rolls Royce of a large new engine, known then as the PV12, which had been derived from the Schneider Trophy Racer 'R' engine. This in turn developed into the 'Merlin'.

In 1933, Camm and his staff had begun to think about a successor to the Fury biplane fighter and studies were initiated using a monoplane wing. Around the same time, increasing fear of war with Germany provided a spur for development of both the Hurricane and Spitfire.

For the original Hawker (Fury) Monoplane, a Goshawk engine was chosen as the power plant. The new fuselage would use the proven tubular braced structure, with some changes to the centre-section to accommodate the low-located monoplane wing. The wing configuration was the key change to achieve the required performance increase.

In August 1933, Camm had a meeting with Air Commodore Cave-Brown-Cave of the Air Staff and Major Buchanan, the Deputy Director of Technical Development, to discuss arming the Fury Monoplane with two guns in the fuselage and two in the wings.

In December of the same year, a three-view drawing of the monoplane was completed by Harold Tuffen of Camm's design staff.

Although Tuffen's drawing only indicates two guns, a hastily formed Air Ministry Armament Research Division had decided in favour of eight 0.300-inch calibre American Browning Guns, modified to take the 0.303-inch British rimmed cartridge. This gun had a high rate of fire and was less prone to stoppages than other contemporary guns.[1]

The Browning installation was fitted into the second set of fabric wings for the Interceptor Monoplane prototype.

The Aerofoil Section for the monoplane wing had a maximum thickness of approximately 18 inches at 30% chord on a 96-inch root chord. This gave a thickness/chord (t/c) ratio of 19%, which was quite a thick wing section.

The Aerodynamics Division at the National Physical Laboratory (NPL) had advised Hawkers that they needed to keep below a 20% t/c ratio, but subsequently, the NPL discovered that due to high wind-tunnel turbulence, it had provided inaccurate drag figures. Nevertheless, the thickness of the wing provided ample space for the retracted undercarriage.

The wing thickness varied only by fractions, when the Interceptor Monoplane design was finalised. The 96-inch chordal dimension was retained at the wing root and continued across the parallel 110-inch span of the centre section. Gross wing areas were 200 square feet for the December 1933 proposal and 257.5 square feet for the Interceptor Monoplane and subsequent Hurricanes.

For installation of the Browning guns in the wings, by chance, the arrangement of the two inboard diagonal rib bracing members of the outer wings enabled the gun mountings and ammunition boxes with their access doors to be fitted in satisfactorily.

Hawkers' metal biplane wings had a range of High Tensile Steel (HTS) strip polygonal-section spar booms, which were produced by a multi-rolling process. These spar booms were joined together with a corrugated stiffened web plate, also produced by rolling methods. This wing spar structure design was considered to be state-of-the-art in the late 1920s.

For the monoplane wing, HTS strip type booms of larger dimensions were created for use on the two-spar outer wing. Similar boom sections were used across the centre section. Enveloping reinforcing rolled sections were also developed and a range of HTS tubular liners, when required, were devised for insertion in the booms.

Much use was made of blind and open-ended 'pop' rivets. However, the web plates used 'thickish' light alloy material, a mixture of rivets and bolts being used for fixing purposes. The webs were stiffened at local details as required, either with angles or channels. Flanged lightening holes were also much used.

The between-spar bracing structure followed a 'zig-zag' pattern in a span-wise manner. These diagonal bracing members had booms which were also made from HTS strip using a smaller section Hawker rolling spar. Again, light alloy web plates were used with lightening holes. The combination of the two-spar layout and diagonal bracing effectively provided a structure for taking the bending and drag loads, whilst at the same time imparting a high degree of torsional stiffness.

Although the gun installation presented no major problem in wing design, it was necessary to modify both of the inboard pair of diagonal bracing members to accommodate the ammunition feed necks for the guns. It was not practical to curve the strip steel rolled section booms of the original bracings, so a curved rib boom, using thicker light alloy angle section was successfully developed.

The ailerons were of the Frise balanced type and employed tubular steel spars with light alloy ribs. Mass balancing by a spanwise steel distributed leading edge was used.

The wing centre section was designed as a separate unit. It was attached to the fuselage, which was provided with saddle fittings, at four positions on the centre section to pick up the front and rear spars. These spars had plug end fittings at their extremities, as did the outer wing spar inner ends, the units being joined together with bushed and tapered joint pins.

The fabric covering and attachment method evoked some controversy outside Hawkers, but was well-trusted in-house. The standard biplane method of using waxed thread for sewing down the fabric also exposed a rather un-aerodynamic external surface to the airstream and was considered unacceptable.

A hidden fixing method was devised and a sample panel was made for examination. The boom of the wing profile ribs (made in light alloy rolled material) was provided with a channel. Into this recess, the fabric, with an inner and outer reinforcing tape, was pulled down by a small flanged channel section. The attachments, at fairly close pitch, were L.A. set screws into clinch nuts of the self-locking type, positioned on the underside of the rib boom recess.

This method of attachment provided an ideal solution. The external recess with its channel and screw heads exposed was finally covered flush at all the rib stations with a doped-on fabric strip. Other flying services – ailerons, tailplane, elevator and the fin and rudder – were similarly designed, but used a smaller recess and channel, in the interest of weight saving. For these smaller and more lightly-loaded units, pop rivets were used instead of set screws for the final attachments. There were no problems in service with this construction.

An engine oil tank, which formed the aerofoil surface, occupied the outer end of the port side section centre section leading edge. Fuel was carried in two 34.5-gallon metal tanks situated between the spars in the centre section and a further fuel tank of 28 gallons' capacity was located ahead of the pilot, behind the fireproof bulkhead which formed the rear of the engine bay. It was inflammation of this tank in combat that caused so many Hurricane pilots to experience horrific burns.

Very wide span wing flaps of the split trailing edge, single surface type were provided. They extended across the entire centre section and onto the outer wings, ending adjacent to the ailerons. Their operation was by a hydraulic jack. Consideration was given to the use of electric motor operation, but aviation-type motors were unknown at that time and commercial-type motors were both too heavy and too bulky. The significance of this decision was that all subsequent Hawker aircraft used hydraulic systems for power actuation of aircraft services, right up to the last successful Kingston design, the Hawk jet trainer.

The main undercarriage with Vickers Ltd oleo legs, hinged on a low-mounted fore and aft member which bridged the spars at each outboard end of the centre section. The legs were braced by struts, lying both fore and aft and sideways.

The lateral strut mechanism, by hydraulic actuation on a knuckle joint, retracted the legs and wheels into the space provided in the centre section and the underside of the fuselage. Fairings attached to the legs completed the aerofoil surface on retraction.

The Hurricane prototype, K5083, was initially fitted with hinged flaps attached to the bottom edge of the doors, carried on the legs, in order to cover the entire under-surface once the wheels had been retracted. However, this mechanism did not produce enough stiffness, resulting in these flaps drooping to become 'daisy cutters'. No suitable alternative operation seemed viable, so after some early flights, the flaps were removed and the wheel bays were left partly open. No performance loss was ever reported from this and all production Hurricanes had these part-open wheel bays (as did Spitfires).

The tubular framed fuselage was covered with wooden formers and stringers and these were covered with Irish linen. At the forward end of the fuselage frame was the engine mounting, which was a detachable unit, attached to the top centre fuselage at two joints and the bottom boom front spar at two other joints. Two side panels, which were connected at the bottom by two cross tubes, supported the engine. The engine feet were supported by four duralumin blocks, the rear pair being offset inboard from the main structure on two subsidiary struts to lower joints.

As well as tubular bracing, wire bracing was also used to strengthen the fuselage centre section. The reserve fuel tank, cockpit and radio were all housed in the centre fuselage. The rear fuselage structure comprised triangular side frames connected by top and bottom cross struts, through plate joints. Wire bracing was again used for the top and bottom panels, with the exception of the rearmost lower panel, which was tubular-braced to support the loads from the tailwheel leg. The tail plane, fin and tail leg shock absorber unit were carried in the tail bay.

The tail unit was of metal construction and again covered with linen. The fixed tailplane was mounted on the rear end of the fuselage, with parallel front and rear spars over its full length. Four bolts secured the tail unit to the rear fuselage. The tail fin was positioned over the tailplane and attached to the fuselage by front and rear fin posts. The elevators and rudder were attached to the tailplane and fin.

K5083 was the only Hurricane to feature a retractable castoring tail wheel and oleo strut. All production aircraft had external fixed castoring tail wheels, which were both lighter and simpler.

In the Kingston design office, staff levels reached one hundred at the end of 1934. On the 21st January 1935, Sydney Camm's diary records a predicted increase in normal loaded service weight of the aeroplane to 4,900 lbs and an estimated maximum speed of 330 mph at 15,000 ft.

On the 21st February, Hawkers received the long-awaited contract for a high-speed monoplane (K5083) to the design submitted in September 1934. It was also known as the Single Seat Fighter, with the specification F.36/34. With the exception of a £5,000 contribution from Rolls-Royce, up to this point, all work on this project had been funded by Hawkers.

On the 20th July 1935, a contract amendment was received which covered work already started on a second set of fabric-covered wings, incorporating the eight Browning machine gun installation. Also in July 1935, Hawkers commenced early investigations into the design of all-metal wings, using stressed skin covering.

In the first quarter of 1935, a mock-up of the structure around the port side four-machine gun installation was constructed. However, this installation was not inspected and approved until the 23rd August. The normal loaded weight with the eight-gun installation was now predicted at 5,200 lbs.

On the 23rd October, the prototype was disassembled and transported to Brooklands Aerodrome, near Weybridge, Surrey. A week later, on the 30th October, the aircraft was weighed and corrected to an 'operational' 5,416 lbs with normal load.

After yet another week, the K5083 first flew on the 6th November 1935. From the formal issue of manufacturing information to first flight had been only 11½ months, a truly impressive performance.

The undercarriage was not retracted for the first flight, which proved uneventful. Chief test pilot P.W.S. 'George' Bulman, who flew the aircraft, was reportedly astonished at the low approach speed and short landing run that he achieved with the aircraft. The cushioning effect of a thick aerofoil section on a low wing monoplane had not been experienced before.

On the third test flight on the 23rd November, the sliding canopy hood detached itself from the aircraft and Bulman lost the hat that he frequently flew in, but suffered no injury. There was minor damage to the hood supporting structure and to the escape panel on the starboard side, under the hood rails. The wood- and fabric-covered fairing adjacent to the hood rear end also suffered slight damage.

The experimental department was already working on a replacement hood, to which had been added another stiffening frame. It is easily possible when examining photographs of K5083 to distinguish the differences between the early hood with its single central frame and the modified structure, with two more intermediate frames.

Distortion of some of the forward underside engine cowling panels was also experienced on early flights and these were subsequently stiffened.

Another design feature of the prototype was that the tailplane was braced with streamline struts, terminating in the vicinity of the junction of the fuselage bottom longeron with the stern post. The tailplane had been designed as a cantilever structure and did not require the bracing struts, but Camm decided to fit them anyway.

In early 1936, while Camm was in hospital having his appendix removed, Roy Chaplin, who Camm had left in charge during his absence, had the struts removed and they were never refitted.

The Air Ministry insisted, even before K5083 had flown, that it should be sent to the Aircraft and Armament Experimental Establishment (A&AEE) at Martlesham Heath, in Suffolk, just as soon as its airworthiness was proven and its claimed performance had been demonstrated by Hawkers. K5083 was thus flown to Martlesham on the 7th February 1936, after only 10 flights, totalling approximately eight flying hours by Hawker pilots.

A&AEE's initial impressions were favourable, except for problems with the PV12 engine. The most serious problem was internal leaks, which led to loss of the coolant. There was also distortion and cracking of the cylinder heads caused by the high temperature running, consequent upon the use of glycol as a coolant. The engine coolant temperature also rose when the flaps were extended.

A&AEE severely criticised the engine in its evaluation report and, on the return of K5083 to Brooklands, Rolls Royce decided that a re-design of the cylinder head was required. The Air Ministry supported Rolls Royce in this decision, but this severely curtailed development flying and advanced production planning.

No Merlin I engines would be available for the planned production aircraft. Instead, the Merlin II would have to be used and these were not planned to be available until the autumn of 1937, which was several months after the first aircraft was due off the production line.

Due to the decision that production Hurricanes now had to use the Merlin II, it was necessary to embody modifications to the engine installation area, caused by changes to the shape of the cylinder head casings. Items affected included cowlings, airscrew hub plate and air intakes, the engine mounted hand starter gear and the header tank and its mounting.

Also around this time, the spinning capability of the aircraft was improved by modifying the fin and rudder shape. These changes were model tested in the then-new spinning tunnel at A&AEE Farnborough in Hampshire. The changes recommended entailed growing a small under-fin adjacent to the fixed tailwheel, combined with a downward extension of the rudder. However, many production aircraft were delivered before these modifications were incorporated.

The undercarriage layout and ease of refuelling and re-arming were design features that were praised by the A&AEE. However, the ailerons and rudder were considered too heavy at high speeds and for aerobatics, although the elevators were deemed light and responsive.

On the 3rd June 1936, the first production contract for 600 aircraft was received by Hawkers and on the 27th June, the name Hurricane was officially approved by the Air Ministry.

On the 2nd February 1937, a conference between Hawkers and the Air Ministry decided the changes that were required for production aircraft, compared to prototype standards.

These changes included a sliding hood and method of operation; the new standard Blind Flying Panel group of instruments, immediately in front of the pilot and full night flying equipment. External venturis had to be fitted on early aircraft to drive the gyro instruments on the blind flying panel.

An engine-driven hydraulic pump on the re-designed Merlin engine was also incorporated. The prototype had used a hand pump system to actuate the undercarriage and flaps, which was quite hard work for the pilot, so this change was considered a real bonus.

A Merlin II engine was installed in the first production aircraft, L1547, on the 19th April 1937, the engine's dry weight being 1,355 lbs. On the 8th September, the aircraft was transported to Brooklands and its first flight was on the 12th October, less than two years before the start of World War II.

L1547 was fitted with the first stage of Rolls Royce-developed ejector exhaust pipes on the 11th November 1937. These replaced the originally-fitted, so-called 'streamlined' exhausts. Early flights on L1547 concentrated entirely on proving the engine/propeller suitability, so that the propeller could be cleared for production.

The Watts fixed-pitch two-bladed wooden propeller was fitted to early Hurricanes, but this had the disadvantage of being too coarse for take-offs and too fine for high speeds. Overspeeding of the engine was also possible in the dive, which could damage the engine. As a result, the Rotol variable-pitch three-bladed propeller was successfully tested on the civil-registered company-owned Hurricane, G-AFKX,[2] by Philip Lucas, who was now chief test pilot, with the first flight on the 24th January 1939.

Following Air Ministry pressure to start equipping the first squadron with the new aircraft, 111 Squadron was selected to become the world's first eight-gun monoplane fighter squadron and started to receive Hurricanes in December 1937.[3]

111 Squadron was based at Northolt, west of London, which was close to both Kingston and Brooklands and thus very easy for supporting the aircraft and problem solving. However, after the squadron had received its full complement of aircraft, in 1938, there were three fatal accidents, which obviously caused much concern. Two pilots dived at high speed through low cloud and flew into the ground. A third pilot hit a flat calm sea in poor visibility.

Subsequent tests discovered that when the aircraft was diving at 400 mph, there was a static pressure error of 1,800 feet on the altimeter. The reason for this was that closed cockpits were new and as with open cockpits, the altimeter was just bolted to the instrument panel with the instrument pipe open to cockpit static pressure.[4] This was resolved by connecting the altimeter pipe to the static side of the pitot-static head feeding the air speed indicator.

Rolls Royce had been experimenting with exhaust systems and they discovered that by ejecting the gas rearwards, instead of sideways, as was the case with the short stub pipes on the prototype, a worthwhile gain of speed was achieved. This increase was of the order of 5 mph on the Hurricane. The so-called streamlined exhaust was fitted to all the original 111 Squadron machines, as well as the aircraft of some other squadrons. The final exhaust configuration resulted when flame damping improvements were required for Hurricane night fighters.

The exhaust exits were in effect wrap-around fishtails with kidney-shaped cross-section exits. Many Hurricanes were fitted with this type of exhaust.

Even before the war started, it was learned that the German BF109 fighter, which was to become the Hurricane's main protagonist in the Battle of Britain, was armed with a large calibre cannon.[5] As a result, it was considered prudent to fit armoured windscreens and armour plate, forward and aft of the cockpit. Not all of the aircraft sent to fight in France were fitted with these improvements, but all aircraft had been converted by the time of the Battle of Britain in 1940.

With the start of hostilities, other urgent modifications became necessary. Gunfire damage could mean that pilots were trapped in their cockpits due to damaged rails. Jettisonable hoods were thus requested and external rear-view mirrors were fitted at the top of the windscreen arch.

Aircraft were also catching fire in combat or were force-landing due to loss of fuel, when fuel tanks were pierced by bullets or flak fragments. Self-sealing fuel tank covers were subsequently introduced on the outside of all the metal fuel tanks.

As the war spread to the Middle East, there was a call for external reinforcing tanks to extend the aircraft's range. These extra tanks were of the fixed type and were so-called non-operational tanks of 45 gallons' capacity, one under each wing. Larger tanks of 90 gallons each were also developed and fitted. Both tank sizes were later developed as jettisonable or 'drop' tanks as the operational requirements demanded.

Hurricane Design and Development

Hurricane prototype K5083 in flight.

A classic photo of K5083 with its modified hood.

Hurricane fuselage and inner-wing section under restoration.

Hurricane fuselage and inner-wing section under restoration.

Inner-wing attachment points.

Uncovered rear fuselage.

Uncovered rear fuselage.

Hurricane Design and Development

Uncovered rear fuselage.

Lower fuselage joint.

Wing section side view.

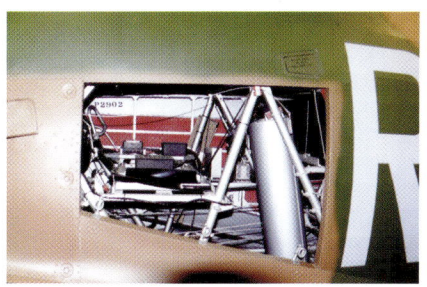

Fuselage with access panel removed.

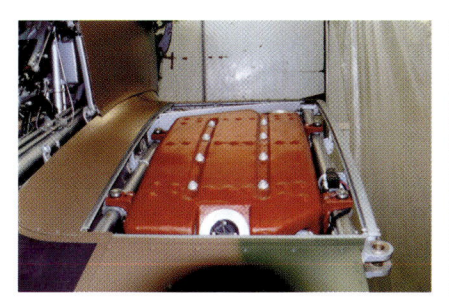

Wing fuel tank.

Undercarriage leg.

Cockpit side access panel removed.

Engine with cowling removed.

Hurricane with outer wing removed.

Fuselage fuel tank.

Engine with cowling removed.

Lower rear fuselage with access panel removed.

Cockpit side access panels removed.

Hurricane Mk. II

Towards the end of the Battle of Britain, the Hurricane I was beginning to be considered outclassed as a pure fighter, so development of the Hurricane II was accelerated. Hawker's initial proposal for this variant had been made to the Air Ministry in February 1940 and having received a rapid approval, the prototype Hurricane Mk. II (P3269) first flew at Brooklands on the 11th June 1940.

The Hurricane Mk. II was fitted with the Merlin XX engine, which had a two speed supercharger of increased efficiency. This led to a power increase to 1,060 hp for the XX engine, against 860 hp of the earlier Merlin II engine.[6] The resulting aircraft speed at this height rose from 300 to 330 mph.

Relatively little change was required to fit the new engine; a slightly longer fuselage – an insert – and a larger coolant radiator. The coolant for the Merlin XX was a mixture of 70% water and 30% glycol, which reduced temperatures by 70 degrees Fahrenheit compared with the pure glycol-cooled Merlin II and it was also non-flammable.

As well as increased performance, the new engine had a longer engine life between overhauls and much greater reliability. All production lines turned to the basic Mk. II configuration as Merlin XX engines became available.

As well as the Merlin XX engine, certain small improvements, including an enlarged rear-view mirror were incorporated, but the normal eight-gun armament was retained, even though the Air Ministry had approved Camm's proposal to add another four Browning machine guns in April 1940.[7]

The first Hurricane Mk. IIA Series 1 was delivered to 111 Squadron in early September 1940 and these were followed in October by the Hurricane IIA Series 2, which had provision for the fitting of auxiliary fuel tanks. These also had an extra fuselage bay and frame immediately forward of the cockpit, which lengthened the nose by approximately seven inches. In addition, behind the Rotol spinner, a deflector oil ring was fitted and a three-blade constant propeller[8] was mounted. The tailwheel undercarriage leg was also modified.

The first production Hurricane Mk. IIB, incorporating the 12-gun wing, flew in August 1940 and service deliveries commenced that autumn, although the real production flow of this version did not begin until January 1941. Although almost identical in performance to the Mk. IIA, the increased weight of the extra guns did reduce the aircraft's rate of roll.

The Hurricane IIB carried a total of 12 .303-inch machine guns, each with 300 rounds of ammunition. Provision was also made for light bomb racks which could carry bombs of up to 250 lbs (113 kgs).

Another armament variation was a version of the aircraft fitted with two 20 mm Hispano or Oerlikon cannons. A trial installation was accomplished very quickly by the Hawker experimental shop, making use of a pair of fabric-covered Mk. I wings which had been returned for repair. For quickness and ease of installation, the guns were only partly buried in the wing, most of the installation being under-slung. These guns used the Chatellerault (linear) ammunition feed, which replaced the original clockwork powered, 30-round drum (although later drum-feed gear became standard).

Piloted by Philip Lucas, L1750 first flew with two Oerlikon cannons on the 24th May 1939 and this particular aircraft made a telling contribution to the Battle of Britain.

On the 14th July, piloted by Flight Lieutenant Smith of 151 Squadron, the aircraft damaged a BF 109, which subsequently crash-landed. Then, on the 13th August, Smith succeeded in shooting down a Dornier DO-17Z of 7/KG2 over Kent, in this aircraft.

L1750[9] was delivered to the A&AEE at Boscombe Down, in Wiltshire, for further trials in October 1940.

Encouraged by the success of L1750's air firing trials, Hawkers converted several other Hurricane Mk. Is which had suffered wing battle-damage, to carry four of the new cannon. One of these, V7360, also fought in the Battle of Britain. On the 5th September, Flight Lieutenant Rabagliati of 46 Squadron shot down a BF 109 of I/JG 54 in this aircraft, near Southend.

The prototype of a new variant, the Hurricane IIC, flew for the first time on the 6th February 1941, piloted by K.G. Seth-Smith. The Mk. IIC had either four Hispano or Oerlikon 20 mm cannon and was powered by the Merlin XX engine, which gave the aircraft a maximum speed of 330 mph and a service ceiling of 35,600 ft. However, in service, two of the cannon were often omitted. Two 44-gallon drop tanks or 250 lbs[10] bombs could be carried by this variant.

Hurricane Mk. IICs started to enter squadron service in late spring 1941 and this was the most-produced variant – in total 4,711 Hurricane IICs were built, including night-fighter versions. These were fitted with small anti-glare shields forward of the cockpit 'quarterlights' to mask flashes from the engine exhaust. Later versions were also fitted with an AI Mk. V radar, which was carried in a fixed fairing.

Both Rolls Royce and Vickers had been developing 40 mm cannon, for use against armoured vehicles since 1939 and in May 1941, the Air Ministry signalled its approval of a project to carry the weapons on aircraft, by asking Hawkers to investigate fitting them under the wings of the Hurricane II. A Hurricane Mk. IIA, Z2326 was fitted with one 40 mm Vickers Type 'S' gun under each wing and it first flew on the 18th September 1941, piloted by K.G. Seth-Smith.

The following day, the aircraft was delivered to Boscombe Down for trials,[11] the pilot for these being Wing Commander Dean of the A&AEE. These trials proved highly successful, with approximately 20 hits from the 28 rounds fired. Each gun only had 15 rounds of ammunition and additionally, each wing retained a single 0.303-inch machine gun, for sighting the larger cannon, usually with tracer ammunition. This variant of the aircraft was immediately ordered into production and designated the Hurricane IID, although it was universally known as the 'tank-buster'.

The top speed of this variant was 304 mph, when fully loaded, but when fitted with the Vokes tropical filter, as most IIDs were, the top speed reduced to 288 mph. The first squadron to operate the Mk. IID in action was 6 Squadron, in Egypt. Aircraft of this squadron first used 40 mm cannon on the 7th and the 8th June 1942, destroying several vehicles, including four tanks. However, the slower speed of this variant, coupled with the very low attack profile used, especially in the desert campaigns, led to high loss rates to light flak, fortunately without heavy loss of life.

The Mk. IIE was a planned version of the aircraft with further wing modifications, but these changes were so extensive that this variant was renamed the Hurricane Mk. IV. The Mk. IIE was to have been a close support variant, capable of carrying a wide range of external stores, including air-launched rockets. An extra 350 lbs of armour plate was also to be added to the forward fuselage and radiator of the Mk. IIE.

Hurricane III

A Hurricane Mk. III was planned, fitted with a U.S. Packard-built Merlin engine, as a fall-back option if the supply of U.K.-built Merlins became restricted. However, by the time that production of this engine was to have started in the U.S., home production of Merlins had increased to such an extent that this variant was considered unnecessary.

Hurricane IV

The last major U.K. production variant of the Hurricane was the Mk. IV, which incorporated the new 'universal wing'[12] that allowed a variety of external ordnance to be carried.

This included bombs of up to 500 lbs, up to eight 25 lbs or 60 lbs unguided rockets, or long-range fuel tanks.[13] This variant could also carry the two Vickers 40 mm cannon and two .303 Browning machine guns of the Mk. IID.

The prototype Mk. IV, KX405, first flew at Langley on the 14th March 1943, piloted by Philip Lucas and had a Merlin 32 engine with a Rotol four-bladed propeller, but production aircraft carried the Merlin 24 or 27, both rated at 1,620 bhp and fitted with a Rotol three-bladed constant-speed propeller. Most Hurricane IVs were also fitted with the Vokes dust filters.

Although early production aircraft were fitted with similar armour protection to the Mk. IID, an additional 350 lbs was added to later Mk. IVs to protect the engine, radiator, fuel tanks and cockpit, during low-level attacks.

The Hurricane IV had a maximum speed of around 330 mph clean, but with external stores, this reduced to around 200 mph. The service ceiling was 32,500 ft.

References

1. e.g. the Vickers gun.
2. Which also had the military serial L1606.
3. Now only 21 months before the start of World War II.
4. There is very different pressure in a closed cockpit.
5. Believed at that time to be either 20 or 37 mm.
6. Both at 20,000 ft.
7. This was postponed so that efforts could concentrate on increased production of Mk. Is.
8. RS5/2 or RS5/3.
9. A Mk. I aircraft.
10. Later 500 lbs.
11. A Vickers Valentine tank was used as the target.
12. Also known as the 'E' wing.
13. Of 45 or 90 gallons' capacity.

CHAPTER TWO

Hurricane Production

The H.G. Hawker Engineering Company[1] was formed in November 1920, immediately after the liquidation of the Sopwith Company. It inherited some of the old Sopwith premises in Canbury Park Road, Kingston, Surrey.

The company supported the Sopwith aircraft in service with the RAF at that time, specifically the Snipe and the Camel. It also refurbished aircraft for the Services and for sale abroad. Sub-contract work was also obtained for other aircraft, including the re-building of D.H. 9s and the manufacture of 130 sets of lower wings for Gloster Grebes and of undercarriages for the Fairy Fawn.

Orders in these early years were normally for one- or two-off prototypes involving a high proportion of handwork and with small demands on manufacturing plant and floor area. However, from 1923–27, 64 Woodcocks were produced for the RAF, plus three Danecocks for Denmark. One hundred and 123 Horsley bombers were also produced in this period, mainly for the RAF, but with small quantities for both Greece and Denmark.

Only a single prototype of the Heron was built in 1925, but it was significant as the first new Hawker type with a primary structure of all metal construction. The steel fuselage tubes were flattened to rectangular or square section throughout their length and the wing spar booms were a three-lobe section of solid drawn tube.

This style was also used in the Tomtit and, by 1927, the tubular metal construction had been developed for heavier duty and employed extensively in the successful Hart biplane and its variants. This construction method was also used in both the Fury and Nimrod single seaters and the larger quantities required of these types resulted in them being produced by Hawkers and eight other companies in the British aircraft industry, as well as under licence in Australia, South Africa and Sweden. The first production Fury flew in 1931 and the Fury Monoplane, which developed into the Hurricane, evolved from this biplane fighter.

For the Hurricane fuselage, a space frame of tubes, mainly of high tensile steel, was connected with stainless steel fish plates and machined fittings at the joints. The tubes were locally rolled to square or rectangular sections where the plates were fitted, and the joints were made with bolts or tubular rivets passing through ferrules, fitted in reamed holes with distance tubes between the squared-off tube walls.

The fuselage structure was made from five sub-assembled units. At the front of the aircraft was the engine mounting, which was later attached to both the centre fuselage and wing centre section. The centre portion of the fuselage was built up to its full rectangular and constant width section and provided the basis for alignment of the rear of the fuselage. The rear fuselage, which tapered in plan, was built up from the top and bottom longerons and diagonal struts, which formed two separate side frames. Behind this was the small tail bay section with tailplane and tail wheel strut attachments.

The complete fuselage was assembled with the centre portion located on a jig representing the centre section spars. The assembly operation consisted of fitting the cross tubes and bracing wires and the tail bay and the adjustment of the bracings to obtain correct alignment at the tail end, which was checked by a plumb bob to a datum plate set in the floor. The fuselage was then, at a later stage, mounted on the wing centre section at the four main fittings in the bottom longerons. The engine mounting, with fireproof bulkhead behind, was then attached and the primary structure completed by the attachment of the diagonal bracing struts to the wing centre section.

The construction of the wings, centre section and tail surfaces was quite different, being based on spars rolled from high tensile strip to form tubular like booms with a series of flat and lipped edges for attachment to the spar or rib web. This method, pioneered by Armstrong-Whitworth and Boulton-Paul, was applied to the original fabric-covered wings planned to be used on the first 300 Mk. 1 Hurricanes, the quantity of which was increased to 500 after the correspondence between F.S. Spriggs, then Hawker's managing director and Air Vice-Marshal A.W. Tedder, the last of these wings arriving at Brooklands for fitting in September 1939.

L2027, the 481st Mk. 1 Hurricane was the first aircraft on the line at Brooklands to receive a metal-skinned wing, although L1877 had been retrospectively fitted with an advance set of metal-skinned wings from Glosters in April. The Hurricane wing was of a size such that, at Kingston, it was convenient to assemble it in wing jigs which were built onto the upright girders of the old furniture depository building. Some production of metal-covered wings was carried out at Kingston, though most were made at Langley.

Hurricane production at its height at Langley.

The metal-skinned wing, initially with 8-gun, then 12-gun and later 4 x 20 mm cannon, armament was interchangeable with the fabric-covered version. Its design and method of construction was completely new and the inevitable delays in its introduction initially were overcome by continued production of the fabric wing. Perhaps this justified the company's cautious approach to this more advanced form of construction. Gone were the spars and diagonal girders with booms of rolled HTS drawn section. These were replaced by light alloy extruded angle sections forming the booms of the main and intermediate spars and ribs with aluminium alloy webs. Various sections rolled from strip were used for the stringers and for the top and bottom booms of the trailing edge ribs, with diagonals of light alloy tube. Nose ribs, inter-spar diaphragms and many detail fittings were pressed from light alloy steel. The whole structure was covered with skin panels prepared with their stringers attached and was flush-riveted. Assembly was mainly carried out in pairs of fixtures with the wing held vertically, with its leading edge down.

Completion of the leading edge and other parts which were more accessible with the wing horizontal was done on trestles. For the cannon-wing, the gun bay was modified and a major change of design came late in production, with the introduction of the 'Universal Wing' for the Mk. IV, for the carriage of all the varied combinations of armament.

It was possible to carry out at floor level much of the installation work on the fuselage at a stage prior to fitting the wooden formers and stringers which faired the top and sides of the centre and rear fuselage to oval section. Later, the fuselage was lifted and lowered onto a wing section. The engine and its mounting, radiator and cowlings were fitted and, at the stage when the undercarriage was ready for test, the aircraft was jacked up for this purpose.

Thereafter the aircraft was moved on its own wheels to the covering and paint shop. It would return to the line for completion of installations, fitting of panels, windscreen, sliding hood and tail surfaces. Some variation of the sequence of assembly was possible and depended on current circumstances. Thereafter, the aircraft was ready for transfer to the flight shed for fitting of the outer wings, armament, radios and preparation for flight testing.

In September 1937, Gloster Aircraft Limited, a Hawker-owned company since 1933, was given a direct contract for 500 aircraft[2] and their first machine flew on the 20th October 1939. A year later, 1,000 Gloster-built Hurricanes had been completed, with an eventual total of 2,750 built, the last being delivered on the 21st March 1942, by which time Typhoon production had replaced the Hurricane in the Gloster shops.

The Canadian Government had agreed to undertake Hurricane production in 1938 and Specification P3 was issued on the 4th January 1939, to cover Hurricanes produced at the Canadian Car and Foundry Co.,

Montreal. Using the Hawker component and tool drawings and with only one set of Hawker-made parts supplied, together with a pattern aircraft and minimum liaison between the companies, considerable detail tooling was ready by February 1939 and the first fuselage structure by July of that year.

Transferred to the airfield on the 8th January 1940, the first aircraft was flown two days later. Production consisted of various versions, Mks. XXI and XII, which were basically Mk. I and II machines adapted for local conditions and the later use of American-made Packard Merlin engines and Hamilton propellers. The Canadian line was terminated in 1943 after 1,451 aircraft had been built.

The Austin Motor Co. were the other major company brought into the Hurricane programme, later producing just one batch of 300 Mk. IIA aircraft in 1940–41 at Longbridge.

Before the war, arrangements had been made for Hurricane manufacture under licence in Belgium, at Avions Fairey. This was terminated by the German assault in May 1940 after only two aircraft had been completed.

A later licence setting up production by Rogozarsky of Belgrade was well-advanced when the German occupation of Yugoslavia took place in 1941 and approximately 20 aircraft had been supplied to the Royal Yugoslav Air Force. It was also planned that the Hurricane should be built at Zemuh by Fabrika Aeroplana I Hydroplana.

The Hawker programme was based on a declared policy to sub-contract 50% of details and sub-assemblies. Output was maintained and expanded by supplies from the many sub-contractors who produced items ranging from single details to complete wings. The metal-covered wing, a completely new design, was supplied to Hawkers by Glosters at 25 sets per month.

Glosters were already making wings for their own Hurricane line. Henry Balfour and Scottish Motor Traction at Airdrie in Scotland and the LMS Railway works at Derby were also brought into the wing supply pool. Problems of delivery from SMT and LMS encouraged larger scale manufacture at Langley and some wings for the Langley production line were also obtained from Austins.

As the Langley site became available from 1939, production at Brooklands was run-down until the buildings were handed over to Vickers in 1941–42, by which time 2,815 Hurricanes had been completed. Hawkers' total Hurricane production was by far the greatest of all the producers of the aircraft and surviving delivery records indicate a figure of 9,920 aircraft plus four aircraft constructed but lost on test and not delivered, plus the prototype, K5083.

Hawker production figures of Hurricanes by quarter

Year/Quarter	Quarterly number	Cumulative total
1937	5	5
1938 Q1	22	27
1938 Q2	28	55
1938 Q3	60	115
1938 Q4	82	197
1939 Q1	139	336
1939 Q2	121	457
1939 Q3	134	591
1939 Q4	140	731
1940 Q1	206	937
1940 Q2	421	1,358
1940 Q3	389	1,747
1940 Q4	315	2,062
1941 Q1	361	2,423
1941 Q2	415	2,838
1941 Q3	486	3,324
1941 Q4	472	3,796
1942 Q1	593	4,389
1942 Q2	725	5,114
1942 Q3	699	5,813
1942 Q4	678	6,491
1943 Q1	716	7,207
1943 Q2	709	7,916
1943 Q3	682	8,598
1943 Q4	634	9,232
1944 Q1	440	9,672
1944 Q2	210	9,882
1944 Q3	38	9,920

The above figures illustrate the big increase in production in the second quarter of 1940, followed by later reductions, the same output level not being recovered until a year later.

Peak production rate from the Langley line of 725 aircraft – eight per day, every day – occurred in the second quarter of 1942, although 1943 produced the highest annual total with a monthly average output of 228.4 aircraft.[3]

At the height of production at Langley, the assembly floor was fed by five lines of fuselage and centre section assemblies, these being on wheeled trolleys which could be moved periodically. One unit was taken off the end of each of these five lines to the Fabric and Paint shop and then back to the final erection track, before going to the Flight Shed. Another five could then be commenced. This change occurred at the end of each day and night shift throughout the week. From the lay-down of the fuselage primary structure to notification of delivery was nominally 45 days.[4] However, material supply and parts manufacturing provisioning ahead of initial assembly occupied the bulk of the total build cycle, which was in the order of 40 to 50 weeks.

Actual man-hour figures for production aircraft are not now available, but Air Ministry/MAP planning in early 1940 for the Hurricane was based on an airframe structure weight of 2,468 lbs, requiring an average of 10,300 man-hours. The comparable figures for the Spitfire were 2,055 lbs and 15,200 man-hours. The resulting figures of 4.17 and 7.4 man-hours per pound respectively for the Hurricane and Spitfire are an indication of the advantages given in production by the much simpler design of the Hurricane.

At the outbreak of World War II in September 1939, the RAF had received 497 Hurricanes, all Hawker-built and all delivered from Brooklands. By the 7th August 1940, when the second phase of the Battle of Britain was beginning, official reports record that 2,309 Hurricanes had been received by the RAF and they equipped 32 squadrons. Comparable figures for the Spitfire were 1,400 aircraft delivered and 19 squadrons equipped.

The Mk. V prototype – only one was converted from a Mk. IV. It was subsequently converted back to a Mk. IV.

References

1. Named after chief test pilot Harry Hawker.
2. Initially.
3. 685 per quarter.
4. Six-and-a-half weeks.

Chapter Three

The Phoney War – United Kingdom

The first enemy aircraft claims by a Hurricane squadron in World War II were on the 21st October 1939, when 46 Squadron intercepted a formation of Heinkel He 115 seaplanes and claimed five shot down, four of which were confirmed. Squadron Leader Barwell, P.O. Frost and Flt. Sgt. Shackley each claimed one, another was shared by P.O. Frost and P.O. Lefevre and the last was shared by Flt. Sgt. Shackley, P.O. Cowles and P.O. Plummer.

Exactly a month later, a DO-17 was claimed by F.O. Davies and Flt. Sgt. Brown of 79 Squadron[1] and an He 111 by Flt. Lt. Lee of 85 Squadron,[2] followed eight days later, on the 29th November, by an He 111 claimed by Squadron Leader Broadhurst of 111 Squadron. The only Hurricane lost to this time in combat was one of 56 Squadron,[3] which was shot down accidentally by a Spitfire on the 6th September, the pilot, P.O. Hulton-Harrop being killed.[4]

The first claim of 1940 was again to 111 Squadron – another He 111 on the 12th January, shared by Flt. Lt. Powell, F.O. Dutton and Sgt. Gunn, but on the 18th, two Hurricanes of 43 Squadron[5] were lost in a collision.[6] However, 43 Squadron made their first claim on the 30th January, another He 111 shared by Flt. Lt. Hull and Sgt. Carey and four days later, on the 3rd February, 43 Squadron claimed a further three He 111s, one of which was the first enemy aircraft to be brought down on the British Mainland in the war. These were shared claims by F.O. Simpson and F.O. Edmunds; Flt. Lt. Townsend, F.O. Folkes and Sgt. Hallowes; and Sgt. Carey and Sgt. Ottewill.

There now followed a series of Hurricane losses, two of 43 Squadron were lost by accident on the 9th[7] and the 21st February[8] and another of 79 Squadron[9] failed to return from a patrol on 16th, F.O. Tarlington being killed. The final claim of February 1940 was another He 111 to 43 Squadron on the 22nd, which was confirmed.

An early production Hurricane Mk.1 with 111 Squadron at Northolt.

No. 111 Squadron at Northolt.

A JU-88 was claimed by F.O. Dutton of 111 Squadron, whilst it was attacking Scapa Flow on the 8th March and 43 Squadron claimed single He 111s on both the 20th[10] and the 28th March 1940[11] in the same area. F.O. Leeson of 605 Squadron also claimed an He 111 on the latter date.[12]

An He 115 seaplane was claimed by F.O. Phillips of 504 Squadron off the Kent coast on the 2nd April, but 151 Squadron lost a Hurricane,[13] which crashed into the sea on a patrol off the east coast, on this date, P.O. Fenton drowning.

The largest battle of this period came on the 8th April, with four He 111s claimed by 43 Squadron[14] and one by 111 Squadron. 43 Squadron claims were by F.O. Edmunds, Sgt. Arbuthnot,[15] Flt. Lt. Townsend and Sgt. Hallowes, while 111 Squadron's claim[16] was shared by F.O. Bruce and P.O. Ferris; *'X' raid, intercepted two He 111s. 'One down in sea'* was reported by Flt. Lt. Townsend, while *'X' raid intercepted two He 111s. 'One down on Drome'* was Sgt. Hallowe's report. Both F.O. Edmunds and Sgt. Arbuthnot recorded *'X' raid, intercepted 'six He 111s. One down in sea'*.[17]

111 Squadron Hurricane Mk.1 aircraft.

Next day, a Hurricane of 229 Squadron[18] crashed into the sea on a convoy patrol off Grimsby. The last claims for April came on the 10th April, single He 111s being claimed by 111[19] and 605 Squadrons,[20] four of the bombers actually being lost by the Germans. Only two more claims were made in May, before the start of the Blitzkrieg, both on the 9th May, DO-17s being claimed[21] by 43[22] and 605 Squadrons.[23]

A total of 29 enemy aircraft were claimed by Hurricane squadrons[24] during the phoney war around the United Kingdom. Eight Hurricanes were lost in this period, none, as far as is known, to enemy aircraft in air combat. In the same period, 21 enemy aircraft were claimed by Spitfire units for only five Spitfire lost, but at least one was a combat loss to an He 111.[25]

References

1   And confirmed.
2   Also confirmed.
3   L1985.
4   L1980 force-landed.
5   L2066 and L1734.
6   Sgt. Mullinger was killed.
7   L1744.
8   L1729.
9   L1699.
10   Sgt. Gough.
11   Shared by Flt. Lt. Hull, Sgt. Carey, Sgt. Ottewill, Sgt. Gough and 605 Squadron.
12   Shared with 43 Squadron.
13   L1799.
14   One of which crashed on Wick airfield. Its victor was Sgt. Hallowes.
15   Unconfirmed.
16   Also unconfirmed.
17   43 Squadron ORB.
18   L1790.
19   Shared by Flt. Lt. Powell, F.O. Ferris and Sgt. Dymond.
20   Shared by F.O. Leeson, P.O. Carter and Sgt. Moffat.
21   And confirmed.
22   Shared by Flt. Lt. Simpson and Sgt. O'Heavill.
23   Shared by F.O.s Edge, Austin and Hope.
24   Fifteen confirmed.
25   Possibly two.

Chapter Four
Phoney War – France

Four Hurricane squadrons were sent to France in September 1939 in support of the British Expeditionary Force (BEF). These were Nos. 1, 73, 85 and 87 Squadrons. These units arrived in France between the 9th and the 15th September. Their first action came on the 30th October when a DO-17P was shot down by P.O. Mould of 1 Squadron. A Hurricane of 73 Squadron was lost to flak next day, Sgt. Phillips escaping unhurt.

Hurricane I, N2358 Z, No. 1 Squadron. France, late 1939.

On the 2nd November, two He 111s were claimed by 87 Squadron,[1] although one of 87 Squadron's Hurricanes was hit by return fire and force-landed. P.O. Mackworth was also unhurt. The claimants were Flt. Lt. Voase-Jeff and, jointly, P.O.s David and Mackworth.

A DO-17 became 73 Squadron's first victory on the 8th November, when F.O. 'Cobber' Kain, who was to become the RAF's first ace of this conflict, opened his account north-west of Metz. This was followed by another two, plus three He 111s claimed by the same Squadron on the 23rd November. Kain claimed one DO-17, the other being claimed jointly by F.O. Scoular and Sgt. Winn. The Heinkels were claimed by F.O. Orton[2] and Sgt. Campbell.

1 Squadron also claimed two DO-17s and an He 111 on this date, but a Hurricane[3] of this unit crash-landed after this combat. F.O. Palmer was unhurt. F.O.s Kilmartin and Palmer shared one of the DO-17s with Sgt. Soper, while the other was shared by Sqn. Ldr. Halahan and F.O. Brown. The Heinkel claim was shared by at least five pilots.[4]

On the 8th November, L1959 of 73 Squadron force-landed in Belgium with oxygen problems. The pilot, P.O. Martin was interned, but escaped. On the 14th November, L1628 and L1813 of 87 Squadron both landed in Belgium and although both Sqn. Ldr. Coope and F.O. Clyde were also interned, again they both escaped.

On the 6th November, a Hurricane of 73 Squadron became the first RAF fighter to encounter the BF109 in an inconclusive combat, but on the 22nd December, a section of three Hurricanes of 73 Squadron were bounced from above by III/JG53 BF109s and two[5] were shot down, killing Sgts Perry and Winn. In return, a BF109 was claimed by P.O. Waller of 73 Squadron, but none was actually lost.

The next decisive Hurricane combat over France was not until the 2nd March 1940, a DO-17 being claimed jointly by P.O. Brown and Sgt. Soper of 1 Squadron, south of Forbach and a BF109 by 'Cobber' Kain of 73 Squadron[6] near Metz, but a Hurricane[7] of 1 Squadron was shot down and another[8] crash-landed, while two Hurricanes[9] of 73 Squadron made crash-landings after combats with BF109s, but were repairable. P.O. Mitchell of 1 Squadron was killed in this combat, whereas F.O. Kain and Sgt. Sewell of 73 Squadron were unhurt.

L1962 of 73 Squadron was lost on the 12th March to an unknown cause and the pilot[10] was killed.

A further BF109 was claimed on the 22nd March at Bouzonville by Flt. Lt. Lovett of 73 Squadron, although one of the Squadron's Hurricanes was lost to a BF109.

Hurricane Mk.Is of No. 73(F) Squadron, 67 Wing, over France early in 1940.

On the 26th March, 73 Squadron claimed no less than six BF109s for one Hurricane[11] shot down, four at Saarlautern and two near Trier. Kain claimed one and one unconfirmed, the others being claimed by P.O. Perry, Sgt. Pyne[12] and F.O. 'Fanny' Orton.[13]

Then on the 29th March, 1 Squadron claimed three BF110s over Metz[14] and a BF109 near Saarbrucken,[15] although only one BF110 was in fact lost. Another 73 Squadron Hurricane was lost to a BF109 on this day, P.O. Perry being killed.

The first claims in April came on the 1st of the month, a further three BF110s being claimed near Thionville by Flt. Lt. Hanks, P.O. Mould and F.O. Clisby[16] of 1 Squadron.

Next day, F.O. Kilmartin and F.O. Clisby of the same squadron claimed a BF109 each over St Avold, for the loss of a Hurricane,[17] although P.O. Palmer was unhurt in this action.

P.O. Ayerst of 73 Squadron claimed a BF109 on the 7th April over Ham-sur-Varburg and three days later, on the 10th, P.O. Cock of

87 Squadron claimed that Squadron's first victory since November, an He 111 off Le Touquet.

On the 18th April, L1637 of 85 Squadron force-landed and was subsequently abandoned in May 1940.

Combats on the 20th April resulted in claims for six BF109s, one He 111 and one DO-17 by 1 Squadron in the Metz and Thionville areas. The '109's were claimed by Sgts Berry[18] and Albonico, P.O. Mould, Flt. Lt. Walker, F.O. Brown and F.O. Drake. The DO-17 was claimed by F.O. Kilmartin and the He 111 by Flt. Lt. Hanks. A Hurricane[19] of 1 Squadron crash-landed after combat, but F.O. Kilmartin was unhurt.

Next day, four BF109s and five BF110s were claimed by 73 Squadron over Merzig, Thionville and Metz. 'Fanny' Orton claimed a BF109 and a BF110, Flt. Lt. Lovett, P.O.s Martin and Scott and Sgt. Pilkingon,[20] also claimed BF110s and Squadron Leader More, P.O. Marchand[21] and F.O. Paul also claimed BF109s. An 85 Squadron Hurricane[22] was damaged on landing on the 21st.

73 Squadron lost a Hurricane[23] to the BF109s on the 23rd April, another of the Squadron's aircraft[24] force-landing. Sgt. Campbell was wounded in the former and Sgt. Pyne in the latter.

The final pre-Blitzkrieg combat on the 9th May led to a BF110 probable being claimed by Sgt. Nowell and P.O. Dunn[25] of 87 Squadron, although a Hurricane[26] of this Squadron was damaged by a DO-17 and overturned on landing.

No Spitfires were sent to France and for a total claim of 50 enemy aircraft by the Hurricane squadrons,[27] 18 Hurricanes were lost, 11 in air combat.

73 Squadron was the highest scoring squadron of the campaign, with some 25 claimed victories, followed by 1 Squadron with 22. 87 Squadron claimed only three victories and a probable, while 85 Squadron had no claims. Twenty-three of the Hurricane claims were for BF109s, although this was clearly a considerable over-claim.

F.O. 'Cobber' Kain was the RAF's first ace of the Second World War, claiming five victories during the 'Phoney War'. F.O. 'Fanny' Orton, also of 73 Squadron, claimed five and one shared before the Blitzkrieg.

References

1. Only one was actually lost.
2. One and one shared with the Armee de L'Air.
3. L1925.
4. Including one of 73 Squadron.
5. N2385 and L1967.
6. Not confirmed.
7. L1971.
8. L1843.
9. L1808 and L1958.
10. Also unknown.
11. L1766?
12. Unconfirmed.
13. The two near Trier.
14. Two by Sgt. Clowes and one shared by Flt. Lt. Walker and F.O. Stratton.
15. Unconfirmed by P.O. Richey.
16. One each.
17. N2326.
18. Unconfirmed.
19. L1843.
20. All unconfirmed.
21. Unconfirmed.
22. N2363
23. N2391
24. P2576
25. Shared
26. N2362
27. Mostly by 1 and 73 squadrons.

Chapter Five

Battle of France

When the German Blitzkrieg against France, Holland and Belgium began on the 10th May 1940, there were six Hurricane squadrons in France, nos. 1 and 73 Squadrons assigned to the Advanced Air Striking Force[1] and nos. 85, 87, 607 and 615 Squadrons with the Air Component of the British Expeditionary Force.[2] 607 and 615 Squadrons were in the process of replacing their Gladiators with Hurricanes.

The Hurricane Squadrons were in action before dawn on the 10th May and fought many air battles during the day. A total of 60 enemy aircraft were claimed this day by the six squadrons, plus nos. 3 and 501 Squadrons, which arrived in France from England during the afternoon of the 10th.[3] Thirty-eight He 111s are included in this claim figure, of which 17 can be confirmed to Hurricanes. Twelve DO-17s,[4] five JU-88s[5] and five HS126 reconnaissance aircraft[6] complete the day's claim. Six Hurricanes were shot down or crash-landed, eight were damaged and two more were destroyed on the ground, the high victory to loss ratio being due primarily to the almost total lack of German fighter opposition this day.[7] This situation was soon to change.

F.O. M.H. 'Hilly' Brown was a Canadian pilot with 1 Squadron. He was number two in a flight of five Hurricanes which encountered DO-215s near Verdun. He reported an *'HE crashed at Longyon.'*[8] 1 Squadron was based at Vassincourt, but moved to Berry au Bac this day. The experiences of this Squadron are typical of those which fought in France in 1940.

On the 11th May, both BF110s and BF109s were encountered by the Hurricane Squadrons. Of the 55 enemy aircraft claimed, 18 BF110s and four BF109s were included, 13 of the BF110s by No. 1 Squadron alone, but this was a considerable over-claim.

Hawker Hurricane – defender of the skies

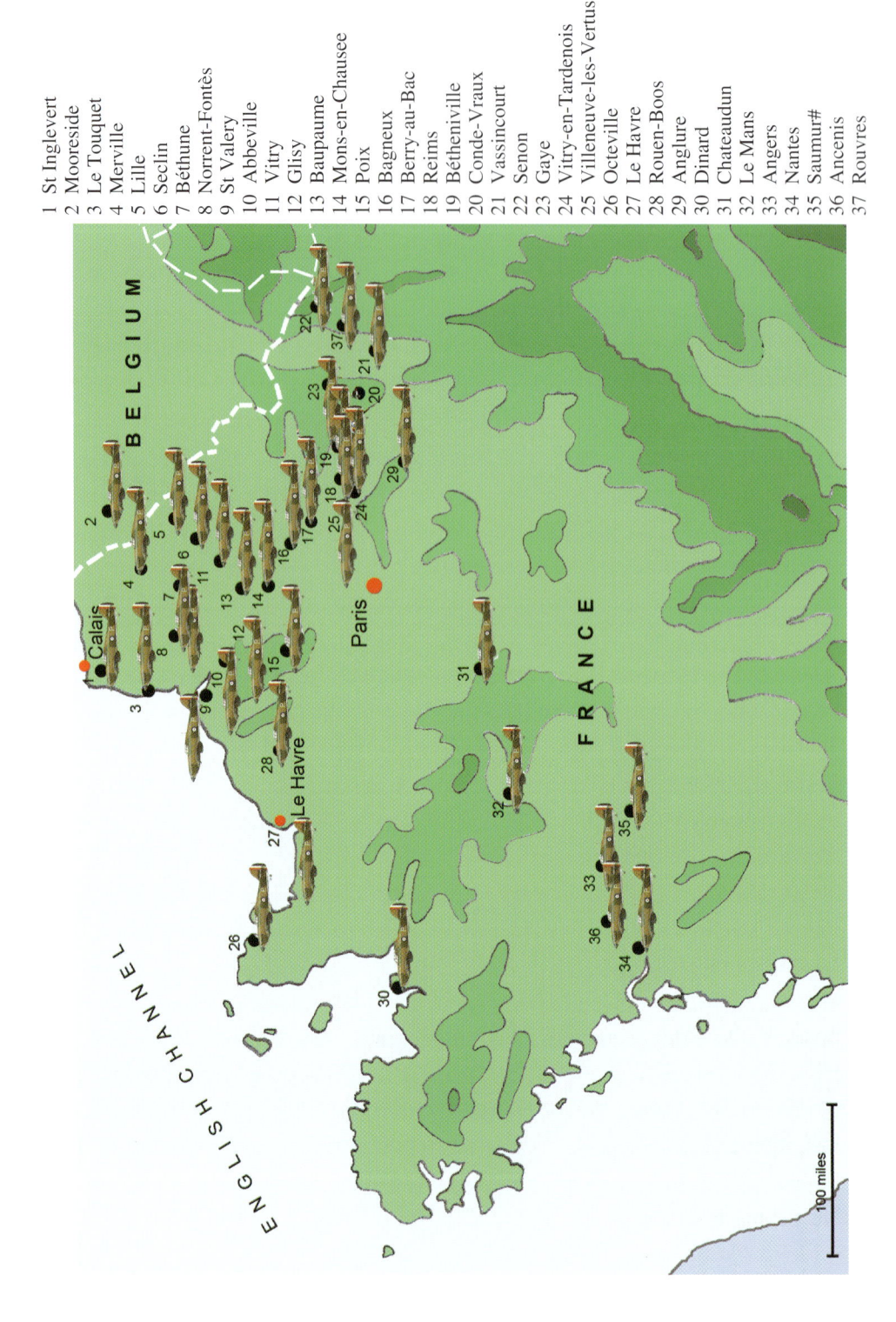

1 St Inglevert
2 Mooreside
3 Le Touquet
4 Merville
5 Lille
6 Seclin
7 Béthune
8 Norrent-Fontès
9 St Valery
10 Abbeville
11 Vitry
12 Glisy
13 Baupaume
14 Mons-en-Chausee
15 Poix
16 Bagneux
17 Berry-au-Bac
18 Reims
19 Bétheniville
20 Conde-Vraux
21 Vassincourt
22 Senon
23 Gaye
24 Vitry-en-Tardenois
25 Villeneuve-les-Vertus
26 Octeville
27 Le Havre
28 Rouen-Boos
29 Anglure
30 Dinard
31 Chateaudun
32 Le Mans
33 Angers
34 Nantes
35 Saumur#
36 Ancenis
37 Rouvres

> *'6 Hurricanes of 1 Squadron met 40 enemy aircraft 15 miles north of their base. A dogfight with 15 ME110s ensued, F.O. Brown claiming one shot down in flames and another crashed. The wreckage of 8 ME110s was reportedly found.'*[8]

Only four BF110s were in fact lost to Hurricanes in the day and only two BF109s. Other confirmed German losses to Hurricanes included four He 111s (13 claimed), four DO-17s,[9] six JU-87s[10] and one HS126.[11]

Five of the Stukas were shot down in one engagement by 87 Squadron. Thirteen Hurricanes were lost on the 11th May,[12] although five of these belonged to 17 Squadron in 11 Group and were lost to I/JG 51 BF109s over Holland.

The bridges over the Albert Canal at Vroenhoven and Veldwezelt, south-west of Maastricht, were attacked during the 12th May by formations of Battles and Blenheims, escorted by Hurricanes. In the course of these and other operations this day, a further 52 enemy aircraft were claimed by the Hurricane squadrons. This total again included mainly bombers, including 20 He 111s,[13] eight DO-17s,[14] 10 JU-87s[15] and one JU-88.[16] Six HS126 recce. aircraft were also claimed[17] of which one can be confirmed. Also, six BF109s were claimed this day, although only one was in fact confirmed lost to Hurricanes.

Twelve Hurricanes were lost on the 12th May, including five to the BF109s and one by accident; reinforcements arrived in the form of 504 Squadron from Debden.

Next day, the Germans crossed the Meuse onto French territory near Sedan. Twenty-six claims were made by Hurricane Squadron, including 11 He 111s[18] and three DO-17s[19] plus five BF109s and five BF110s, although none of the former and only two of the latter can be confirmed. Two HS126s were also claimed this day, none being confirmed, together with two HS123 biplanes which were confirmed. In return, 10 Hurricanes were lost, including two in a collision, two to BF110s and four to BF109s. AOC Fighter Command was now authorised to send a further 32 replacement Hurricanes to France.

> *'1 Squadron despatched 8 aircraft to provide cover over Maastricht, F.O. Brown getting badly shot up.'* [8]

Tuesday the 14th May has come to be known as 'the Day of the Fighters.' Hurricanes were tasked with escorting the bomber formations attacking the German forces around Sedan. In doing so, many combats with German fighters resulted and heavy losses were suffered by the Hurricane Squadrons. Twenty-seven Hurricanes were shot down, 13 by BF109s and nine by BF110s. 3 and 504 Squadrons both lost five Hurricanes, 73 Squadron lost four and 607 Squadron lost three. On the credit side, 60 enemy aircraft were claimed, including 18 JU-87s and 20 fighters. In reality, 31 enemy aircraft were destroyed, of which 11 were JU-87s, seven BF109s, two HS123s, one HS126 and 10 bombers.

On the 15th May, the Hurricane Squadrons continued operations along a line connecting Gembloux, Wavre and Louvain in Belgium, to protect the BEF and French 1st Army. Although this day was quieter than the previous day, nevertheless, 35 enemy aircraft were claimed by Hurricane Squadrons, of which 10 were confirmed. This confirmed total included one He 111, two DO-17s, one JU-87, one HS126, one BF109 and four BF110s. Twenty-one Hurricanes were lost this day, 11 to BF110s and three to BF109s.

The next day was quieter still, with only 14 claims of which one JU-88, two FW 189s, one BF109 and one He 111 were confirmed. In return, 13 Hurricanes were lost in the air, six by 85 Squadron alone. In addition, five damaged Hurricanes of 73 Squadron were abandoned and set on fire, as were reportedly two of 1 Squadron at Conde/Vraux and several of 615 Squadron at Vitry. At least two Hurricanes of 501 Squadron were also left behind at Betheniville.

> *'6 Hurricanes of 1 Squadron patrolled over Sedan, F.O. Brown claiming one ME109 and one JU-87 in flames.'* [8]

Air Chief Marshal Dowding, C-in-C Fighter Command, famously sent a letter to Churchill this day, urging against sending further Hurricanes to France.

> *'I must point out that within the last few days the equivalent of 10 Squadrons have been sent to France, that the Hurricane Squadrons remaining in this country are seriously depleted, and that the more Squadrons that are sent to France the higher will be the wastage and the more insistent the demands for reinforcements.'*

However, the British War Cabinet agreed that four more Hurricane Squadrons were to be sent to France as soon as possible. Fighter Command was actually ordered to despatch eight separate flights of Hurricanes, six of which arrived on the 16th, from 56, 229, 242, 245, 253 and 601 Squadrons. Responding to pressure from above, further reinforcements were sent by 11 Group Fighter Command on the 17th May.

A second flight of 601 Squadron and single flights from 111 and 213 Squadrons, together with 151 and 32 Squadrons were despatched to France to operate there during the day and return to the U.K. at dusk. 17 Squadron also arrived in France mid-afternoon, before returning to Hawkinge.

Thirty-nine Luftwaffe aircraft were claimed by Hurricane Squadrons during the 17th May, of which 20 were confirmed. Included in this total were 10 JU-87s,[20] of which seven were shot down by 151 Squadron and three by 17 Squadron. Although seven BF109s and five BF110s were also claimed, only three of the latter type were in fact lost to Hurricanes. Sixteen Hurricanes were lost on the 17th May, including four by accident. Seven of the losses were to BF109s.

> *'Having moved earlier this day to Conde/Vraux airfield, 6 aircraft of 1 Squadron met 15 ME110s North of Reims, F.O. Brown claiming one in flames, 8 miles West of that city.'*[8]

Next day, amid much confusion as to the extent of the German advance, heavy losses were experienced by the Hurricane Squadrons. At least 33 were shot down or force-landed and eight more were destroyed on the ground. 253 Squadron lost five Hurricanes in the air and four on the ground at Vitry. 56 Squadron lost three in the air and one on the ground and 229 Squadron lost four in the air. However, 57 enemy aircraft were claimed, of which 13 were confirmed. No less than 21 BF110s were claimed by Hurricane squadrons, although only two can be confirmed. A large number of bombers were also claimed but here the claims were more accurate – 11 He 111s claimed,[21] 12 DO-17s claimed,[22] one JU-88 claimed and confirmed. In addition, four BF109s were claimed,[23] together with an HS126.

'10 Hurricanes of 1 Squadron moved to Anglure this day.'[8]

The focus of the air battle now switched to the city of Lille and its surrounding airfields. For the heavily outnumbered Hurricane Squadrons, this was the climax of their resistance to the German onslaught. Seventy-four German aircraft were claimed by Hurricane Squadrons on the 19th May, the highest day's total of the campaign. Thirty-four of these were He 111s, although only 10 were confirmed, including eight from KG 54 alone.

Seven BF109s were also confirmed,[24] the highest total of this type destroyed in any day of the campaign. But in return, 87 Squadron was the hardest hit, losing four aircraft. Before the end of the day, these Squadrons were ordered to evacuate to Merville. At least 23 of the 34 Hurricanes lost this day were victims of the BF109s. Unserviceable Hurricanes were also destroyed at Lille and Vitry.

On the 20th May the situation had become so critical that the decision was made to withdraw most of the Hurricane Squadrons from France. From Norrent-Fontes, nine of 615 Squadron's Hurricanes and four of 607 Squadron were evacuated to RAF Kenley. Three unserviceable aircraft of 615 Squadron were also sent back independently to Kenley. Six Hurricanes of 504 Squadron were evacuated to RAF Manston, with a further two non-operational aircraft going directly to Croydon. Five Hurricanes of 3 Squadron also returned to Croydon, as did four unserviceable aircraft of 607 Squadron, where, due to battle damage, they were scrapped.

From Merville, three Hurricanes of 242 Squadron were ordered back to Manston and 213 Squadron 'B' flight flew to Northolt. An unserviceable aircraft of 87 Squadron flew directly to England, while the rest of the Squadron followed as transport escorts. 85 Squadron only had two or three Hurricanes left and returned to RAF Debden.

Armourers prepare ammunition belts during the Battle of France. The Hurricane is an 85 Squadron aircraft.

In spite of the evacuation, 23 enemy aircraft were claimed by Hurricane Squadrons, including six by 87 Squadron.[25] Of that total, nine were confirmed, including four bombers,[26] an HS 126 reconnaissance aircraft and two BF109s. In return, 13 Hurricanes were lost, six to flak.

> '1 Squadron started for Merville, but met heavy flak at St. Quentin. Sgt. Albonico was reported missing, but F.O. Brown claimed an H.S.126.'[8]

On the 21st May, the Germans reached the channel coast. Only one He 111[27] and two HS 126s were shot down by Hurricane units this day, for the loss of three Hurricanes.

> '6 aircraft of 1 Squadron met 16 He 111s North of Reims and the battle extended to Chateau-Thierry. 2 He 111s were claimed, one 10 miles North-West of Reims and another 10 miles West of Chateau-Thierry, from which 3 crew got out.'[8]

Combats continued on the 22nd May, with 23 claimed by Hurricane squadrons, including four HS 126s and seven JU-87s. In reality, two of the HS 126s were destroyed, as were four Stukas. However, four Hurricanes of 605 Squadron were lost, as well as one of 56 Squadron.

On the 23rd May, three abandoned Hurricanes were made serviceable at Merville and returned to England. Seven BF109s were claimed by Hurricane units[28] for the loss of seven Hurricanes. An He 111 and three BF110s were also claimed this day. Next day, a BF110 was claimed by 73 Squadron, for the loss of two of that Squadron's Hurricanes. Two of 242 Squadron's aircraft were also lost in a collision.

On the 25th May, 17 Squadron claimed three JU-87s,[29] one DO-17[30] and an HS 126, while 605 Squadron claimed four JU-87s and two HS 126s. 151 Squadron lost two aircraft,[31] without making any claims. 73 Squadron claimed a DO-17 and 242 Squadron claimed a BF110, but this was actually a DO-17P.

Also this day,

> 'twelve aircraft of 1 Squadron were providing cover near Laon, F.O. Thom in P2880 being hit by flak. He subsequently flew North instead of South and was taken prisoner.[8] He was actually a 73 Squadron pilot, but on secondment to 1 Squadron at the time.'[8, 32]

The Battle of France did not end with the evacuation from Dunkirk. The three AASF Hurricane Squadrons, 1, 73 and 501 continued their struggle against an overwhelmingly superior enemy air force, as they moved south, from base to base. They were ably assisted by several Squadrons from Fighter Command, two of which, nos. 17 and 242 Squadrons, moved to France on the 7th June 1940.

Battle of France

On the 3rd June, a JU-87 was claimed by 17 Squadron,[33] but a Hurricane of that Squadron was shot down by a BF109, killing F.O. Meredith. Two BF110s were also claimed by Flt. Lt. Nicholls of 73 Squadron, an aircraft of 9/ZG26 being lost to this Squadron or the French GC I/5. P.O. Hawken of 73 Squadron was shot down and killed by BF109s of I/JG76.

'Twelve aircraft of 1 Squadron moved to Chateaudun this day.'[8]

Next day, 1 Squadron claimed a DO-17, three He 111s[34] (plus one unconfirmed) and three BF110s, but no Luftwaffe losses can be matched to these claims. Two Hurricanes of 1 Squadron were written-off on landing after combat with BF110s,[35] although this may have been on 5th June.

1 Squadron were again in action on the 5th June,

'twelve aircraft meeting about 75 enemy aircraft over Boos,'[8]

claiming two He 111s and these were indeed aircraft of 3/KG27 lost this day.

'A DO-17 was also claimed in flames by F.O. Brown after having a time to outwit ME110s.'[8]

However, a 1 Squadron Hurricane was shot down over Rouen by He 111s or BF110s, P.O. Shepherd being killed.

501 Squadron claimed two BF110s and three He 111s, but two JU-88s were in fact lost, either to 501 Squadron or the French GC II/10. A Hurricane of 501 Squadron was also shot down over Rouen by He 111s or BF110s, P.O. Claydon being killed. Squadron Leader More and F.O. Kain of 73 Squadron despatched a DO-17 of 3(F)/22 between them.

On the 6th June, 17 Squadron claimed a BF109 plus two unconfirmed, an aircraft of 3(J)/LG2 actually being shot down south-east of Abbeville by Flt. Lt. Toyne. In return, however, a Hurricane of 17 Squadron[36] failed to return, with Sgt. Holman missing. 111 Squadron claimed heavily this day – three BF109s[37] and an HS126, but none of these claims can be confirmed.

A Hurricane of 111 Squadron[38] was lost to BF109s however, Sgt. Brown being injured. 501 Squadron engaged DO-17Zs South of Abbeville early in the morning, an aircraft of 7/KG76 being shot down by P.O. Lee.

The next day saw several combats near Le Treport, as Hurricanes fought to protect retreating British Troops. 43 Squadron claimed six BF109s and a BF110, whilst in fact destroying two BF109s of 4/JG26 near Dieppe. Four BF109s of JG3 can also be confirmed to 32 and 79 Squadrons, which claimed two and three (plus four unconfirmed) respectively. However, no fewer than seven Hurricanes of 43 Squadron[39] were shot down by JG3, 20 and 26, two of the pilots, F.O. Edmonds and F.O. Wilkinson, being killed.

17 Squadron also lost two Hurricanes[40] with both Squadron Leader Emms and P.O. Whittaker missing, as did 601 Squadron,[41] F.O. Robinson being wounded and F.O. Hubbard unhurt. 151 Squadron also lost an aircraft[42] to BF109s, P.O. Pettigrew being missing.

Tragically this day, 'Cobber' Kain was killed while flying an aerobatic routine[43] over Echemines airfield. He was credited with 16 enemy aircraft[44] at the time of his death. Unconfirmed claims this day include two BF109s by 17 Squadron, two BF109s and an He 111 by 32 Squadron, a BF109 by 56 Squadron, an HS126 by 79 Squadron, four BF109s by 111 Squadron and a BF109 and BF110 by 601 Squadron.

32 and 79 Squadrons engaged a formation of He 111s of I/KG1 and BF109s of III/JG26 on the morning of the 8th June. Four of the former[45] and three of the latter were claimed by 32 Squadron, one He 111 and two BF109s also being claimed by 79 Squadron. Two He 111s were in fact lost in this combat, together with two BF109s. Three Hurricanes[46] of 32 Squadron were lost to the BF109s, however, P.O.s Cherrington and Kirkaldie being killed. Two BF109s were also claimed by 151 Squadron and one BF109[47] by 501 Squadron this day, but no corresponding losses can be confirmed. A Hurricane[48] of 151 Squadron was shot down by flak, without injury to the pilot, P.O. Blomely.

On the 9th June, two BF109s[49] were claimed by 242 Squadron, but an aircraft of this Squadron[50] was shot down by BF109s, P.O. MacQueen being killed. 17 and 501 Squadrons both had Hurricanes force-land and written-off, P.O. Leahy[51] being unhurt, but Sgt. Lacey of 501 Squadron was injured.

Next day, 111 Squadron claimed a BF109 and a DO-17, but these aircraft cannot be confirmed. However, a BF109 of I/JG76 was shot down by P.O. Gibson of 501 Squadron near Le Havre, although Gibson was hit by return fire and bailed out unhurt.

Two HS126s[52] were claimed on the 11th by 32 Squadron, a DO-17 by 73 Squadron, an He 111 by 145 Squadron and a BF109 by 615 Squadron, but none of these can be confirmed. However, 111 Squadron engaged BF109s of 2/JG3 North of Le Havre, early in the afternoon and shot down three. The only Hurricane loss this day was an aircraft of 32 Squadron,[53] which force-landed in France after attacking an HS126 over Dieppe. The pilot, Sgt. Jones, was believed captured unhurt.

On the 12th June, five He 111s were claimed by 17 Squadron and three by 242 Squadron. Three He 111s of Stab/KG54 were actually lost in this combat. Next day, P.O. Eliot of 73 Squadron claimed an He 111 and although this crash-landed, it was repairable.

An He 111 was also claimed by 1 Squadron on the 14th June, but this cannot be confirmed. However, a BF109 of 3/JG54 is believed to have been shot down by 17 Squadron. Three BF109s were also claimed by 242 Squadron, but in fact, two BF110s of 9/ZG26 are believed to have been lost in this action, North of Conches-en-Ouche. Two Hurricanes of 1 Squadron were lost this day – Flt. Lt. Warcup was captured but Flt. Lt. Brown was unhurt. A Hurricane of 242 Squadron was also lost in a forced landing, P.O. Stansfeld also being unhurt.

On the 15th June, a Hurricane of 73 Squadron was shot down by a BF109, wounding Sgt. McNay. Another He 111 was claimed by 1 Squadron on the 17th June, but no He 111s were listed as lost this day.

However, next day, an He 111 of 5/KG1 was shot down over the Channel by Wing Commander Beamish of 151 Squadron, but two Hurricanes of this Squadron[54] were shot down by He 111s, P.O. Wright and Sgt. Aslin both being killed. Three Hurricanes[55] of 1 Squadron and three of 242 Squadron[56] were burned on the ground on evacuation. That night, an He 111 was claimed by 605 Squadron.

Two BF109s were claimed by 3 Squadron on the 19th June, one aircraft of 5/JG3 actually being lost south of Cherbourg to P.O. Carey. An He 111 was also claimed by 79 Squadron.

On the 20th June, a Hurricane[57] of 501 Squadron was lost on evacuation. Five more were lost on the 21st June.[58]

On the 22nd June, 615 Squadron claimed three He 111s,[59] two BF110s[60] and an unconfirmed JU-52. An He 111 of III/KG1 crash-landed but was repairable. A Hurricane[61] of 615 Squadron was shot down by a BF110 of 7/ZG26 West of Rouen, P.O. Lloyd being killed.

242 Squadron's stay in France was brief, as it was evacuated from France on 18th June, along with 1 and 73 Squadrons. 17 and 501 Squadrons, which had temporarily moved to the Channel Islands, followed on the 21st June. From the 3rd June until they evacuated, 1 Squadron claimed 11 enemy aircraft[62] without loss; 73 Squadron claimed five, but lost three Hurricanes and 501 Squadron claimed eight,[63] also without loss.

From Fighter Command, 242 Squadron claimed eight,[64] including five[65] Bf109s, for one Hurricane shot down; 17 Squadron also claimed eight,[66] including five He 111s on the 12th June, but four of the Squadron's Hurricanes were lost.

Other Fighter Command Hurricane Squadrons were active over or near to France in June 1940 and claimed a further 59 enemy aircraft[67] for the loss of 23 Hurricanes. Included in this claim were 40 BF109s, a considerable over-claim.[68]

Of 452 Hurricanes sent to France, 386 were lost by the end of the 20th May: 173 of these were lost in air combat, 12 were lost to flak, 10 were destroyed on the ground and a further 13 were lost accidentally. In addition, 178 were abandoned as the Germans advanced across France, most having been left in an irreparable condition by their squadrons.

After the 20th May,[69] at least another 39 Hurricanes were lost in air combat up to the end of the French campaign on the 30th June.

Hurricane Squadrons claimed 499 enemy aircraft in combat during the 12 days, 10th–21st May inclusive. Of these, 299 can be confirmed to the Hurricane units. A further 197 enemy aircraft[70] were claimed from the 22nd May to the 30th June, inclusive, when in fact only 23 of these can be confirmed.

The top scoring Hurricane pilot of the Battle of France was F.O. Leslie Clisby of 1 Squadron, with 16 and one shared, although since the battle, research has cast doubt over this total, which has been reduced to 11 or nine and three shared by certain historians.

Although Hurricane losses in the Battle of France had been high, a creditable victory/loss ratio had been achieved in air combat against vastly superior odds and the experience gained by surviving pilots proved invaluable in the forthcoming Battle of Britain.

Restored Hurricane P3551. Ex-New Zealand, now based in France.

References
1   AASF.
2   BEF.
3   Together with 79 Squadron which did not claim.
4   Six confirmed.
5   None confirmed.
6   Two confirmed.
7   Only one BF110 damaged was claimed by 87 Squadron.
8   Extract from F.O. M.H. 'Hilly' Brown Log Book.

9	Nine claimed.
10	Seven claimed.
11	Two claimed.
12	Including one on the ground.
13	Seven confirmed.
14	Two confirmed.
15	Three confirmed.
16	Confirmed.
17	Three by No. 3 Squadron.
18	Two confirmed.
19	None confirmed.
20	Eleven claimed.
21	Six confirmed.
22	Two confirmed.
23	One confirmed.
24	Of 21 claimed.
25	Two confirmed.
26	One He 111, two DO-17s and one DO-215.
27	Two claimed.
28	Four confirmed.
29	All confirmed.
30	Confirmed.
31	In a collision.
32	*See* Chapter Eight for Dunkirk.
33	Wrongly.
34	Plus one unconfirmed.
35	P.O.s Hillcoat and Hancock were unhurt.
36	P3660.
37	Plus one unconfirmed.
38	P2885.
39	L1931, L1847, L2116, N2585, L1726, L1737 and L1608.
40	P3472 and P2905.
41	P3484 and P3490.
42	P3529.

43	In L1826.
44	Plus one damaged.
45	Plus one unconfirmed.
46	P3353, N2582 and N2406.
47	Plus two unconfirmed.
48	P3315.
49	Plus one unconfirmed.
50	P2767.
51	17 Squadron.
52	Plus one unconfirmed.
53	N2533.
54	P3313 and P8324.
55	L1757, L1974 and P3045.
56	N2381, P3683 and P3779.
57	P3347.
58	L1624, L1911, P3450, P3491 and P3542.
59	Unconfirmed.
60	Plus one unconfirmed.
61	P2764.
62	Plus five unconfirmed.
63	Plus three unconfirmed.
64	Plus one unconfirmed.
65	Plus one unconfirmed.
66	Plus three unconfirmed.
67	Plus 24 unconfirmed.
68	Only 13 can be confirmed.
69	Excluding the Dunkirk evacuation.
70	Including 60 unconfirmed.

Chapter Six

The Desert Air Campaign 1940–1942

Hurricanes were operated throughout the Desert Air Campaign, from June 1940 to May 1943. It was in this campaign that the Hurricane really matured as a ground attack aircraft with the specialist Hurricane 2D, armed with 40mm cannon, being particularly effective as 'tank busters'. Hurricanes were used in greater numbers than any other allied combat aircraft in this theatre and although superseded in the air superiority role by Tomahawks in late 1941, Kittyhawks in early 1942 and then by Spitfires in the second half of 1942, Hurricane pilots still managed to claim more enemy aircraft shot down than pilots in any of those other fighters. In fact, up to the end of 1942, after which most Hurricane squadrons were relegated to rear area operations, Hurricane squadrons had claimed over five times as many victories as Spitfire-equipped units. Of course, Spitfires were not despatched to the desert until late April 1942 when 145 Squadron started to receive their aircraft, but as in the Battle of Britain, the number of Hurricanes that had been available to allied air commanders, during the desert campaign, was decisive to its eventual outcome.

Although Hurricanes were originally available in small numbers in the latter half of 1940, they completely dominated the Italian Air Force that opposed them and maintained air superiority until the first gruppe of JG 27 began claiming victories in April 1941 with their BF109s.

Up to the end of 1940 some 78 Italian aircraft were claimed by 33, 73, 80 and 274 Squadrons for the loss of a maximum of 10 Hurricanes in air combat (eight of which were force-landed). In reality, only 28 Italian aircraft (16 CR-42s and 12 SM-79s) were admitted lost, but the Hurricanes clearly had the edge over the CR-42 biplane fighters used by the Italians. A further 32 Italian aircraft were claimed in January 1941 for the loss of three Hurricanes in air combat and three to flak. Seven CR-42s, three SM-79s and a G-50 were actually lost by the Italians.

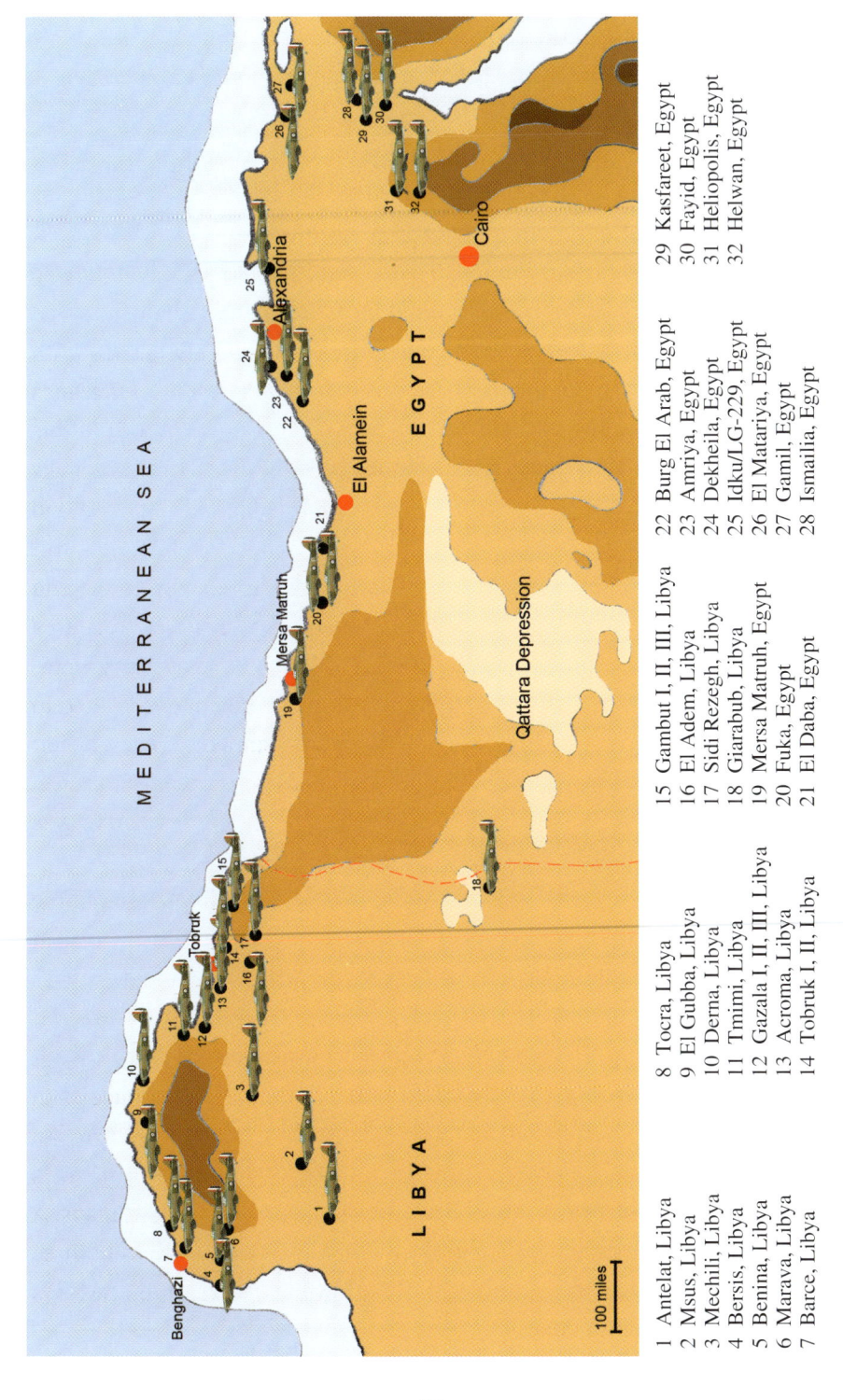

The Desert Air Campaign 1940–1942

1 Antelat, Libya
2 Msus, Libya
3 Mechili, Libya
4 Bersis, Libya
5 Benina, Libya
6 Marava, Libya
7 Barce, Libya
8 Tocra, Libya
9 El Gubba, Libya
10 Derna, Libya
11 Tmimi, Libya
12 Gazala I, II, III, Libya
13 Acroma, Libya
14 Tobruk I, II, Libya
15 Gambut I, II, III, Libya
16 El Adem, Libya
17 Sidi Rezegh, Libya
18 Giarabub, Libya
19 Mersa Matruh, Egypt
20 Fuka, Egypt
21 El Daba, Egypt
22 Burg El Arab, Egypt
23 Amriya, Egypt
24 Dekheila, Egypt
25 Idku/LG-229, Egypt
26 El Matariya, Egypt
27 Gamil, Egypt
28 Ismailia, Egypt
29 Kasfareet, Egypt
30 Fayid, Egypt
31 Heliopolis, Egypt
32 Helwan, Egypt

In February 1941, Luftwaffe aircraft started appearing over the front, but the arrival of BF109s in April dramatically changed the situation in the air. Only a single Gruppe of JG27 (I/JG27) was available from April to October 1941 (when II/JG27 arrived with their improved BF109Fs), although one other Staffel (7/JG26) arrived on the 1st June, to assist them.

The BF109s not only had a better high altitude performance than the Hurricanes but were also employed with superior tactics. Operating in small numbers, they sat high above allied formations, using dive and zoom tactics to attack. Allied fighter formations were often too loosely controlled and suffered heavily to the BF109s. Allied fighter losses, especially Hurricanes, were heavy and during the period April to September 1941 inclusive, some 82 Hurricanes were claimed by I/JG 27 BF109s, of which 69 were actually lost.

Refuelling a Hurricane at Burg el Arab in July 1941.

Over the same period, 26 (possibly 28) BF109s were claimed by Hurricane squadrons, of which only 10 were confirmed.

Fifty-six JU-87s were also claimed by Hurricane pilots; however, and again, though certainly an over claim (46 of these were claimed from April to June inclusive, of which only 12 can be confirmed lost, plus six force-landed), this still represented a significant loss to the Africa Korps of its close air support capability – only two Stuka Gruppen were available at the start of 'Operation Battleaxe'.

Recovering a wrecked Hurricane in the desert.

October and early November 1941 were quiet over the desert. Three BF109s and two Italian G.50s were claimed by 1 SAAF Squadron for the loss of at least 13 Hurricanes (of several Squadrons) in air combat. However, on the 18th November, 'Operation Crusader', the biggest allied offensive of the war so far, commenced.

Operation Crusader

This campaign involved heavy air activity until the middle of February 1942, during which time 97 enemy aircraft were claimed by Hurricane units, including 28 BF109s (nine confirmed), 19 JU-87s, at least 15 JU-88s, eight MC 202s, seven G.50s and six CR.42s, but at a heavy cost – 96 Hurricanes were shot down in air combat (23 of these either forced or crashed-landed), almost all by BF109s. Eleven Hurricane units were available from the start of 'Crusader' including the Royal Navy Fighter Unit (RNFU) and two PRU, far more than were available of any other allied type.

Believed to be an RNFU Sea Hurricane in the desert.

On the first day of the operation, a Ghibli was claimed destroyed on the ground by 33 Squadron, the same Squadron claiming three CR-42s in the air (P.O. Wade (2), the other was claimed by several pilots). A Hurricane of 451 Squadron was reportedly shot down. Two days later, Sub. Lt. Charlton of the RNFU claimed three 'Stukas', but his Hurricane (W9327) force-landed after being attacked by a Tomahawk, Sub. Lt. Charlton being unhurt. A Hurricane of 1 SAAF Squadron was shot down by flak and another aircraft of that Squadron failed to return. Lt. Kershaw was wounded in the former and 2nd Lt. Currin was unhurt in the later. A Hurricane of 33 Squadron was also lost to flak this day, P.O. Winsland force-landing. W9357 of 208 Squadron was also a flak victim, P.O. Lomas crash-landing unhurt.

The next day saw more flak victims, two Hurricanes (one was Z5141) of 229 Squadron being shot down (Sgt. Boyde was reported missing), an aircraft (Z4175) of 80 Squadron also force-landing, Sqn. Ldr. Morgan being wounded. A Hurricane (Z4108) of 33 Squadron was also lost, although Sgt. Stammers was reported safe, while another aircraft (V7561) of this unit landed by mistake at a German aerodrome (F.O. Jewell was

The Desert Air Campaign 1940–1942

presumably taken prisoner). Another Hurricane of 451 Squadron was also reportedly shot down.

On the 22nd November, two JU-88s and an SM-79 were claimed by 33 Squadron, but two Hurricanes of this Squadron were destroyed on the ground by JU-88s. An aircraft of 238 Squadron was shot down by flak (Sgt. Matthews was unhurt), while one of 237 Squadron (Z4841) was shot down by an MC 200 or G-50, Flt. Lt. Hutchinson also being unhurt. Three Hurricanes (Z4033, Z4426 and Z4619) of 80 Squadron also failed to return, Sgts. Smith, McVean and Cross all being reported safe. Another Hurricane of an unknown unit was abandoned in the desert.

Next day, Stuka formations were engaged by 229 and 238 Squadrons, three plus three probables being claimed by the former unit (Sgt. Wesson (1), Sqn. Ldr. Smith (1+1), P.O. Marland (0+1), P.O. Ravn (1), Flt. Lt. Johns (0+1), W.O. Hoare (0+1)) and a further three claimed by the latter, Flt. Lt. Forsyth of this Squadron also claiming a G-50, while a BF109 probable was also claimed by this Squadron. However, both Squadrons suffered heavily to the BF109s, two aircraft of 229 Squadron (BD898 and Z5269) being shot down, with another (Z5328) force-landed and written-off. P.O. Stideford was reported missing. Four Hurricanes of 238 Squadron were also shot down, with all four pilots missing (Sgt. Pike, F.O. Sulman, P.O. Outhwaite and P.O. Frost) and a further aircraft was shot down later by a BF109, P.O. Sellar also being missing. Four Hurricanes of the RNFU were also lost, again with four pilots missing (Sub. Lts Talbot and Willis, Lt. Cox and an unknown pilot), for two BF109 probables claimed (by Sub. Lts Astin and Henderson). 33 Squadron also had a Hurricane (V7772) force-land this day, while claiming a BF110. II/JG27 claimed four fighters on this date, including two Hurricanes, while admitting the loss of two BF109s. Fourteen victories were also claimed by Italian fighters.

On the 24th November, 1 SAAF Squadron claimed four BF110s (not in ORB) and one shared (Sgt. Comfort) with 80 Squadron, which also claimed another BF110 (Sgt. Foskett), but an aircraft (Z4796) of 80 Squadron was shot down by a BF110 (of ZG26) and another (Z4648) failed to return. F.O. Tulloch was missing in the former, but Sgt. Crouch was believed safe in the latter. An SM-79 was claimed by 33 Squadron (P.O. Wade/

Sgt. Inglesby), which lost an aircraft on take-off (P.O. Edy was unhurt).

A G-50 was also claimed by Lt. Palm of 94 Squadron, while a Hurricane (Z4766) of 237 Squadron was shot down by flak (Flt. Lt. Spence was unhurt).

The following day, two BF109s were claimed by 229 Squadron (not according to the ORB), while an aircraft ('A') of the RNFU was shot down by flak, Lt. Johnston being reported missing. A Hurricane (Z4251) of 33 Squadron also force-landed, but F.O. Tofield was safe.

238 Squadron was hit hard by BF109s on the 26th November, losing three Hurricanes shot down and two force-landed. Sgt. Knappett was reported missing, Sgt. Kay, F.O. Kings and P.O. Currie were all unhurt and Sgt. Fairbairn was wounded. An aircraft (W9351) of 33 Squadron was shot down by CR-42s, P.O. Winsland being missing and another (Z5314) of 274 Squadron crashed on landing due to flak damage (although Sgt. Persse was believed to be uninjured).

On the 27th November, an SM-79 and a BF109 probable (confirmed on fire) were claimed destroyed on the ground by F.O. Vos of 94 Squadron. A Hurricane of 260 Squadron failed to return, with P.O. Wyley missing. Two Hurricanes were claimed by I/JG27 this day. Next day, a BF110 was claimed by Lt. Moolmanof of 94 Squadron, but three Hurricanes (Z4614, Z4427 and Z4930) of that Squadron were shot down by a II/JG27 BF109, P.O. Muhart being wounded and F.O. Vos and Lt. Palm both being missing. An aircraft of 1 Squadron was also shot down, probably by a BF110, Capt. Wiebenberg becoming a PoW.

The second half of February 1942 and the first half of March 1942 were affected by bad weather, which considerably reduced air activity. In fact, the operational tempo did not pick up again until late May 1942. From mid-February to mid-May, only 13 enemy aircraft were claimed by Hurricane Squadrons, three of which were BF109s (one confirmed), and three MC 202s. Fourteen Hurricanes were lost in air combat during the same period and a further eight were crash- / force-landed.

There was a major re-organisation of the Desert Air Force in March 1942. 243 Wing now included 33, 73, 80, and 274 Hurricane Squadrons.

A new axis offensive started on the 26th May 1942, which resulted in the surrender of Tobruk on the 21st June and on the 24th June, axis forces crossed into Egypt. Allied forces had fallen back to defensive positions on the Alamein line and although Rommel launched an attack against these positions on the 1st July and subsequently, allied counter-attacks also occurred during July 1942, by the end of that month, the activity had ground to a halt as both sides consolidated their positions and re-equipped.

The Hurricane squadrons had been used primarily in ground attack and bomber escort roles during these operations and this inevitably led to high losses to the BF109s. From mid-May to the end of July 1942, 98 Hurricanes were lost in combat or crash- / force-landed.

However, Hurricane squadrons nevertheless managed to claim 122 enemy aircraft in air combat during this period, including 44 BF109s (only five confirmed), 41 JU-87s, 13 JU-88s, 11 CR-42s and nine MC202s.

August 1942 was relatively quiet in terms of air activity over the desert. Only nine enemy aircraft were claimed by Hurricane Squadrons, three of which were BF109s, also, three JU-88s and three JU-87s (two confirmed). In return, at least 22 Hurricanes were lost in air combat, of which six crash- / force-landed.

Alam El Halfa

The next Africa Korps offensive commenced on the 31st August at Alam El Halfa and lasted until the 4th September, when Rommel decided to withdraw.

The Germans attacked at dawn on the 31st August, with formations of Stukas supporting the ground assault.

213 Squadron intercepted one of these formations, P.O. Barnes, Flt. Sgt. Stephenson and Flt. Sgt. Rebstock each claiming one, two JU-87s actually being confirmed. However, P.O. Barnes was shot down (in BP451) and wounded. A BF109 was shot down by a Hurricane of either 213 or 7 SAAF Squadron and a JU-88 was reportedly claimed by 73 Squadron (although not recorded in the ORB). A Hurricane ('H') of 238 Squadron crash-landed after a flak hit, P.O. Hay being unhurt and another aircraft of this squadron belly-landed.

A Hurricane of 127 Squadron was destroyed on the ground this day and an aircraft of 1 SAAF Squadron crash-landed after combat with BF109s of II/JG27. In addition, one other Hurricane was reported missing this day (from an unknown unit). Two Hurricanes were claimed by I/JG27 BF109s and another by III/JG53.

Next day, 213 Squadron was in action again, claiming three JU-88s, but losing five aircraft (BP342, HL704, BN273, BP409 and BP499 – although two of these crash-landed and were assessed as Cat. II damaged), with F.O. Wollaston killed, Sgt. Potter missing and F.O. Avise, Flt. Sgt. Ross and Sgt. Garrood unhurt. They had been the victims of I/JG27, for whom Hauptmann Marseille claimed 17 victories in the day! A Hurricane (possibly HL568) of 208 Squadron, flown by Wg Cdr Rogers also failed to return, probably being one of I/JG27's victories. Aircraft (Z9666) of 238 and 1 SAAF Squadrons were also lost to the BF109s this day, the fate of F.O. Matthews being unknown in the former and Lt. Bailey being wounded in the latter. Nine Hurricanes were lost this day, but not one allied bomber was lost to German fighters, a testimony to the protection afforded by the Hurricanes (and other allied fighters).

On the 2nd September, Hurricanes of 127 and 274 Squadrons disrupted further Stuka attacks, the former Squadron claiming five and two probables. Claimants included Sqn. Ldr. Pegge (1), Flt. Lt. Lawrence (2), P.O. Rebman (1), W.O. Raises (1 + 1 probable) and P.O. Terry (1 probable). For 274 Squadron, Flt. Sgt. Neill claimed one and a probable, Sgt. Carter also claiming a probable.

Three of the Stukas were actually seen force-landing. Sgts Carter and Ott of 274 Squadron also claimed a BF109 each, with Flt. Lt. Wade of 33 Squadron claiming a probable. Flt. Sgt. Reynolds of 127 Squadron (in BM979) force-landed with engine trouble (cat. II damaged) and an aircraft (BG966) of 274 Squadron was shot down by BF109s of I/JG27 - Sgt. Carter was safe. 33 Squadron also lost a Hurricane (--908) to II/JG27 BF109s, P.O. Dibbs being reported missing and an aircraft (BE681) of 238 Squadron was shot down by ground fire, Sgt. Webb's fate being unknown.

There were no Hurricane claims on the 3rd September, but 33 Squadron lost an aircraft (--334) shot down (possibly two) by BF109s, Flt. Sgt. Bellau being reported safe. Three Hurricanes of 7 SAAF Squadron were also shot down and crash-landed by BF109s of I/JG27 (four were claimed), with one pilot killed.

During the four-day battle, 17 Hurricanes were lost (at least 15 in air combat), for a claim of 15 enemy aircraft.

All operations for the rest of September were at a slower pace, although 7 SAAF Squadron experienced such losses (10, of which six crash-landed) that it was withdrawn from the front on the 9th. Six enemy aircraft were claimed by Hurricane units from the 4th September to the end of the month, of which two were confirmed BF109s, for the loss of nine Hurricanes in air combat.

The most significant operation of early October occurred on the 9th, when raids were launched on the Daba and Fuka advanced landing grounds. No claims were made by Hurricane squadrons, but nine Hurricanes were lost (one to flak). Overall, up to and including the 23rd October, only three BF109s were claimed for the loss of 11 Hurricanes to BF109s during the month.

Hurricanes at El Alamein

The night of the 23rd October 1942 saw the beginning of the decisive Battle of El Alamein.[1] Hurricane units involved included 80, 127, 274 and 335 (Greek) Squadrons in 7 SAAF Wing, 1 SAAF, 33, 213 and 238 Squadrons in 243 Wing, 73 Squadron,[2] 6 and 7 SAAF Squadrons with Hurricane 2Ds and 40 SAAF and 208 Squadrons for tactical reconnaissance. The Hurricane thus represented the most numerous type available to the allies.[3]

73 Squadron was active from the start of the battle, but mainly in a ground attack role. On the 24th October, a BF109 was claimed by Flt. Lt. Ayerst of 33 Squadron in the late afternoon and another[4] of II/JG27 was claimed by Bobby Pryde of 1 SAAF Squadron, west of Sidi abdel Rahman. In return, a Hurricane of 1 SAAF Squadron was force-landed, the pilot being safe.[5a]

Four Hurricane IIDs of 6 Squadron, together with two of 7 (SAAF) Squadron took off at 1055 hrs to attack enemy armour in the Southern Sector. Six 'Honeys' were claimed hit by 6 Squadron. A subsequent mission commenced at 1225 hrs, again with four aircraft of 6 Squadron and two of 7 (SAAF) Squadron; this time, eight 'Honeys' and two Crusaders were claimed hit.[6]

No claims or losses were reported on the 25th, but next day, two JU-87s and two probables were claimed by 213 Squadron. The Squadron was airborne on 'decoy patrol' from 1735 to 1820 hrs, during which time six plus Stukas were seen diving from 15,000 to 6,000 ft. F.O. Houle claimed two and a probable, with P.O. Carrick claiming the other probable.[7]

A Hurricane[8a] of 274 Squadron was shot down by BF109s and listed as Cat. II, but the pilot, F.O. Graves, was unhurt. A Hurricane of 1 SAAF Squadron was force-landed by flak, again without injury to the pilot, Lt. Alexander.

BN110 of 127 Squadron was lost by accident, killing Sgt. Stoddard and HL547 of 208 Squadron crash-landed.[9] In addition, a Hurricane[10a] of 238 Squadron crashed on landing, injuring P.O. Rylands. 6 Squadron was again in action, three of its aircraft, together with three of 7 (SAAF) Squadron taking off at 1010 hrs and claiming two 'Honeys', two Crusaders, one unidentified tank, five armoured cars, a semi-tracked vehicle and a lorry.[6]

The 27th saw a CR-42 and two probables claimed by 213 Squadron. Twenty-four of the Italian biplanes were spotted flying east at 12,000 ft, with an escort of eight plus MC202s at 15,000 ft and five miles further south. P.O. McKay made the claim and P.O. Smith and Sgt. Sweney claimed the probables.[7a]

33 Squadron flew top cover for 213 Squadron and west of El Alamein, Flt. Lt. Kallio claimed a JU-87 as did P.O. Peterson, with Flt. Sgt. Belec claiming a probable. However, a Hurricane[7b] of 213 Squadron failed to return[7c] and two of 33 Squadron were shot down by BF109s. Sqn. Ldr. Lloyd and P.O. Gardner of that Squadron were also both reported missing. Only one Hurricane was claimed by II/JG27, however.

Next Day, 335 (Greek) Squadron was in action, but lost a Hurricane, probably to flak and another crash-landed.[11a] P.O. Xydis was unhurt, but P.O. Kartalamakis was reported missing.

Six Hurricane IIDs of 6 Squadron took off at 1446 hrs and claimed two

Mk.13 tanks, seven lorries, two semi-tracked vehicles and a wireless truck. Six aircraft were ordered to be available at landing ground 37 (LG37) by 0700 hrs next morning to support 9th Australian Division. In fact, seven aircraft of 'A' Flight took off at 0645 hrs on 29th October and flew to LG 37. Subsequently, six Hurricanes took off at 0905 hrs and claimed hits on three lorries and a semi-tracked vehicle. P.O. Jones' aircraft was hit by flak and he force-landed inside allied lines, but was rescued unhurt.[6]

On the penultimate day of October, 33 Squadron took off at 0850 hrs to patrol the line with 238 Squadron as top cover. Fifteen plus Stukas were seen bombing the line and engaged by 33 Squadron, Sgt. Francis claiming a probable, but one of the Squadron's Hurricanes failed to return, probably a victim of flak. P.O. Peterson was reported missing.[12]

No claims or losses were reported on the last day of October by the Hurricane Squadrons, but on the 1st November, an aircraft[7d] of 213 Squadron force-landed after its engine failed. Its pilot, P.O. Thrift, was unhurt.

Next day, General Montgomery launched Operation 'Supercharge', his planned breakout. The Germans attempted to counter with Stukas attacking the British Armour, but they met several Hurricane squadrons, which disrupted their plans.

Eleven Hurricanes of 335 Squadron took off at 0915 hrs and flew top cover for 274 Squadron on a Northern Sector patrol. Flt. Sgt. Soufrilas had the honour of claiming the Squadron's first victory, a BF109.[11b]

A JU-87 was claimed by Captain Phillips and a probable by F.O. Gilbert of 33/238 Squadrons – 33 Squadron was flying as top cover at 1150 hrs on an Anti-Stuka patrol of 12 aircraft.[12a]

Three JU-87s and three probables were also claimed by 213 Squadron, which had scrambled at 1540 hrs and saw 20-plus bandits approaching at 17,000 ft from the south-west. Squadron Leader Oliver claimed one and a probable, P.O. Carrick and Sgt. Usher also claimed one each, with P.O. Luxton and Sgt. Jones both claiming probables. Sgt. Bird of 213 Squadron also claimed a BF109 probable,[7a] as did 274 Squadron.[8b]

At 1545 hrs, 1 SAAF Squadron, with 213 Squadron as top cover, took off and encountered a 'Stuka Party', 25 JU-87s and 22-plus BF109s being seen approaching 1500 ft below at 6,500 ft, three JU-87s and a probable being claimed.

Hannes Faure claimed one and a probable, Bobby Pryde claimed one and another was shared by Captain Viljoen and Robinson. A BF109 was also claimed by Bill Rabie.[5]

Two Hurricanes[8c] of 274 Squadron failed to return, possibly the victims of III/JG27 Bf109s, with both pilots, Flt. Sgt. Howie and Sgt. Robertson, missing. A Hurricane of 238 Squadron also failed to return and another was force-landed[10b] by flak. Two fighters were claimed by I/JG27. Sgt. Allen was killed, but F.O. Gilbert was unhurt. HL657 of 208 Squadron also belly-landed after a flak hit, wounding Captain Becourt-Foch.

127 Squadron flew as top cover for 80 Squadron on the 3rd November, encountering 24 JU-87s and 15 BF109s over the Northern Sector. The Squadron was badly hit, losing six Hurricanes[13a] to II/JG 27 and JG 77. In return, Flt. Sgt. Moulden and Sgts Trench and Willshaw each claimed JU-87 probables and a BF109 was seen to spin in and crash.[13b]

80 Squadron was more successful, claiming seven JU-87s and nine probables, nine Stukas actually being lost, for one Hurricane[14a] force-landed. It was observed that several of the Stukas had no rear gunners![14b]

A JU-87 was also claimed by Sgt. Cordwell of 238 Squadron and another by Flt. Lt. Kallio plus probables by Flt. Sgt. Belleau and Sgt. Cowley of 33 Squadron. A Hurricane of 33 Squadron was force-landed[12b] and two others of that Squadron failed to return, one from a cannon test. Two Hurricanes of 1 SAAF Squadron also failed to return, with Lt. James reported missing and Balley killed. Two Hurricanes[7e] of 213 Squadron also failed to return, both force-landing,[7f] wounding P.O.s Aitken and Luxton.

6 Squadron were given permission to hunt for targets in the Southern Sector, seven aircraft taking off between 1500 and 1510 hrs. No armour was found, but 12 lorries, three semi-tracked vehicles and a transporter were claimed destroyed. Sgt. Paton's Hurricane failed to return, but he was safe and his aircraft was believed salvageable.[6]

On the 4th November, a general breakthrough was made on the ground by the Eighth Army. The Afrika Korps now retreated in full flight along the coast, harried by air attacks.

Only one claim was made this day by the Hurricane Squadrons, for a BF109, 20 miles west of Alamein, by Flt. Lt. Ayerst, now of 238 Squadron, but at least nine Hurricanes were lost; two of 33 Squadron[12c] were probably shot down by BF109s – P.O.s Steward and Turner were both missing; two of 1 SAAF Squadron, one to a BF109 and one to flak;[5b] four of 238 Squadron,[10c] two shot down by BF109s,[15] Flt. Sgt. Ayerst and Sgt. Blachford were both wounded, Sgt. Wise also failing to return and a Hurricane of 213 Squadron was shot down by flak. An aircraft of 40 SAAF Squadron was also shot down by flak, with Captain Webb missing.

Next day, the pace reduced for the Hurricane Squadrons. An Fi-156 was claimed by Flt. Sgt. Burman of 274 Squadron and a BF109 out to sea West of Fuka by F.O. Mackinnon of 127 Squadron. The former unit lost a Hurricane[8d] shot down by a BF109 as did 80 Squadron,[14c] P.O. Wilson being reported missing.

Twenty-nine air claims were made by the Hurricane squadrons from the 24th October to the 5th November, including 20 JU-87s and six BF109s, for the loss of up to 19 Hurricanes to BF109s. At least nine JU-87s can be confirmed. In addition, 60 vehicles were claimed destroyed on the ground by 6 Squadron Hurricane IIDs.

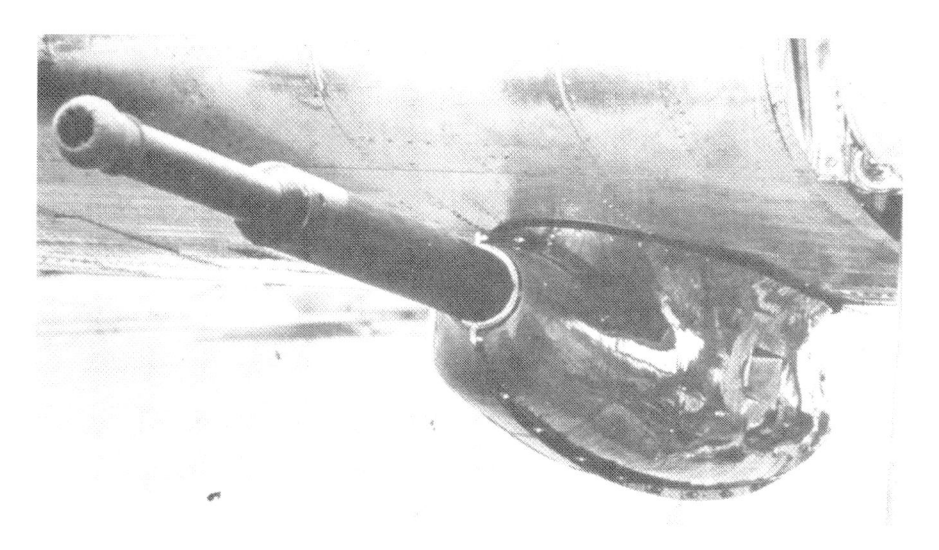

Installation of the Vickers 40mm K gun under the wing of a Hurricane Mk.IID.

As the axis forces retreated from El Alamein, most of the Hurricane squadrons were left behind on defensive duties, the exceptions being 73 Squadron (for night intruder operations) and 40 SAAF Squadron for tactical reconnaissance. From the 10th November through to the end of 1942, only 11 enemy aircraft were claimed by Hurricane squadrons in air combat, including eight JU-88s (five by 73 Squadron), for the loss of four Hurricanes (three of 40 SAAF Squadron), to BF109s.

From June 1940 to December 1942 inclusive, 549.5 enemy aircraft were claimed in combat by Hurricane pilots in the desert. Fairly accurate real loss figures of axis aircraft are available up to the end of June 1941. For this period, against a figure of 214 claimed, 95 enemy aircraft were actually shot down or force-landed. On the debit side, 682 Hurricanes were shot down, crash- or force-landed (between June 1940 and December 1942), of which 389 were in air combat. However, mention should be made of the excellent RAF Repair and Salvage organisation which recovered literally hundreds of aircraft, in particular Hurricanes, which had crashed or force-landed in the desert. Many of these aircraft were subsequently returned to service.

During the period of June to December 1942, inclusive, 102 claims were made by the Spitfire units engaged in operations over the desert (92, 145, 601 and 1 SAAF Squadrons, plus 103 Maintenance Unit), of which some 43 can be confirmed, for loss of 71 Spitfires, including 58 in air combat.

References

1   Or the Battle of Daba as it was less famously known.
2   Night fighters.
3   Only three Spitfire squadrons were available to the Western Desert Air Force.
4   Wrongly.
5   1 SAAF Squadron ORB.
5b   Pryde missing, Faure safe – 1 SAAF Squadron ORB.
6   6 Squadron ORB.
7a   213 Squadron ORB.
7b   HL613 of 213 Squadron failed to return – 213 Squadron ORB.

7c Flt. Sgt. Brook was reported missing – 213 Squadron ORB.
7d HL725 – 213 Squadron ORB.
7e BP583 and HL613 – 213 Squadron ORB.
7f One at least due to flak – 213 Squadron ORB.
8a HL774 – 274 Squadron ORB.
8b 274 Squadron ORB.
8c BE705 and BP438 – 274 Squadron ORB.
8d BH287. W.O. Neil was safe – 274 Squadron ORB.
9 Flt. Lt. Barlow was unhurt – 208 Squadron ORB.
10a 'L' – 238 Squadron ORB.
10b 'N' and 'U' – 238 Squadron ORB.
10c 'A' 'G' 'H' and 'T' – 238 Squadron ORB.
11a BP155 and BD834? – 335 (Greek) Squadron ORB.
11b 335 (Greek) Squadron ORB.
12a 33 Squadron ORB.
12b P.O. Maxwell – 33 Squadron ORB.
12c --354 and --501 – 33 Squadron ORB.
13a BN406, BP289, BP292, HL629, HL773 and HM130. Flt. Lt. Lannere?, P.O.s Melville and Rebman? and Sgts Mayze, Thomas and Andrews were all reported missing (ORB is not legible here) – 127 Squadron ORB.
13b 127 Squadron ORB.
14a BP337. Flt. Lt. Foskett was unhurt – 80 Squadron ORB.
14b 80 Squadron ORB.
14c BM985 – 80 Squadron ORB.
15 Three claimed by I/JG77 and one by flak.

CHAPTER SEVEN

East Africa

Although involving only small numbers of aircraft on both sides, the campaign in East Africa was fought over a vast area which included the Sudan, Eritrea, Abyssinia, Kenya, British and Italian Somaliland. At the start of the war with Italy in June 1940, the South African Air Force had only one fighter squadron, No.1 SAAF Squadron, equipped initially with Gladiators, based at Nairobi in Kenya and a flight of Hurricanes, which were based at Mombasa, for harbour protection.

In the first offensive fighter sorties on the 19th June, two Hurricanes took off before dawn to escort three JU-86 bombers in an attack on Yavello aerodrome in South-West Abyssinia. The raid was intercepted by Italian fighters and a CR-42 was claimed by Captain St Elmo 'Saint' Truter of 1 SAAF Squadron in one of the Hurricanes.[1] Unfortunately, the other Hurricane, flown by 2nd Lt. B.L. Griffiths was shot down by a fighter or by flak, the pilot being killed.

On the 1st October 1940, 1 SAAF Squadron's scattered detachments in Kenya were re-designated as 2 SAAF Squadron, equipment then comprising nine Furies, nine Gladiators and five Hurricanes. On 24th October, 3 SAAF Squadron, equipped with nine Hurricane 1s also arrived in Kenya. Next day, Flt. Lt. Robert Blake and Lt. D.H. Loftus of 2 SAAF Squadron borrowed two of 3 Squadron's Hurricanes and intercepted an Italian bombing raid over Lokitaung in Northern Kenya. Operating from the advanced landing ground at Lodwar, two of the three SM-81s were claimed and confirmed shot down, one to each pilot.

3 SAAF Squadron's first engagement was on the 22nd November, when three CA.133s raiding Bura were intercepted. One CA.133 was shot down by Lt. Allan and another crash-landed, having been attacked by 2nd Lts. Glover and Kershaw, the third being damaged by these two pilots.

On the 5th December, four Hurricanes left Kenya for 1 SAAF Squadron

East Africa

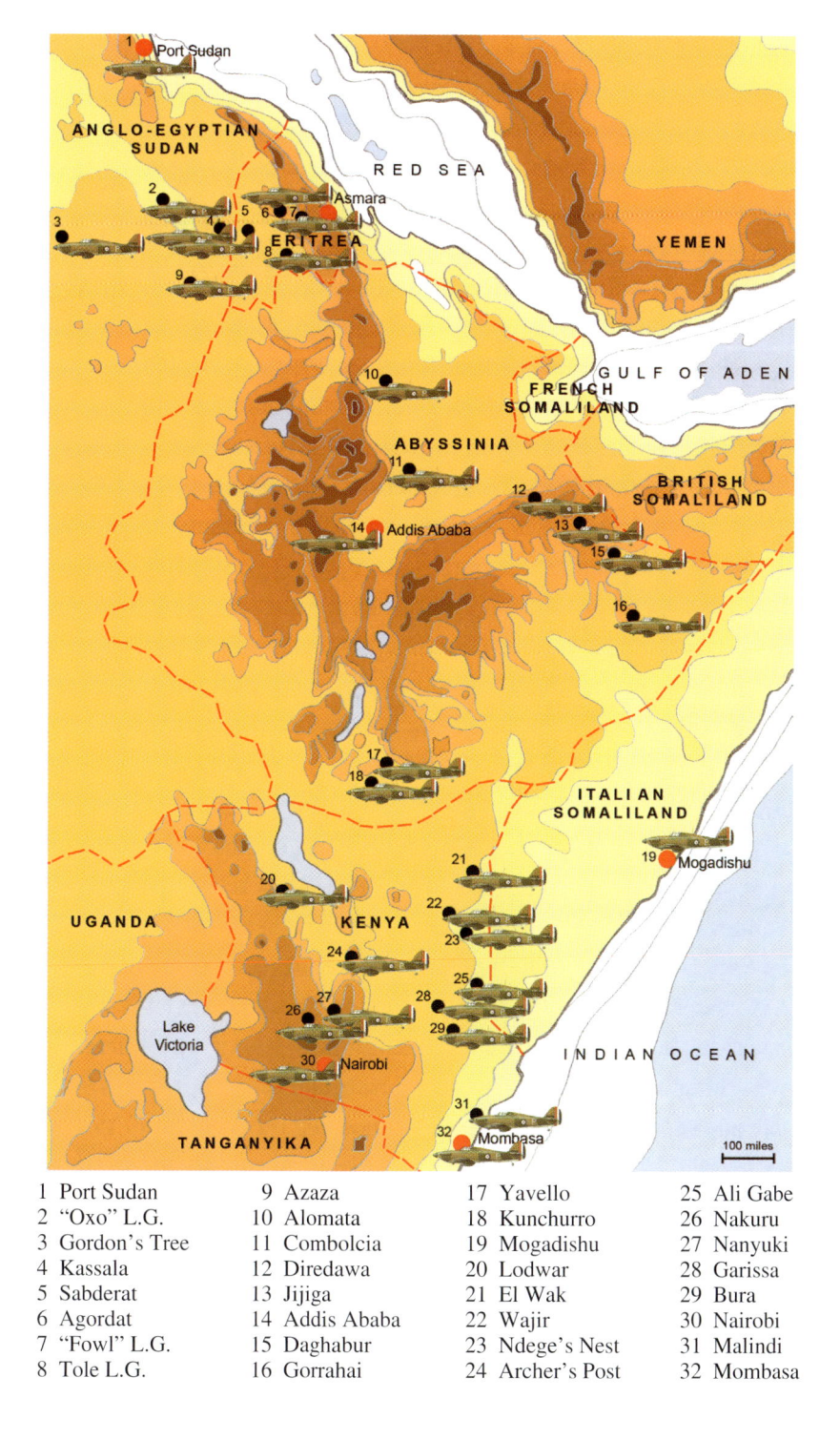

1 Port Sudan	9 Azaza	17 Yavello	25 Ali Gabe
2 "Oxo" L.G.	10 Alomata	18 Kunchurro	26 Nakuru
3 Gordon's Tree	11 Combolcia	19 Mogadishu	27 Nanyuki
4 Kassala	12 Diredawa	20 Lodwar	28 Garissa
5 Sabderat	13 Jijiga	21 El Wak	29 Bura
6 Agordat	14 Addis Ababa	22 Wajir	30 Nairobi
7 "Fowl" L.G.	15 Daghabur	23 Ndege's Nest	31 Malindi
8 Tole L.G.	16 Gorrahai	24 Archer's Post	32 Mombasa

in the Sudan. Although the air war had commenced in the north of the region on the 11th June 1940, only a small number of Gladiators had been available in the Sudan to counter the numerically superior Italian force that opposed them. Whilst the Gladiators had held their own, the Hurricanes would now give the imperial forces a decisive edge.

On the 16th December, two of the former 2 SAAF Squadron Hurricanes that had been flown up to Port Sudan by Major Wilmot and Captain Ken Driver of 1 SAAF Squadron engaged three SM-79s and claimed one shot down and another damaged.[2] Next day, another SM-79 was claimed damaged by Captain Driver.[3]

However, on the 29th December, four Hurricanes of 'A' flight of 2 SAAF Squadron left Ndege's Nest in Eastern Kenya to strafe the Italian aerodrome at Badera in Italian Somaliland. Three S81s were hit on the ground, one of which caught fire (the other two were claimed to be badly damaged), but three CR-42s took off from a nearby satellite airfield and shot down two of the Hurricanes. Lt. J.A. Cock was slightly wounded, whereas Flt. Lt. Bob Blake was more seriously wounded and both became PoWs until liberated later in the campaign. One of the CR-42s was claimed damaged by Lt. Colenbrander.

On the 22nd January, a formation of three CA.133 bombers was engaged late morning by 1 SAAF Squadron,[4] which was patrolling over 'Gazelle Force,' near Wachia-Keru. One of the CA.133s was jointly claimed by Lts. Burger and Coetzee in Hurricanes,[5] with another claimed damaged by Burger. That afternoon, Lts. Burger and Hewitson of 1 SAAF Squadron jointly claimed a CA.133 destroyed at Agordat airfield.

On the afternoon of the 29th January, an attack on Gura was made by 1 SAAF Squadron Gladiators with six Hurricanes of the same Squadron as top cover. One SM-79 was claimed shot down by Captain Driver and confirmed. An SM-79, or 81, was then strafed and destroyed on a field near Teramni, also by Driver.

Next day, further strafing attacks on Adi Agri and Teramni landing grounds by four Hurricanes of 1 SAAF Squadron resulted in two SM-79s being claimed destroyed on the ground.[6] On the last morning of January 1941, Captain Driver flew an escort mission from Sabdaret, engaging an

SM-79 which he claimed shot down.[7]

In the south, meanwhile, an offensive into Abyssinia had commenced on the 31st January. On the 2nd February, a CA.133 was strafed by Captain 'Jack' Frost of 3 SAAF Squadron at Afmadu and claimed destroyed. Next day, in a feat of outstanding airmanship, Captain Frost shot down three CA.133s and a CR-42 near Dif.[8] Later the same morning, in strafing attacks on Gobwen and its satellite airfield, three Hurricanes of 3 SAAF Squadron claimed three more CA.133s and two CR-42s destroyed on the ground. A CR-42 was also claimed in the north during the morning by Captain le Mesurier of 1 SAAF Squadron (either in a Gladiator or Hurricane).

On the 4th February, in a strafing attack on Bahar Dar airfield, another CA.133 was claimed destroyed by Captain Driver in a Hurricane of 1 SAAF Squadron.

The next 11 days proved very successful for 1 SAAF Squadron Hurricanes in air combat. On the 5th February, Captains Driver and Le Mesurier both claimed CR-42s shot down near Asmara landing ground.[9] On the 8th February, Driver claimed another CR-42, 40 kilometres west of Asmara airfield and two days later, Driver and Boyle both claimed CR-42s.[10]

On the 13th February, Lt. Duncan claimed a CR-42 South East of Asmara, seeing the pilot bail out. Major Wilmot and Captain Boyle also shared a claim for a CR-32, which was seen to crash East of Asmara, the pilot bailing out.[11] Both aircraft were admitted lost by the Italians.

Then on the 15th February, Captains Boyle and Driver each claimed CR-42s, Boyle's crash-landing in the Gura area and Driver's crashing on the southern edge of Asmara landing ground.[12]

Escorting a Wellesley raid on Gura airfield on the 16th February, six Hurricanes of 1 SAAF Squadron strafed the field, claiming two SM-79s destroyed on the ground. In two similar attacks on Asmara on the 19th, three SM-79s, three CR-42s and two CA.133s were claimed destroyed on the ground by 1 SAAF Squadron.[13]

Next, on the 21st February came an attack on Massawa, where a large number of CR-42s had been reported by reconnaissance. Six CA.133s and a CR-42 were claimed destroyed in the open, on the ground by the seven 1 SAAF Squadron Hurricanes.[14] Other aircraft were attacked in hangars on the airfield, the result being unknown. Unfortunately, a Hurricane[15] was shot down by flak during the attack, killing Lt. J.J. Coetzer.

Makale airfield was the target on the 23rd February, where, for the loss of another Hurricane[16] force-landed by a CR-32, five SM-79s and three CR-32s were claimed destroyed on the ground and a CR-32 was shot down by Lt. Andy Duncan of 1 SAAF Squadron. An S-82 transport was also claimed destroyed on the ground this day at Zula landing ground by Captain Duncan of the same Squadron.

By the end of February 1941, 1 SAAF Squadron was fully equipped with Hurricanes as the advance into Eritrea continued. On the 11th March, an SM-79 was claimed on fire at Keren aerodrome by Captain Driver and Lt. Hewitson of this squadron.

Meanwhile in Abyssinia, on the 13th March, Captain Veron of 3 SAAF Squadron engaged and claimed an SM-79[17] north-east of Dagah Bur and in company with Lt. Venter of the same Squadron, successfully shot down two CR-42s over Dagah Bur,[18] but a Hurricane (283) was shot down by the CR-42s, Lt. Dudley being killed.

Two days later, Diredawa Main and satellite airfield were attacked in the morning by six Hurricanes of 3 SAAF Squadron. In the air, two CR-32s and a CR-42 were claimed destroyed[19] and two SM-79s, one CA.133, two CR-32/42s/RO-37s and an RO-37 were claimed on the ground.

That afternoon at 1540 hrs, the raid was repeated, but two Hurricanes were shot down by flak, Captain Harvey being killed, although Captain Frost force-landed and was courageously rescued by Lt. Kershaw. Two SM-79s were claimed destroyed in the second attack on the ground at Diredawa Main airfield by Captain Theron. Five aircraft were admitted destroyed on the ground by the Italians.

Back in Eritrea, the assault on the mountain fortress of Keren had begun on the 15th March. In an attack on the Damba landing ground on the 17th, an S-82 was claimed destroyed on the ground by Lt. Pare of 1 SAAF Squadron. At 0530 hrs on the 18th March, five CR-42s, followed 20 minutes later by two SM-79s, attacked Agordat and destroyed a Hurricane[20] between them.

On the 21st March, early morning offensive patrols by two flights of three Hurricanes each in the Keren area met at least four CR-42s, three being claimed by 1 SAAF Squadron[21] and next day, two more CR-42s were claimed by this Squadron near Asmara as two Hurricanes engaged three CR-42s.[22]

In an attack on Diredawa on the 24th March, 3 SAAF Squadron claimed two SM-79s destroyed on the ground, while near Keren on the 25th March, two Hurricanes of 1 SAAF Squadron encountered two CR-42s, both of which were claimed shot down by Lt. Pare,[23] followed by another CR-42 next day, also near Keren.[24] Keren was taken on the 27th March.

In a surprise attack on Jijiga main airfield on the 29th March, a 3 SAAF Squadron Hurricane was destroyed on the ground by CR-42s and CR-32s, but in pursuit of the attackers, two CR-42s were claimed by Lt. Venter and Captain Frost of 3 SAAF Squadron. In fact, one CR-42 and a CR-32 were destroyed.

On the 31st March, in a patrol near Teclesan by two Hurricanes of 1 SAAF Squadron, one of three SM-79s encountered was wrongly claimed by Captain Driver, but the Hurricane flown by Lt. Van der Merwe[25] was hit by return fire from one of the SM-79s and shot down, Van der Merwe being killed.

Another Hurricane[26] of 1 SAAF Squadron was lost on take-off next day at Tole landing ground, 2nd Lt. Marais being killed. Asmara, the capital of Eritrea, fell the same day.

1 SAAF Squadron's final operation in East Africa was on the 5th April. Forty-eight enemy aircraft were claimed shot down by 1 SAAF Squadron (at least 21 by Hurricanes, of which nine can be confirmed) and a further 53 were claimed destroyed on the ground. Thirty-three of these are recorded above, of which 13 can be confirmed.

In support of the advance towards Addis Ababa, the Italian colonial capital of Abyssinia, a series of attacks on its airfield commenced on the 4th April. An SM-79 and a CA.133 were claimed destroyed on the ground by Captain Theron and Lt. Upton of 3 SAAF Squadron in the afternoon.

Next day, five SM-79s and three CA.133s were claimed destroyed at the same target by 3 SAAF Squadron.[27] Addis Ababa was occupied by allied troops on the 6th April, remaining Italian aircraft then being concentrated at Dessie, Jimma and Shashamanna airfields.

In an attack on Dessie airfield that day, three CR-42s, three SM-79s (or CA.133s) and a CA.133 were claimed destroyed on the ground by 3 SAAF Squadron.[28] Two CR-42s were also claimed shot down by 3 SAAF Squadron from a flight of three, returning from a front strafing mission.[29] The third aircraft force-landed.

Shashamanna and Jimma were the targets on the 10th April, where 11 ground victories were claimed by 3 SAAF Squadron.[30] In addition, a CR-42 and a CR-32 were claimed shot down, the former shared by Captain Frost and Lt. Howitson and the latter by Lts. Upton and Glover. All of the ground claims were acknowledged by the Italians as were the two air claims, although in fact they were both CR-32s.

At Jimma on the 13th April, an RO37 and a CA.133 were strafed and claimed burnt by Captain Frost of 3 SAAF Squadron,[31] while on the 16th, five CR-42s, a CR-32 and an SM-79 were claimed destroyed on the ground at Dessie.[32]

2 SAAF Squadron left East Africa on the 17th April, leaving 3 SAAF Squadron as the sole remaining operational fighter unit in the region.

On the 24th April, two CR-42s were set on fire in a hangar at Combolcia airfield,[33] but a 3 SAAF Squadron Hurricane (282) was shot down by flak at Jimma, Lt. Howitson being killed. Next day, a CA.133 was set on fire by Lt. Glover of 3 SAAF Squadron at Bonaia airfield near Lekemti. Dessie fell on the 27th April and on the 30th, an SM-79 was claimed shot down by Captain Frost. He also set a CR-32 on fire at Jimma.

3 SAAF Squadron had now claimed 25 air (17 are known and recorded above) and 77 ground victories.[34] The sole remaining ground claim in the campaign by Hurricanes was the CA.133 ambulance aircraft at Jimma on the 19th May by Lt. Upton of 3 SAAF Squadron. This aircraft had been used as a bomber. Five SAAF Squadron Hurricanes were, however, subsequently lost to various causes up to mid-August 1941. At least 48 air combat victories were claimed by the three SAAF Hurricane squadrons in the East African campaign, against five, or possibly six, Hurricanes lost to enemy aircraft in combat. Twenty-one of the air claims can be confirmed.[35] Captain Ken Driver was the top scoring South African Air Force pilot of this campaign with nine victories and one damaged, plus four ground claims (one shared).

References

1 This was actually a CR-32 and was the first enemy aircraft shot down by the South African Air Force in this campaign.
2 Driver claimed an SM-79 destroyed, from which two crewmen were seen to bail out. Wilmot's claim was for a damaged SM-79 with one engine on fire.
3 One of this SM-79's engines was claimed to have been stopped by Driver.
4 1 Squadron formation comprised two Gladiators and two Hurricanes.
5 Four crewmen were seen to bail out.
6 In reality three SM-81s were destroyed.
7 The pilot and four other crewmen were seen to bail out.
8 The three CA.133s and CR-42 were all confirmed, 11 prisoners being taken.
9 A formation of four Hurricanes and two Gladiators had engaged Six CR-42s.
10 Six Hurricanes on an offensive patrol met five CR-42s near Asmara. The pilot was seen to bail out of Boyle's CR-42 claim.
11 Five Hurricanes on patrol over Asmara met four CR-42s just before 1300hrs.
12 Three Hurricanes on an offensive patrol to Gura met three CR-42s, then four Hurricanes and two Gladiators on offensive patrol to Asmara met six CR-42s. One CR-42 was claimed in each patrol.
13 One CR-42, one SM-79 and two CA.133s were actually lost by the Italians.
14 In fact, three CA.133s and two SM-81s were lost by the Italians.
15 This was V7658.
16 V7733? Major Wilmot was captured and became a PoW.
17 This claim was in error – the SM-79 returned to its base.
18 Captain Theron and Lt. Venter each shot down a CR-42. One pilot was seen to bail out but later died.
19 Captains Frost and Theron each claimed a CR-32 and the CR-42 was a shared claim by Lts. Morley and Venter. In fact, three CR-32s had engaged the Hurricanes and all landed safely, although one was a

forced landing.
20. This was V7471.
21. One by Captain Driver and two by Lt. Pare. Both of Pare's claims were seen to bail out.
22. One by Lt. Theron and the other by Lt. White.
23. One pilot was seen to bail out.
24. By Major Theron of 1 SAAF Squadron.
25. This may have been V7733.
26. This was V7668.
27. Captain Frost claimed four SM-79s and two CA.133; Lt. Kershaw claimed one SM-79 and one CA.133.
28. Captain Frost claimed two SM-79s and two CR-42s; Lt. Glover claimed a CA.133; Captain Veron, Lt. Van Ginkel and Lt. Venter jointly claimed an SM-79 and a CR-42. Nine aircraft were admitted destroyed by the Italians, though not all were by Hurricanes.
29. One CR-42 was claimed by Captain Veron and the other by Lt. Van Ginkel. One of the pilots was seen to bail out.
30. At Shashamanna, Lt. Howitson claimed two S.81s and Captain Frost claimed two CA.133s. At Jimma, Captain Frost claimed a CA.133 and a CR-32; Lts. Glover, Marsh and Upton each claimed a CA.133 and Lt. Howitson claimed two enemy aircraft.
31. The CA.133 was actually a CA.148.
32. Captain Frost claimed two CR-42s and one CR-32, Lt. Howitson claimed three CR-42s and one SM-79.
33. By Captain Veron and Lt. Venter.
34. Fifty-eight of the ground claims are recorded in the above text, of which 24 can be confirmed.
35. This total includes six CR-42s, six CR-32s, two S.81s; two SM-79s and five CA.133s.

NOTE: The primary source of the above text was *Springbok Fighter Victory, Volume 1*, by Michael Schoeman.

Chapter Eight
Dunkirk

The RAF's performance over Dunkirk during 'Operation Dynamo', as the evacuation from Dunkirk was known, was seen as a victory by both commanders and politicians alike. Lasting for nine days from the 26th May to the 3rd June inclusive, this was the first major operation in which both the Spitfire and Hurricane were involved and both aeroplanes achieved very similar claims to loss ratios. However, there was inevitably much over-claiming and only 33 Luftwaffe aircraft can be confirmed lost to Hurricanes during the period of the evacuation.

On the first day of the evacuation, Sunday 26th May, single JU-88s were claimed by each of 17,[1] 32[2] and 605 Squadrons,[3] the latter two being confirmed – aircraft of 7 and 9/KG54.

605 Squadron also claimed a DO-17[4] and 17 Squadron, a BF109.[5] The only other claim this day was for an He 111 by P.O. Parrott of 145 Squadron. None of these can be confirmed from German records. However, a DO-17P of 3 (F)/10 was shot down near Gravelines by Flt. Lt. Adye, P.O.s Whittaker and Manger and possibly Flt. Lt. Toyne of 17 Squadron, having only been claimed as damaged.

In return, four Hurricanes were downed – one of 17 Squadron[6] failed to return, Flt. Sgt. Jones being killed; another of 17 Squadron[7] was shot down by BF109s;[8] a 605 Squadron Hurricane[9] was shot down by a BF110, P.O. Muirhead being unhurt and P.O. Parrott of 145 Squadron[10] was force-landed near Dover by the He 111 that he claimed, Parrott also being unhurt and the aircraft being repairable.

The tempo increased the next day with several Hurricane squadrons claiming impressive victory scores. Squadron Leader Knowles of 56 Squadron claimed an He 111 near Ostend and another was shared by three of the Squadron's pilots.[11] Later the same afternoon, Knowles claimed two BF110s,[12] but three Hurricanes[13] were lost to flak. F.O. Fisher was wounded, the other pilots being unhurt.

213 Squadron claimed four BF109s[14] near Gravelines without loss, those claimed by Wight both being confirmed from 5/JG2. 79 Squadron claimed five BF110s and two probables[15] again without loss, but none of these can be confirmed.

Other Hurricane squadrons were less successful on this day. 601 Squadron claimed three BF110 and two probables[16] and two BF109s,[17] none of which can be confirmed, for two Hurricanes[18] shot down. F.O. Lee-Steere was killed in one.

145 Squadron claimed three BF110s plus two more 110s or JU-88s[19] but lost six aircraft shot down[20] with three pilots killed; P.O. Elsen, Sgt. Bailey and P.O. Rainier. None of the claims can be confirmed, but the BF110s were possibly from ZG52. 605 Squadron lost three Hurricanes[21] without scoring. Sqn. Ldr. Perry and F.O. Danielson were killed and F.O. Forbes became a PoW. A DO-17 was also claimed by Flt. Lt. Meredith of 17 Squadron and confirmed, while another claimed as damaged by Sgt. Steward was also lost, both of these aircraft coming from 9/KG2.

213 Squadron was again in the thick of things next day, claiming five BF109s[22] a BF110 and a JU-88,[23] but losing five Hurricanes.[24] P.O. Stone and Flt. Lt. Winning were killed, Sgt. Lishman was wounded, whereas F.O. Boyd and Sgt. Butterfield were unhurt. Only one BF109 of 8/JG3 can be confirmed to 213 Squadron – the claim by Flt. Lt. Wright.

A BF109 was also claimed by 229 Squadron for the loss of one aircraft[25] and its pilot, Sgt. Hillman, who was killed. P.O.s Turner and Willie McKnight of 242 Squadron claimed a BF109 each[26] for the loss of two Hurricanes.[27] P.O. Jones was killed, whereas P.O. Deacon was taken prisoner. None of these claims can be confirmed.

213 Squadron's prolific scoring continued on Wednesday the 29th May. Sgt. Llewellyn claimed two BF109s, an He 111 and a probable, while Flt. Sgt. Grayson claimed a JU-87 and an He 111 probable and P.O. Atkinson another He 111 probable, without any loss. Four He 111Hs of KG1 were actually lost in this engagement.

However, 229 Squadron suffered a heavy defeat on this day, losing five Hurricanes[28] to BF109s, while claiming two 109s.[29] Flt. Lts. Clouston and

Brown and Sgt. Harrison were killed, while F.O. New and P.O. Linney were unhurt.

56 Squadron also lost two aircraft[30] while claiming two BF109s[31] and a JU-87.[32] The two BF109s were from I/JG27 and were confirmed lost.

P.O. McKnight of 242 Squadron claimed a BF109 and a DO-17, other BF109s being claimed by Flt. Lt. Plinston, P.O. MacQueen and P.O. Latta of that Squadron which lost a Hurricane[33] in a take-off crash, injuring P.O. Howitt. None of the claims can be confirmed.

151 Squadron claimed a BF110[34] near the French coast and a JU-88[35] for two Hurricanes lost,[36] in which F.O. Newton was unhurt and P.O. Courtney wounded. The JU-88 was confirmed as an aircraft from 6/LG1.

P.O. Manger of 17 Squadron claimed a DO-215, which crashed in a field south of Calais and F.O. Harper of the same Squadron claimed a BF110 without loss to this unit. A BF110C of 5/ZG76 was believed lost in this attack.

It has been reported that, wherever possible, Squadrons were being advised to operate in wing formations, rather than as single units, to counter the large German formations they were encountering. However, whether this advice came from Group/Sector level,[37] or from within the Squadrons themselves, is not clear.

The 30th May marked the mid-point in the evacuation and was a day of reduced air combat. A DO-17 was claimed by Blue Section of 213 Squadron and another by Flt. Lt. Norman of 245 Squadron.[38] The DO-17 claimed by 213 Squadron was confirmed as being from 5(F)/122, while a I/KG3 machine was confirmed to 245 Squadron. Although no Hurricanes were lost this day, three of 245 Squadron's aircraft[39] were forced to land after combat.

The action increased again next day and 213 Squadron was again heavily involved, claiming six BF109s[40] but losing five Hurricanes.[41] Flt. Lt. Wight claimed two BF109s, Sgt. Butterfield claimed one and a probable and Sgt. Norris, P.O. Sizer and F.O. Robinson each claimed one. F.O. Gray and Sgt. Boyd were killed, the other pilots[42] being unhurt. Two BF109E-1s of JG26 were actually lost to 213 Squadron or 264 Squadron Defiants.

111 Squadron also claimed impressively – five BF109s, two He 111s

and a JU-88 – but without loss. BF109s were claimed by F.O.s Ferriss and Bruce, P.O. Walker and Sgts Craig and Brown, while Sgt. Dymond claimed the two He 111s. The JU-88 was claimed by Sgt. Robinson and was possibly an aircraft of 7/KG4 that ditched offshore.

242 Squadron recorded claims for three BF110s,[43] one JU-88[44] and a DO-17,[45] for one Hurricane[46] lost to a BF109, P.O. Stewart being killed. Three BF109s of JG20 were actually downed by 242 Squadron this day, while a JU-88 of 8/KG4 that was lost may be Plinston's claim.

229 Squadron claimed four BF110s,[47] for two Hurricanes[48] shot down by BF110s, Sgt. Edgehill being wounded. The only other Hurricane loss this day was a 245 Squadron machine[49] that force-landed without injury to the pilot. Other claims were made by P.O. Manger of 17 Squadron[50] and Flt. Lt. Dutton of 145 Squadron[51] without loss to these squadrons. Manger's claim was an aircraft of 2/JG26 which crashed west of Nieuport, while a BF109 of Stab I/JG26 was believed to be the shared 145 Squadron claim.

The 1st June saw the highest claims of the evacuation by Hurricane squadrons. A total of 14 BF109s[52] were claimed by 43 Squadron,[53] 245 Squadron,[54] 145 Squadron[55] and 242 Squadron,[56] a further eight BF109s[57] being claimed by Spitfire squadrons. However, only two BF109s of 6/JG26 can actually be attributed to 43, 145 and 245 Squadrons.

For 43 Squadron, BF109 claims were made by Flt. Lt. Simpson,[58] Sgt. Ottewill,[59] Sgt. Hallowes,[60] F.O. Edmunds and a probable each to F.O. Wilkinson and P.O. Woods-Scaven. Succesful 245 Squadron pilots included P.O. Southwell,[61] P.O.s Edward-Hill and Redman, while P.O. Mowat claimed two probables. Flt. Lt. Dutton claimed two BF109s for 145 Squadron and Flt. Lt. Miller of 242 Squadron claimed two probables, one more being claimed by P.O. Turner of the same Squadron.

In addition, six BF110s were claimed by 145 Squadron,[62] four BF110s[63] by 43 Squadron and three JU-87s[65] and two BF110s by 242 Squadron. A single JU-87 was also claimed by P.O. Smith of 229 Squadron[67] and a JU-88 probable by 151 Squadron. No BF110s can be confirmed to Hurricane Squadrons, but two JU-87Bs of TrGr.186 were lost in combats which included 229 and 242 Squadrons.[68]

Six Hurricanes were lost – two each by 43[69] and 245 Squadrons[70] and single aircraft by 17[71] and 145 Squadrons.[72] Pilot losses included Sgt. Gough,[73] P.O.s West and Treanor[74] and P.O. Dixon,[75] all killed in action.

Next day, 111 Squadron was in action again, F.O. Ferriss claiming one BF109 and a probable, F.O. Powell claiming a BF109, P.O. Simpson a BF110 probable, and Flt. Lt. Connors and F.O. Bruce each claiming an He 111 probable. One of 111 Squadron's Hurricanes[76] was shot down by a BF110, although P.O. Wilson was unhurt. Sqn. Ldr. Donaldson of 151 Squadron claimed a BF110 and a probable was also claimed by an unknown pilot of that unit, as was a JU-87 probable, while P.O. Smythe of 32 Squadron claimed a JU-88 and a BF109 probable. Sgt. Flynn of that Squadron was shot down[77] and taken prisoner. None of the Luftwaffe losses this day can be confirmed to Hurricanes.

The 3rd June was the last day of the evacuation and only one claim was made, for a JU-87 by P.O. Hanson of 17 Squadron,[78] while a Hurricane[79] of 17 Squadron was shot down by BF109s of 5/JG3, its pilot, F.O. Meredith being killed.

Fourteen Hurricane Squadrons made air combat claims over and around Dunkirk. 213 Squadron was the top scorer with 19 confirmed kills, followed by 242 Squadron,[80] 145 Squadron,[81] 43 Squadron[82] and 111 Squadron.[83]

Top scoring Hurricane pilot of the nine days of Operation Dynamo was Willie McKnight of 242 Squadron, with seven victories, closely followed by Flt. Lt. Wight,[84] with six.

References
1   P.O. Bird-Wilson.
2   Flt. Lt. Crossley.
3   P.O. Cooper-Slipper.
4   F.O. Edge.
5   P.O. Whittaker.
6   N2528.
7   P3483.
8   Flt. Lt. Adye was missing.

9   N2346.
10 In N2589.
11 Both confirmed.
12 Several were lost.
13 P3311, P3355 and P3478.
14 Flt. Lt. Wight (2), Flt. Lt. Winning and P.O. Atkinson.
15 F.O. Davies – one+one probable; P.O. Stones – one+one probable; F.O. Duus, P.O. Clift and P.O. Steven – one each
16 P.O. McGrath – one+one; F.O.s Hubbard and Clyde – one each and F.O. Cleaver – one probable.
17 Flt. Lt. Robinson (two).
18 P3486 and P2568?
19 Flt. Lt. Boyd - two+one; P.O. Storrar (one) and P.O. Forde – one unconfirmed.
20 N2710, N2711, N2713, P2713?, P2723 and P3314.
21 L2119, P3423 and P3581.
22 Sgt. Butterfield (two), Flt. Lt. Wight, Sgt. Lishman and P.O. Atkinson.
23 Both by Sgt. Butterfield.
24 P2721, P2792, P2817, P2834 and P3354.
25 N2551.
26 Plus one probable by Flt. Lt. Miller.
27 L1746 and N2651.
28 N2473, N2521, P2636, P2876 and P3489.
29 One by P.O. Clifford Brown, but none confirmed.
30 L1972 and N2659.
31 By F.O. Greminsky and Flt. Sgt. Higginson.
32 By Sgt. Smythe.
33 L1756.
34 P.O. Blomeley.
35 Shared by Sqn. Ldr. Donaldson and P.O. Kamar.
36 P3303 and P3321.
37 Or above.
38 Plus two probables by P.O.s Southwell and Pennington.
39 N2496, N2709 and P2597.

40 Plus one probable.
41 P2763, P3361, P3419, P3424 and P3482.
42 Sqn. Ldr. McGregor, F.O. Robinson and P.O. Sizer.
43 P.O. Stansfeld claimed one, which crashed onto the beach and P.O. Willie McKnight claimed two.
44 Flt. Lt. Plinston.
45 P.O. Mac Queen.
46 P2732.
47 None of which can be confirmed.
48 L1982 and P3553.
49 N2702.
50 One BF109.
51 Two BF109s – one shared with P.O. Newling.
52 Plus eight probables.
53 Seven plus three.
54 Four plus two.
55 Three.
56 Three probables.
57 Plus two probables.
58 Two.
59 Two.
60 Two plus a probable.
61 Two.
62 Flt. Lt. Boyd (two), Flt. Lt. Dutton, P.O.s Yule, Newling and Weir one each.
63 Plus one probable.
64 F.O. Edmonds, Sgt. Hallowes and two unknown pilots – one each, Sqn. Ldr. Lott claiming the probable.
65 Plus two probables.
66 Willie McKnight claimed two of the Stukas and P.O. Stansfeld the other, north-west of Dunkirk harbour; P.O. Turner claimed a BF110.
67 Plus two probables – one by P.O. Bary.
68 Plus Spitfires.
69 N2584 and L1758.

70	N2658 and N2709.
71	P3476.
72	P2952.
73	Of 43 Squadron.
74	Of 245 Squadron.
75	Of 145 Squadron.
76	L1564.
77	In P2727.
78	None was reported lost.
79	P3477.
80	Seventeen.
81	Fifteen.
82	Eleven.
83	Nine.
84	213 Squadron.

Chapter Nine

Battle of Norway

The German interest in Scandinavia and its material resources was well-known to the British Government. The build-up of invasion forces by the Germans in early April 1940 prompted plans to be initiated by the British to counter the expected imminent invasion. An expeditionary force was planned to be despatched to Norway, in order to control the Baltic and prevent the Germans from seizing valuable materials. However, on the 9th April, the Germans landed their forces in Southern Norway before the British Carrier Group set sail. In response, the first Anglo-French landing was at Harstad, near Narvik in the north of the country on the 15th April.

The 18 Hurricanes of 46 Squadron flew from the carrier H.M.S. *Glorious* to Skaanland, in Norway, on the 26th May 1940. Their role was to protect the amphibious forces landing at Narvik.

> *'The first flight landed at Skaanland at 2130 hrs – one accident occurred due to the soft surface of the aerodrome.'*[1]

On arrival of the second flight, another accident occurred for the same reason and the decision was then made to send the remaining aircraft to Bardufoss, 60 miles north. These aircraft arrived safely at Bardufoss. The Hurricanes had no ground radar to assist them and had to fly wasteful standing patrols, in order to give adequate protection to the land and naval forces.

On the 28th May, on a three-aircraft patrol[2] F.O. Lydall destroyed a JU-88 of 6/KG30 over Tjelboten. Early evening the same day[3] another section of three Hurricanes attacked two DO-26 flying boats on Rombaksfjord, as they disembarked troops.

> *Both machines burst into flames.*[4]

NORWEGIAN SEA
Tromso
Senja
Bardufoss
Skaanland
FINLAND
Hinnoya
Narvik
SWEDEN
Trondheim
NORWAY
Bergen
Oslo
50 Miles

This was great airmanship, as the enemy aircraft were moored under the edge of a cliff at a very narrow part of the fjord.[5]

At 0040 hrs on the 29th May, Flt. Lt. Jameson claimed a JU-88 and P.O. Drummond claimed an He 111, but Drummond was shot down by return fire from the Heinkel. Both victories were confirmed by H.M.S. *Firedrake*, which also rescued Drummond. At 1540 hrs the same day, P.O. Banks claimed a 'four-engined Junkers' which was bombing Tromso.

> *'In the evening, 26 enemy aircraft approached Vestfjord from the South and split up into formations of five aircraft. Nine 46 Squadron aircraft were on patrol at the same time and in the subsequent encounters with superior forces, F.O. Lydall and P.O. Banks were shot down and killed. Flt. Sgt. Shackley shot down one JU-88[6] and two more enemy aircraft were destroyed, probably by F.O. Lydall[7] and P.O. Banks.'*[4]

Four Hurricanes were lost this day,[8] three at least to He 111s.

The next combat was on the 2nd June, when Sgt. Taylor and P.O. Drummond, on patrol over Narvik, spotted two JU-87s dive-bombing a destroyer.

> *'They attacked and 87s separated and made off, twisting and turning. The pilots waited for their chance and shot them down south-east of Narvik. The gunner of the JU-87 that Drummond attacked used the rear gun after this aircraft had crashed.'*[4]

A further Hurricane[9] was lost this day when it suffered a collapsed undercarriage on landing at Skaanland, but the pilot was safe.

Next day, the weather was bad. Two patrols were attempted but not completed. On the 4th June, seven patrols were flown and on the 5th, patrols were carried out over Narvik and Harstad.

On the 6th June, patrols were carried out over Narvik, Skaanland, Lodingen and Harstad. Two aircraft also provided an escort for five Walruses bombing in the neighbourhood of Norfold.

The last actions of this short campaign occurred on the 7th June. Two early morning patrols this day[10] resulted in F.O. Knight and P.O. Drummond each claiming an He 111, while Squadron Leader Cross and P.O. Lefevre shared another.

> *'At 1810 and 1815 F.O. Mee and P.O. Drummond returned from a patrol over Narvik, during which they had engaged four He 111s. Each pilot claimed to have shot down one enemy aircraft and P.O. Drummond attacked and damaged the other two.'*[4]

These claims gave 46 Squadron a total of 14 enemy aircraft claimed destroyed in the air, plus two on a fjord. Four Hurricanes had been lost in combat and a further three had been wrecked on landing (the fate of one more is unknown). P.O. Drummond was the top 46 Squadron scorer in this campaign, with a creditable four enemy aircraft.

> *'The pilots were warned that they would have to evacuate Norway that night and volunteers were asked to fly on to H.M.S. Glorious. 100% volunteered.'*[4]

Extra weight was carried in the tail of each Hurricane, to prevent them bouncing on landing.

The surviving 10 Hurricanes were re-embarked on H.M.S. *Glorious* on the 7th and 8th June, a tremendously difficult task without arrestor hooks, but tragically, all were subsequently lost on the 8th,[11] when the battle cruisers *Scharnhorst* and *Gneisenau* found and sank H.M.S. *Glorious*.

Eight of 46 Squadron's pilots were lost with *Glorious*.[12] Only two pilots survived, having been rescued after three days adrift – Squadron Leader Cross, the C.O. and Flt. Lt. Jameson. However, other pilots had left earlier on the Arandora Star merchantman.

References

1. Sqn. Ldr. Cross had also bent his airscrew on landing, but the aircraft was repaired. 46 Squadron ORB.
2. From 1015 to 1205 hrs. 46 Squadron ORB.
3. From 1715 to 1900 hrs. 46 Squadron ORB.
4. 46 Squadron ORB.
5. *Hurricane: The War Exploits of the Fighter Aircraft*, by Adrian Stewart.
6. Which he confirmed with his own cine photos.
7. This was confirmed by the crew of three of an He 111 who said they had been shot down by a 'Spitfire' three miles south of Andenes Point.
8. Including L1816, L1988 and L1794?
9. N2543.
10. From 0340 to 0455 hrs and from 0350 to 0420 hrs. 46 Squadron ORB.
11. Serials were L1853, L1961, P2632, P2633, L1793, L1804, L1805. L1806, L1815 and L1980.
12. Flt. Lt. Stewart, F.O. Cowles, F.O. Frost, F.O. Knight, F.O. Mee, P.O. Bunker, Sgt. Shackley and Sgt. Taylor.

Chapter Ten

Battle of Britain

The Battle of Britain was, arguably, the Hurricanes' finest hour. It is common knowledge that Hurricanes shot down more enemy aircraft than the rest of Britain's defences combined. A total of 1,392 were claimed by Hurricane Squadrons in the four months of the battle, whereas 1,065 claims were submitted by Spitfire Squadrons. In reality, of course, there was much over-claiming in the heat of the battle and in the final analysis, 661 enemy aircraft were credited to Hurricane Squadrons and 518 to Spitfire units.

Much has been written about the Battle of Britain and it is not the purpose of this book to repeat old material or analysis. The principal reason for the Hurricane's position as the most effective air defender was the number available. In 11 Group, which bore the brunt of the battle, there were 16 Squadrons of Hurricanes available on the 1st July 1940, against only eight Squadrons of Spitfires. On the 1st September, despite some re-organisation, there were still 14 Hurricane Squadrons in 11 Group and only six of Spitfires.

A total of 1,715 Hurricanes flew with Fighter Command during the Battle of Britain, far in excess of all other British fighters combined. This fact was due entirely to a fateful decision made by T.O.M. Sopwith and the other members of the board of directors of Hawker Aircraft in March 1936. Before any production contract for Hurricanes was forthcoming by the Air Ministry, the board of Hawkers decided to commence production scheduling. As a result, Hawkers were able to issue production drawings to the shops only five days after receipt of the first Air Ministry contract, for 600 aircraft, on the 3rd June 1936. Production was thus started 3 months earlier than it otherwise would have been.

The crucial nature of this decision can be seen by the fact that at the start of the battle, Hurricane production was running at over 400 aircraft per quarter year. A similar number of Hurricanes[1] had already been lost

Battle of Britain

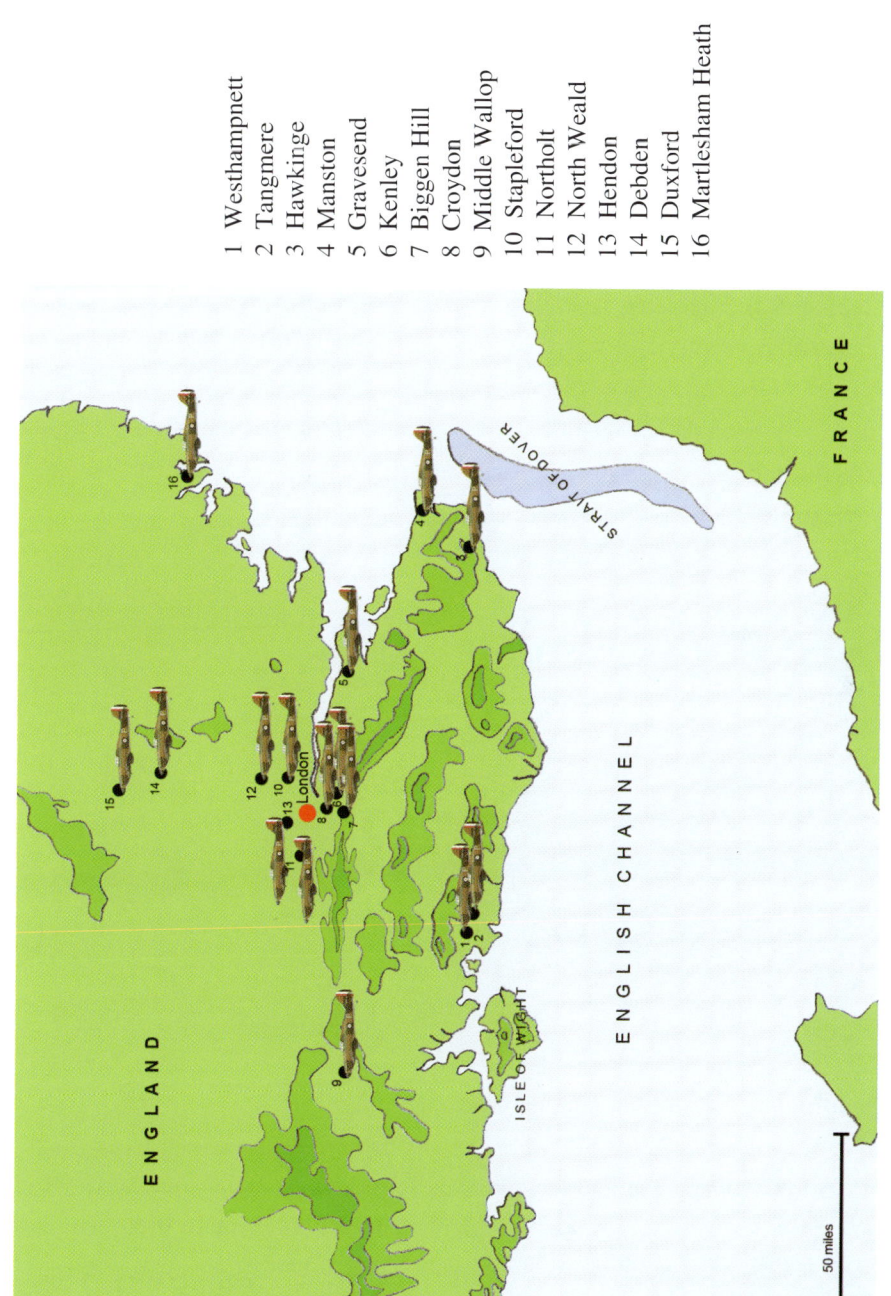

1 Westhampnett
2 Tangmere
3 Hawkinge
4 Manston
5 Gravesend
6 Kenley
7 Biggen Hill
8 Croydon
9 Middle Wallop
10 Stapleford
11 Northolt
12 North Weald
13 Hendon
14 Debden
15 Duxford
16 Martlesham Heath

Hurricane bases in South-East England during the Battle of Britain

during the Blitzkrieg of May and June 1940 in France, so if the Royal Air Force had had a further 400 Hurricanes fewer available during the battle, it seems highly likely that the outcome would have been very different. The three months that the decision by Hawkers bought the defences were vital in ensuring that sufficient fighters were available to meet the German onslaught.

In addition, the Hurricane was 'right technically'. It needed minimal testing and was approved by the Aircraft and Armament Experimental Establishment[2] in a few weeks. It was easy to build, making use of tried and familiar manufacturing techniques developed at the Hawker factory for the earlier and very successful series of 'beautiful biplanes'. The Spitfire, by contrast, was a more complex aeroplane to build, having a light metal stressed-skin monocoque structure. It was also less robust than the Hurricane and not able to sustain as much battle damage.

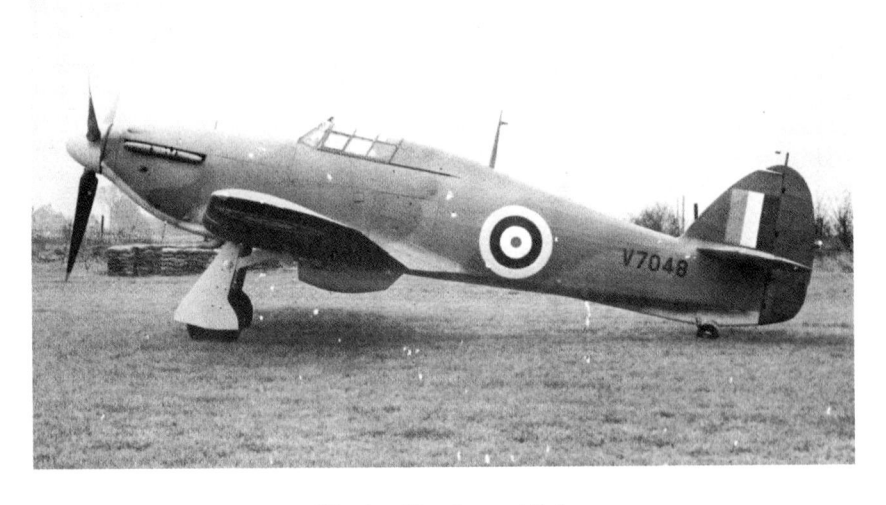

Hawker Hurricane Mk.1.

The Spitfire was also subjected to a longer and more intensive pre-production test programme than the Hurricane, another factor that resulted in fewer Spitfires being available in the summer of 1940.

Although the Battle of Britain officially started on the 10th July, a day when enemy aerial activity certainly increased, the first nine days of July had resulted in 20 German aircraft being claimed by Hurricane Squadrons, for the loss of 11 Hurricanes, although only six of the Hurricanes were lost in combat. Fourteen of the claimed victories were, in fact, confirmed, only one of which was a BF109.

During July as a whole, 173 enemy aircraft were claimed by Hurricane Squadrons, of which 75 were actually lost. In return, 61 Hurricanes were lost, but 32 of these losses were in accidents. One-hundred-and-fifty-six German aircraft were claimed by Spitfire Squadrons during the month, of which 71 are confirmed, for 50 Spitfires lost.[3]

Hurricane of 245 Squadron – Aldergrove.

79 Squadron had suffered heavily in the previous two months and was withdrawn to Acklington in July, to rest and train new pilots. It was not to be the last Hurricane Squadron withdrawn from 11 Group during the battle.

August was the month when the major air assault really started. The first seven days of the month saw only limited aerial combat, but on the 8th August, determined attacks were made against a channel convoy, codenamed 'Peewit'. Having claimed only seven enemy aircraft from the 1st to the 7th August for the loss of five Hurricanes,[4] 23 German aircraft were claimed by Hurricane squadrons on the 8th,[5] but 14 Hurricanes were shot down.

Although 'Adler Tag', the start of the campaign to eliminate the Royal Air Force by attacking its airfields, was to have commenced on the 10th August, unfavourable weather caused its postponement to the 13th August. The airfield attacks on this day caused few problems for fighter command – only one Spitfire being destroyed on the ground. In return, 45 enemy aircraft were claimed by Hurricane squadrons[6] for the loss of 12 Hurricanes.

The next day saw the withdrawal of two more Hurricane Squadrons to quieter sectors. 145 Squadron had lost five Hurricanes on the 8th, a further four on the 11th and three on the 12th. 238 Squadron had lost three on the 8th, four on the 11th and two on the 13th and was replaced by 249 Squadron in 10 Group.

The 15th of August saw the heaviest day's fighting of the entire battle, with concentrated attacks against the north as well as the south of England. At least 106 enemy aircraft were claimed by Hurricane squadrons[7] for the loss of 18 Hurricanes. Only 52 claims were made by Spitfire squadrons[8] for the loss of 11 Spitfires. A total of 79 German aircraft were lost on this day to all causes.

Three days later, on the 18th August, came the decisive defeat of the JU-87 'Stuka' dive-bomber in this campaign. On this day, 14 Stukas were claimed by Hurricane squadrons and 15 by Spitfire units, although in reality, a total of 18 were lost.[9] The Stuka was withheld from major[10] attacks in the Battle of Britain after this date.

The marginal weather of the next five days resulted in sporadic raids of a lesser strength, but on the 24th August, the crucial period of the battle commenced, a two-week period during which Fighter Command had to fight for its very survival. From the 24th August to the 6th September, 323 claims were made by Hurricane units, as against 233 by Spitfires. In reality, 154 enemy aircraft can be confirmed to Hurricanes and 70 to Spitfires. Hurricanes were thus responsible for destroying more than twice as many Luftwaffe aircraft as were Spitfires in this most decisive phase of the Battle of Britain. One-hundred-and-sixty-one Hurricanes were lost in this period and 109 Spitfires.

Another Hurricane Squadron was relieved from 11 Group on the 27th August. 32 Squadron, which had lost 15 Hurricanes between the 12th and 25th, including four on the 18th and five on the 24th, was withdrawn; its place in the line was taken by 79 Squadron. This was followed on the 29th August by 615 Squadron, which had only 10 remaining Hurricanes, having lost 16 between the 14th and the 28th August.[11] 253 Squadron replaced 615 Squadron in 11 Group. Then, on the 1st September, 56 and 151 Squadrons were removed from 11 Group to quieter sectors. 56 Squadron had suffered 23 Hurricanes lost from the 11th August to the end of that month[12] while 151 Squadron had lost 15 during the same period. 85 Squadron was next to go, on the 3rd September, with eight aircraft left, the Squadron having lost 17 Hurricanes from the 18th August to the 1st September.

The tactical change by the Luftwaffe to attack London on the 7th September has been widely recorded as a great mistake that relieved the pressure on Fighter Command. It was also seen as somewhat of a surprise to the defenders, but nevertheless, 52 claims were made by Hurricane Squadrons this day as against 25 by Spitfire Squadrons. Due to the large number of aircraft engaged in combat, it has not proved possible to attribute claims to actual losses by the Luftwaffe on the 7th, but 41 German aircraft were lost, 16 of which were BF109s. Seventeen Hurricanes and 15 Spitfires were also lost.

Another relatively quiet period followed this massive assault, from the 8th to the 14th September and then, on the 15th September the battle reached its crescendo.[13]

The tremendous air battles that occurred during further major attacks on London resulted in a claim by Fighter Command of 185 enemy aircraft being broadcast by the BBC, although in fact, 124 were claimed by Hurricane Squadrons and 72 by Spitfire Squadrons. Again, due to the large numbers of aircraft involved, accurately tying losses to claims is impossible, but the Germans lost 60 aircraft. Twenty-one Hurricanes were lost on the 15th and seven Spitfires.

Although there were two more days of heavy combat in September, on the 27th and 30th, these were not on the same scale as the large attacks of the 7th and 15th. From the 16th to the 30th September, 200 claims were made by Hurricane units, including 87 on the 27th and 28 on the 30th. Forty-nine of those claims were confirmed,[14] but 87 Hurricanes were lost.[15] One-hundred-and-fifty-six enemy aircraft were claimed by Spitfires during the same period, of which 65 can be confirmed, including 27 on the 27th, for the loss of 58 Spitfires to enemy action.

So ended the decisive month of the battle, a month during which Hurricane Squadrons had claimed more enemy aircraft and suffered greater losses than Spitfire units, but the higher numerical availability of the Hurricanes had been the crucial factor. Of the Hurricane Squadrons that had commenced the battle in the vital 11 Group sector at the beginning of July, only four[16] had fought continuously to the end of September without being rested. Ten decimated Hurricane Squadrons that had borne the brunt of the battle were relieved, yet another indicator of the Hurricane's vast contribution to the battle.

October 1940 was a month of less intense aerial combat, as the Germans again altered their tactics. The medium bombers were mainly re-assigned a night bomber role, leaving bomb-carrying high altitude BF109s to spearhead the attacks on England. Although Fighter Command had to counter these attacks and suffered serious losses on several days in October, the raids were, in reality, of no strategic importance and of only nuisance value, in comparison to the large-scale assaults of September.

Exactly 100 enemy aircraft were claimed by Hurricane Squadrons during October, of which 55 were confirmed. Spitfire units claimed 112 in October, of which 58 were confirmed, so the two British fighters achieved near parity in both claims and actual confirmed kills. One-hundred-and-eleven Hurricanes were lost in October, but 39 of these were in accidents rather than by enemy action. Sixty-five Spitfires were lost in the month, 19 by accident.

Six-hundred-and-nineteen Hurricanes were recorded as category three or total losses during the 18 weeks ending on the 2nd November 1940, as against 373 Spitfires. At least 113 of the Hurricanes lost[17] were by accident.

Hawker Hurricane purchased for £5,000 by public appeal in Croydon in 1940.

References

1. Three-hundred-and-eighty-six.
2. A&AEE.
3. Fifteen in accidents.
4. Four by accident.
5. Plus 28 unconfirmed.
6. Twenty-five actually lost.
7. Thirty confirmed.
8. Eleven confirmed.
9. Six to Hurricanes and 12 to Spitfires.
10. But not all.
11. Including six destroyed on the ground on the 18th.
12. Including four on three occasions.
13. On the 8th September, 111 Squadron left 11 Group, with seven remaining Hurricanes, having lost 21 aircraft since the 11th August. 43 Squadron, with 11 aircraft remaining, left the same day, having lost 24 aircraft including four on the ground, since the 8th August.
14. Nineteen on the 27th and 10 on the 30th.
15. Fourteen by accident.
16. Nos.1, 257, 501 and 601 Squadrons
17. 18%.

Biography – Josef Frantisek

Josef Frantisek was a Czech who flew with 303 (Polish) Squadron in the Battle of Britain and, flying Hurricanes throughout the Battle, he became the RAF's top-scoring Ace of that campaign.

303 Squadron officially became operational on the 31st August 1940 (although on the previous day, the Squadron had claimed its first 'kill', before becoming operational).

Frantisek started scoring victories on the 2nd September 1940, by destroying a BF109 near Dover (not confirmed).

This was the first of 17 enemy aircraft plus one probable that Frantisek claimed by the end of September 1940. Of this total, 10 were BF109s, five were He 111s and single examples of the He 113 (!), JU-88 and BF110 were also claimed.

Interestingly, five of Frantisek's claims were shot down in the Horsham area and all but three were claimed after midday.

On the 8th October, on a routine patrol, Frantisek's Hurricane (R4175) crashed at Cuddington Way, Ewell, Surrey, the cause never being known. Frantisek died in the crash. He had a reputation for being an individualist and frequently broke away from the Squadron to hunt on his own.

He was awarded the Polish cross of Valour (Virtuti Miltari) and three bars and the Czech Military Cross. He was posthumously promoted to the rank of S-Lieutenant. His only British award was the DFM.

Chapter Eleven

Malta

The first four Hurricanes to arrive on Malta landed on the 28th June 1940 to form the 'Fighter Flight' and the first decisive encounter involving Hurricanes occurred on the 3rd July, F.O. Waters, in P2614 engaging one of two S.79s[1] on a reconnaissance mission over Malta and destroying it. Unfortunately, Waters was attacked by the escorting CR.42s[2] as he returned to land and crash-landed, although he was unhurt.

Four days later, the dockyard was targeted by two formations of S.79s with CR.42 escort, F.O. Woods successfully engaging and destroying one of the bombers.[3] On the 10th July, 20 SM.79s missed the rendezvous with their escorting CR.42s but proceeded to attack several targets and were intercepted by Hurricanes. F.O. Taylor shot down an SM.79,[4] as did F.O. Woods.[5]

The next air combat was on the 16th July, 12 CR.42s of the 23rd Gruppo on another reconnaissance mission being intercepted by a Hurricane[6] and a Gladiator. Flt. Lt. Keeble in the former was shot down and killed, but apparently not before he destroyed one of the CR.42s. Twelve reinforcement Hurricanes were flown to the island from the carrier H.M.S. *Argus* on the 2nd August 1940. These were amalgamated with the remaining Hurricanes of the 'Fighter Flight' to form 261 Squadron.

A heavy air raid on the 6th August destroyed two of the newly arrived Hurricanes on the ground. Then, on the 13th of this month, in a night interception, F.O. Barber claimed an SM.79 probable and this bomber[7] failed to return to Sicily. Two days later, 10 SM.79s escorted by 18 CR.42s were intercepted by four Hurricanes, one of which[8] was shot down, Sgt. O'Donnell being killed.

In another decisive encounter on the 24th August, six SM.79s,[9] escorted by 17 CR.42s of the 23rd Gruppo, were engaged by four Hurricanes of 261 Squadron. F.O. Taylor claimed a CR.42 and P.O. Balmforth claimed a

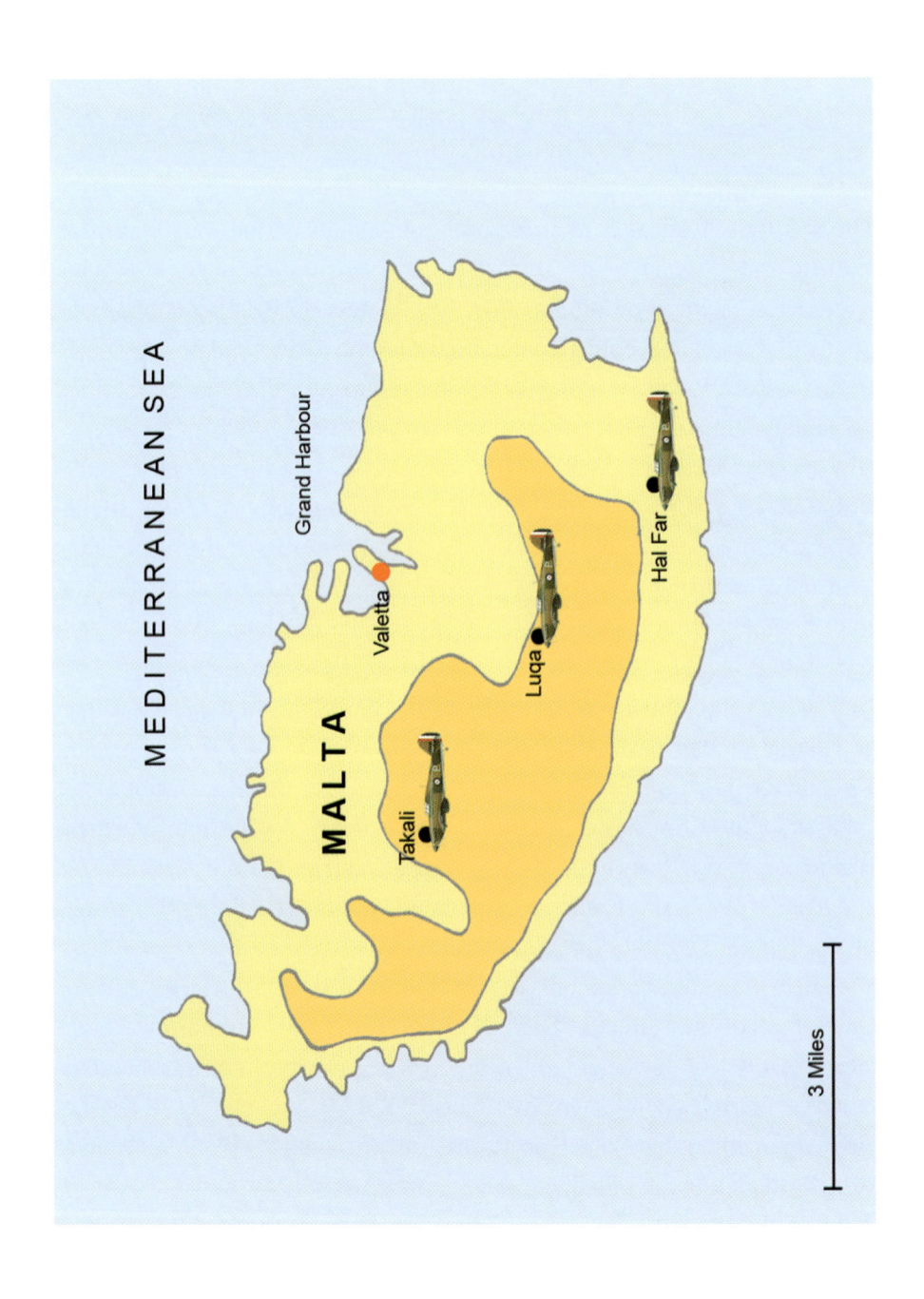

probable, although only one CR.42 was lost.

On the 5th September, eight SM.79s of the 34th Stormo with an escort of 10 CR.42s of the 23rd Gruppo, were met by Hurricanes, Flt. Lt. Greenhalgh, P.O. McAdam and Sgt. Hyde each claiming one of the fighters, while Sgt. Ayre claimed a probable.

Two were seen to fall by observers, but none were admitted lost by the Italians. Two days later, Valetta was raided by 10 SM.79s of the 36th Stormo with 17 CR.42s of the 23rd Gruppo as escort. Three Hurricanes and three Gladiators engaged this formation, an SM.79 being jointly claimed by Flt. Lts. Greenhalgh and Lambert and F.O. Barber, an aircraft of 258th Squadriglia, 109th Gruppo being lost.

A raid by 12 JU-87s[10] with 21 CR.42s of the 23rd Gruppo and six MC200s of the of the 36th Stormo as escort on the 17th September, was intercepted by three to four Hurricanes, one of the Stukas[11] falling to F.O. Barber, while F.O. Woods destroyed a CR.42.[12]

Twelve days later, three Hurricanes and two Gladiators scrambled to intercept a reconnaissance formation of nine MC200s of the 6th Gruppo, one being claimed by F.O. Taylor and a probable being claimed by Sgt. Robertson, one of the fighters actually being lost.

The first combat of October occurred on the 4th, when an MC200 formation from the 6th Gruppo was engaged by 261 Squadron, an unnamed pilot claiming one of the Macchis. The bombers returned on the 8th, when five SM.79s of 36th Stormo attacked at night, F.O. Taylor shooting one down.

Another SM.79 was claimed on the 16th by Flt. Lt. Waters, but there is no Italian record of this combat. The last action in October by Hurricanes was on the 27th, when nine MC200s of the 6th Gruppo were intercepted by six Hurricanes and two Gladiators. F.O. Taylor claimed a probable, which was confirmed.

On the 2nd November, 20 SM.79s of 34th Stormo with 11 MC200s[13] and five CR.42s[14] as escort raided Malta, being intercepted by either one or two Hurricanes and a Gladiator. One of the MC200s[15] was shot down by an unnamed pilot of 261 Squadron.

Ten days later, 12 MC200s of the 6th Gruppo flew a reconnaissance over the island, one being shot down by P.O. Balmforth.

On the 14th, two SM.79s and eight CR.42s were intercepted north of Gozo by five Hurricanes, F.O. Barber claiming a CR.42 probable. Twelve more reinforcement Hurricanes were flown off H.M.S. *Argus* on the 17th November, but due to an error in the launch point, eight ran out of fuel and only four reached the island.

On the 26th, three CR.42s[16] on another reconnaissance mission over Malta were engaged by two Hurricanes. On this occasion, however, although Sgt. Ashton shot down a CR.42, he was in turn shot down[17] and killed. On the 28th November, an afternoon raid of 10 SM.79s of the 30th Stormo escorted by 12 CR.42s of the 23rd Gruppo and 10 MC200s of the 6th Gruppo, were attacked by Hurricanes, Sgt. Robinson claiming an SM.79 probable, which was later upgraded to a confirmed kill. Flt. Lt. Greenhalgh was also believed to have claimed a CR.42.

The only decisive Hurricane combat in December was on the 18th, at night, an SM.79[18] being despatched by Sgt. Robertson.

In 1940, Hurricane pilots flying from Malta claimed nine SM.79s plus a probable, eight CR.42s plus three probables, four MC200s plus two probables and one JU-87. In return, four Hurricanes were shot down by CR.42s and a further two were destroyed on the ground. The air-to-air combat ratio was a very creditable five-and-a-half to one in favour of the Hurricanes.

Crash-landed Hurricane on Malta.

The first action over Malta in 1941 saw 16 MC200s of the 6th Gruppo attacking Luqa airfield on the 9th January, being intercepted by five Hurricanes of 261 Squadron. Three were claimed shot down, two by Flt. Lt. Machlachlan and one by F.O. Taylor, but in reality, only two of the Macchis were lost. A Hurricane[19] was lost by accident on the 11th, resulting in the death of Sgt. Timms.

With the badly damaged aircraft carrier, H.M.S. *Illustrious* now the target, a large raid on the 16th January included 17 JU-88s, 44 JU-87s, 20 BF110s, 10 MC200s and 10 CR.42s as the Luftwaffe attacked in strength for the first time.

Seven Fulmars and Hurricanes scrambled to intercept, four JU-88s[20] and one JU-87[20] were claimed, although possibly all by the Fulmars. One JU-88[21] was actually lost and a further three crash-landed. Two days later, another raid by JU-87s, escorted by MC200s targeted Hal Far and Luqa airfields, the latter being put out of action temporarily. Five Hurricanes and five Fulmars intercepted, claiming seven Stukas and two probables. Flt. Lt. Burges of 261 Squadron claimed a probable, Sgt. Ayre claimed one, plus a probable, F.O. Taylor claimed two and Sgt. Bamberger one. Only one JU-87,[22] one JU-88[23] and one MC200[24] were actually lost this day.

Next day, there were several raids against *Illustrious*, countered by six Hurricanes, one Fulmar from *Illustrious*, and one Gladiator. Around 40 JU-87s and JU-88s raided first at 0830 hrs, followed 90 minutes later by 20 Stukas with 24 CR.42s as escort. These were engaged over Grand Harbour by six Hurricanes, a JU-87 and a CR.42 probable being claimed by Sgt. Robertson of 261 Squadron.

Late morning the same day, a Cant Z.506B of the 612th Squadriglia was shot down by Flt. Lt. Machlachlan and an early afternoon raid by six Stukas with around 12 CR.42s of the 23rd Gruppo as escort was intercepted by five Hurricanes, Sgt. Robertson claiming a CR.42 and a probable. Flt. Lt. Burges claimed two JU-87s this day and Sgt. Bamberger claimed one. Flt. Lt. Machlachlan also claimed two JU-87s and a probable, plus one JU-88. Actual German losses were three JU-87s[25] and two JU-88s.[26] A Hurricane[27] of 261 Squadron was lost, possibly shot down by a JU-87, Sgt. Kelsey being killed. This ended the attacks on H.M.S. *Illustrious*, which left for major repairs in the U.S.A. on the 23rd January. Six more Hurricanes arrived from Cyrenaica on the 30th January.

On the 1st February, an SM.79 of the 193rd Squadriglia, escorted by four CR.42s of the 156th Gruppo, flew a reconnaissance sortie over Malta, these being engaged by three Hurricanes. Sgt. Robertson and F.O. Whittingham each claimed one of the fighters, although only one CR.42 was lost. Just before dark, JU-88s with fighter escort attacked one of the airfields, one[28] being claimed by F.O. Peacock-Edwards and destroyed in a crash-landing at Catania. Three days later, another dusk raid against the airfields by JU-88s was engaged by eight Hurricanes and two Fulmars.

One of the bombers was claimed by Sgt. Robertson, while P.O. Pain claimed a probable. Three JU-88s of II/LG1 actually crash-landed on return to Catania[29] although none were lost.

On the night of the 8th February, an He 111[30] and a JU-88[31] were shot down by Flt. Lt. Machlachlan.

Hurricane destroyed on ground by air attack on Malta.

The BF109Es of 7/JG26 had now reached Sicily and they first appeared over Malta on the 12th February, shooting down two Hurricanes,[32] killing Flt. Lt. Watson and wounding P.O. Thacker. This was a grim portent of things to come.

The tactics used by the BF109s were simple but very effective. If they could not begin combat with a height advantage, they refused battle. Normally, however, they would dive from altitude[33] onto the Hurricanes, which were often caught climbing. After an attack they would then zoom back up to high-altitude, before re-assessing, then re-attacking or withdrawing.

Four days later, Flt. Lt. Machlachlan[34] was also shot down and wounded by the BF109s. Flt. Lt. Teddy Peacock-Edwards of 261 Squadron noted this day,[35]

> *'Scramble. Shot up by ME109. Landed with numerous shell and bullet hole and starboard aileron shot away.'*

On the 17th February, P.O. Hamilton claimed a DO-215, but this may have been a BF110D[36] that was lost this day over Malta.

Another Stuka raid on the 23rd February led to one of the dive-bombers also being claimed by P.O. Hamilton, an aircraft of III/StG1 being lost.

On the 25th February, eight Hurricanes intercepted four raiders, reportedly DO-215s and claimed three, one each to Flt. Lt. Whittingham, P.O. Hamilton and F.O. Hilton Barber. In fact, a BF110 of 2(F)/123 was lost in the area and a case of misidentification is thought likely. That afternoon, a Hurricane was lost, killing P.O. Walsh, possibly another victim of the BF109s.

Early the next afternoon, a large raid targeted Luqa. This included 38 JU-87s, 12 JU-88s, 10 DO-17/215s and 10 He 111s escorted by up to 30 fighters.[37] Eight Hurricanes intercepted, P.O. Eliot and F.O. Foxton each claiming a JU-87 plus a probable, F.O. Taylor a probable, P.O. Pain a DO-215 probable and unnamed pilots claiming a DO-215 and JU-88 probables. At least three and possibly as many as five Hurricanes[38] were shot down by the BF109s, P.O.s Kearsey and Langdon and F.O. Taylor all being killed. Three JU-87s of II/StG1 were lost by the Germans, but two of these may have been the victims of AA gunners.

On the 5th March, eight Hurricanes scrambled against a late afternoon raid of up to 70 German aircraft, Sgt. Robertson claiming a JU-88 and a BF109. Sgt. Ayre also claimed a JU-88 and shared a DO-215 with P.O.s Rippon and Pain. P.O. Rippon also claimed a JU-87, as did Sgt. McDougal, but both Sgt. Ayre and Sgt. McDougal were shot down by BF109s,[39] the latter being killed. P.O. Pain also claimed a BF110 probable. Actual German losses to Hurricanes were one JU-88,[40] one BF110, two JU-87s[41] and another JU-87 jointly with the AA gunners. Two days later, Sgt. Jessop[42] was shot down and wounded by a BF109 while trying to protect a returning Maryland.

On the 9th March, a Hurricane was destroyed on the ground at Takali by a JU-88 escorted by four BF110s.

Another Hurricane destroyed on ground by air attack on Malta.

On the night of the 10th, a DO-215 was claimed, probably by P.O. Rippon, although this was likely to have been a BF110C that was reported lost.

Hurricanes were scrambled again on the 18th, meeting some 15 CR.42s.[43] P.O. Pain claimed two of the enemy fighters. Six more replacement Hurricanes arrived this day from North Africa.[44]

The 22nd of March was another very bad day for 261 Squadron. A morning raid by five JU-88s was met by four Hurricanes, with no decisive results, but in the afternoon, 10 JU-88s with an escort of 12 BF109s were intercepted by eight Hurricanes, five of which[45] were shot down by BF109s.[46] P.O.s Foxton, Knight and Garland, F.O. Southwell and Sgt. Spyer were all killed. P.O. Whitney claimed a BF109 but none were lost.

However, on the 23rd, as a convoy from Alexandria arrived, mid-afternoon, a raid of JU-87s[47] escorted by 15 MC200s[48] attacked the ships in harbour and was engaged by 14 Hurricanes, no fewer than nine Stukas and a probable being claimed by the Hurricane pilots. Sgt. Robertson, Flt. Lt. Peacock-Edwards and P.O. Rippon each claimed two, with Sqn. Ldr. Lambert, P.O. Whitney and Sgt. Ayre claiming one each. The probable was claimed by unnamed pilots. Sgt. Robertson[49] was shot down by a JU-87, but bailed out unhurt. Actual losses were four JU-87s, at least one by AA fire.

Flt. Lt. Teddy Peacock-Edwards of 261 Squadron recorded:[35]

> *'Scramble – Interception. 1 JU-87 destroyed – 1 damaged. Very good sport – JU-87s were picked off like flies – Sqdn. bag 14 bandits. Sgt. Robertson shot down.'*

A Cant Z.501[50] was also lost this day, reportedly to fighters from Malta, but the pilots are unknown. On the afternoon of the 28th March, Sgt. Goode of 274 Squadron was shot down[51] by BF109s and severely wounded, Sgt. Livingston also force-landing after being shot up.

April 1941 started with 12 more Hurricanes flown off H.M.S. *Ark Royal* on the 2nd.[52] During the mid-morning of the 11th April, a force of 12 MC200s,[53] six CR.42s and some BF109s[55] flew a fighter sweep over Malta as cover for a recce JU-88.

Hurricanes were scrambled to meet this sweep, the JU-88 being claimed as a probable by P.O. Kennett and Sgt. Waghorn in Hurricane IIs, but both pilots were immediately shot down[56] by BF109s and killed.

Late that morning, eight Hurricanes intercepted a formation of around 20 MC200s and BF109s. Sgt. Deacon claimed a BF109, but was then forced to land[57] by another BF109 and wounded. P.O. Mortimer[58] was also shot up, slightly wounded and crash-landed, as was P.O. Whitney,[59] at least one of their Hurricanes being written-off. P.O. Whitney was unhurt and claimed a BF109. No BF109s were lost, but a BF-110C[60] was reportedly shot down by fighters. Unnamed pilots were also credited with two CR.42 probables.

On the night of the 11th/12th April, a JU-87 was claimed by P.O. Hamilton, but this aircraft was also claimed by AA gunners, the Stuka[61] being lost. Next day, Hurricanes intercepted two of four raids on Malta, a BF109 being claimed by Flt. Lt. Mason, but Mason was then shot down[62] and wounded. Flt. Lt. Peacock-Edwards also claimed a BF109, but he was also hit and crash-landed,[63] though he was unhurt. He recorded in his log,[35]

Scramble. F/O Mason attacked 4 ME109s. Got one and shot down with wounds.'

Again, no BF109s were reported lost.

On the 20th April, three SM.79s raided and were escorted by nine CR.42s and 15 MC200s, but only two Hurricane IIs intercepted. Two CR.42s were claimed by F.O. Laubscher and one by P.O. Pain, but only one was actually lost. Two days later, 261 Squadron engaged BF109s, Sgt. Hyde claiming one, although again, no BF109s were lost. Next day, an evening recce sortie over Malta was escorted by BF109s which shot down and killed F.O. Auger.[64] On the 23rd April, 23 reinforcement Hurricanes were flown to Malta from H.M.S. *Ark Royal*. On the 28th April, 261 Squadron again fought BF109s, F.O. Westmacott claiming one, but yet again, none were lost.

On the penultimate day of the month, a raid of JU-88s[65] was escorted by BF109s, P.O. Rippon and P.O. Hall jointly claiming a JU-88. One JU-88[66] was indeed lost, but possibly to flak. Three Hurricanes were claimed by the BF109s and two Hurricanes of 261 Squadron are believed to have been lost, although the identity of the pilots is unknown.

On the 1st May, Hurricanes and BF109s clashed again, two Hurricanes[67] being shot down, P.O. Innes and Sgt. Walmsley both being wounded. From the 28th April to the 1st May inclusive, six Hurricanes were admitted lost by AHQ Malta, probably all to BF109s. On the 2nd May, Sgt. Ottey was killed[68] in an accident and on the morning of the 5th May, a JU-88[69] was spotted over Kalafrana Bay by two patrolling Hurricanes and jointly claimed by P.O. Hall and Sgt. Jolly, this aircraft being confirmed as lost. Next day, four He 111s[70] escorted by BF109s[71] attacked at noon, being intercepted by a flight of Hurricanes. F.O. Westmacott claimed an He 111 probable, one He 111 being lost. However, three Hurricanes[72] were shot down by the escort, P.O.s Dredge and Gray and Sgt. Branson all being wounded. Later, Sqn. Ldr. Whittingham intercepted a night raid claiming one plus a probable, actual losses being one JU-88[73] and another He 111[74] which crash-landed. Next day, Sgt. Jennings was killed and Sgt. Walker slightly injured when their aircraft[75] were lost in a collision.

A Stuka raid[76] on the 9th May was intercepted by Hurricanes, one being claimed jointly by Sgt. Davies and an unidentified pilot, with another jointly by Sgt. Jordan and F.O. Laubscher, one JU-87[77] being confirmed lost.

185 Squadron was formed with 18 pilots on the 12th May and next afternoon, four of its Hurricanes engaged BF109s,[78] Flt. Lt. Westmacott being shot down[79] and wounded. An aircraft[80] of 261 Squadron was also shot down, killing P.O. Thompson.

Next day, an afternoon clash between 185 and 261 Squadrons and the BF109s[81] resulted in another loss[82] to 185 Squadron, P.O. Hamilton being killed. Hamilton was an ace with six victories, all scored on Hurricanes. A similar engagement the following day saw yet another Hurricane[83] of 185 Squadron shot down by BF109s,[84] Sgt. Wynne being killed. The same day, P.O. Pain claimed an He 111, which may have been one of two SM.79s[85] lost by the Italians.

On the 20th May, it was 261 Squadron's turn to lose a Hurricane[86] to the BF109s of III/JG27, P.O. Reeves being wounded.

Next day, 47 more Hurricanes reached the island, most flying onto Egypt, but enough remained to equip 249 Squadron, replacing 261 Squadron, which disbanded. 261 Squadron had taken a heavy beating from the BF109s, losing at least 33 Hurricanes to the German fighters.

On the 25th May, early afternoon, BF109s of 7/JG26 strafed Takali airfield, destroying two of 249 Squadron's Hurricanes on the ground. Six days later, 7/JG26 left Sicily, having claimed at least 42 air combat victories, without any operational losses, 12 of its pilots having claimed victories over Malta. With the departure of Luftwaffe units from Sicily, Italian aircraft became more prominent again over Malta in June 1941.

On the 3rd June, an SM.79[87] was claimed over Malta by Sqn. Ldr. Barton of 249 Squadron and confirmed, for the squadron's first victory over the island. On the night of 5th/6th June, an He 111 was claimed as a probable by Flt. Lt. Hancock of 185 Squadron, which had been re-designated as Malta's night fighter unit. On the 6th June, a further 16 Hurricanes of 46 Squadron arrived on Malta. Early on the morning of the 7th June, 14 MC200s of the 7th Gruppo strafed Hal Far airfield and claimed two fighters destroyed on the ground, but no details of any losses are available.

The next night, Sqn. Ldr. Barton of 249 Squadron shot down a BR-20M,[88] while F.O. Beazley and P.O. Palliser jointly claimed a probable, but this bomber returned only damaged.

On the 9th June, four Hurricanes of 249 Squadron were despatched to intercept four SM.79s[89] out over the sea. Sgt. Livingstone claimed one of the bombers, which was confirmed lost.

46 Squadron had their first combat on the 11th June. Early that morning, a reconnaissance SM.79, with 17 MC200s[90] as escort were intercepted before they reached Malta by seven Hurricanes. The SM.79 was shot down jointly by Sgt. Walker and Sqn. Ldr. Rabagliati, F.O. McGregor and P.O. Grant, but one Hurricane[91] was shot down by the MC200s, Flt. Lt. Burnett being killed.

Early next morning, another reconnaissance SM.79,[92] escorted by 30 MC200s[93] was intercepted by 18 Hurricanes of 46 and 249 Squadrons, Flt. Lt. Neil of the latter unit claiming a BF109 and Sgt. Livingston a probable. P.O. Rathie and Sgt. Johnston of 46 Squadron jointly claimed a CR.42 or MC200, with Flt. Lt. Lefevre also claiming an MC200. One MC200 was actually lost by the Italians, but two Hurricanes of 249 Squadron were shot down by the MC200s, P.O. Saunders being wounded, but P.O. Rioch Munro was killed.

That afternoon, a Cant Z-506B[94] escorted by two CR.42s[95] was engaged by 46 Squadron Hurricanes, Sgt. Main shooting down the floatplane and one of the CR.42s. Sqn. Ldr. Rabagliati claimed another CR.42 and Sgt. Hackston claimed an MC200. Only one CR.42[96] was lost, but a Hurricane of 46 Squadron was shot down by a CR.42, killing Sgt. Walker. Another Cant Z-506B escorted by nine CR.42s[97] and 24 MC200s[98] was also despatched and intercepted by seven Hurricanes of 249 Squadron, the Cant being shot down by Sgt. Etchells.

On 4th June, tragedy struck when, of 48 Hurricanes flown off *Ark Royal* and *Victorious*, only 11 reached Malta safely, due to a navigation error.

In the early afternoon of the 18th June, nine MC200s[99] were engaged by Hurricanes of 249 Squadron to the North of the island. P.O. Palliser and Sgt. Sheppard claimed an MC200 and a probable between them, one MC200 actually crash-landing on return. One Hurricane[100] was shot down by the MC200s, Sgt. Livingston being killed.

Four days later, early in the morning, 17 Hurricanes intercepted a reconnaissance Cant Z-1007 bis, escorted by 30 MC200s, one of which was claimed by Sqn. Ldr. Rabagliati, although no MC200s were lost this day.

On the 25th June, however, an SM.79[101] with 36 MC200s[102] as escort, was intercepted by 46 Squadron Hurricanes, the SM.79 being claimed as a probable by Sqn. Ldr. Rabagliati and three MC200s being claimed by P.O.s Anderson and Main and Sgt. Copp.[103] Two MC200s[104] were actually lost by the Italians.

Further batches of Hurricanes arrived on the 27th and the 30th June. Mid-morning on the 27th June, 10 Hurricanes of 46 Squadron engaged another SM.79 escorted by 24 MC200s, Sgt. Copp claiming an MC200 and a probable, P.O. Anderson also claiming an MC200, one MC200 being lost. Late morning, another formation of one S.79[105] with 22 escorting MC200s[106] was also engaged by 46 Squadron, Sqn. Ldr. Rabagliati claiming an MC200 and P.O. Barnes claiming two of the fighters. Sgt. Jolly also claimed one MC200 and a probable. Sgt. Hackston made a claim for an MC200 on the 26th June, but this may actually have been during this combat on the 27th. Two MC200s[107] were actually lost by the Italians in this engagement.

On the 28th June, 46 Squadron was re-numbered as 126 Squadron with immediate effect. Two days later, the new unit had its combat debut, just after midday, when formations of MC200s[108] were intercepted by six Hurricanes, F.O. Carpenter claiming one of the fighters and Sgt. Mackie claiming another, one MC200 actually being lost. Hurricane losses declined considerably in June, only five being lost in combat, plus one by accident.

The MC200s were back on the 4th July, 58 of 54th Stormo's aircraft escorting a reconnaissance Cant Z-1007 bis,[109] which turned back before reaching Malta, but the Macchis were engaged by four Hurricanes of 185 Squadron. Flt. Lt. Jeffries and Sgt. Jolly each claimed an MC200, again, only one being actually lost.

A night raid on the 8th/9th July by 10 BR-20Ms[110] and six SM.79s[111] was engaged by F.O. Cassidy of 249 Squadron, who claimed one of the former, but in fact an SM.79 was lost by the Italians.

On the afternoon of the 9th July, four Hurricanes of 126 and 185 Squadrons attacked the seaplane base at Syracuse, six seaplanes being claimed destroyed on the water. One Cant Z-501[112] and a Cant. Z-506D[113] were actually lost in this attack. Two days later, a large formation of 53 MC200s[114] attacked Hal Far airfield and were intercepted by at least 12 Hurricanes.

Sqn. Ldr. Mould, P.O. Barnwell and Flt. Lt. Jeffries of 185 Squadron each claimed an MC200, but none were actually lost. On the 17th July, a reconnaissance Cant Z-1007 bis was escorted by 49 MC200s[115] over the island, 19 Hurricanes of 185 and 249 Squadrons intercepting. Sqn. Ldr. Barton and P.O. Leggett of the latter unit both claimed MC200s and two Macchis[116] were indeed lost, but Sgt. Guest was shot down (in Z2818) and killed.

On the morning of the 25th July, a Cant Z-1007 bis on a reconnaissance mission was escorted by 47 MC200s[117] and 22 Hurricanes of 185 and 249 Squadrons scrambled to intercept them. The Cant was claimed as a BR-20 by six pilots of the two squadrons and shot down. The escort was engaged by 249 Squadron, for whom Sqn. Ldr. Barton, P.O. Hill and P.O. Matthews each claimed MC200s, two[118] being lost.

In the early hours of the 26th July, Italian naval units attacked Malta and at dawn were engaged by Hurricanes of 126 and 185 Squadrons. These were in turn attacked by MC200s,[119] which were supporting the attack, P.O. Winton of 185 Squadron being shot down by the Macchis, but bailing out unhurt. However, Sgt. Haley of 126 Squadron claimed two MC200s and P.O. Thompson of 185 Squadron claimed one, two Macchis[120] actually being lost by the Italians.

Next morning, two SM.79s were intercepted over the sea by four Hurricanes of 185 Squadron, P.O. Thompson and P.O. Bailey jointly claiming one and Flt. Lt. Hancock and Sgt. Cousens jointly claiming the other, but only one SM.79[121] can be confirmed lost.

July resulted in a better claims-to-losses ratio for the Hurricanes. Sixteen enemy aircraft were claimed[122] for two Hurricanes lost in combat. Two Hurricanes of 126 Squadron were also lost in accidents on the 4th[123] and the 19th July, resulting in the deaths of Sgt. Hackston and Sgt. McCracken respectively. Z3492 of 249 Squadron also crash-landed on the last day of the month, wounding Sqn. Ldr. Barton.

At the end of July, the Malta Night Fighter Unit[124] was formed at Takali, with 12 Hurricane IIBs and Cs. This unit had its first victories on the night of the 5th/6th August, when a raid against Valetta by eight BR-20Ms[125] was intercepted by two Hurricanes, F.O. Cassidy claiming one and P.O. Barnwell two, two of the bombers[126] being lost.

Next morning, four Hurricanes reportedly engaged three MC200s flying a reconnaissance mission, one of the Macchis being claimed by an unknown pilot. On the 10th August, a Cant Z-506B was claimed by Sqn. Ldr. Rabagliati of 126 Squadron, the floatplane being seen to land on the sea and sink by him. On the night of the 11th August, a raid by BR-20Ms,[127] SM.79s[128] and JU-87s against Malta, was engaged by four MNFU Hurricanes, one of the BR-20Ms being claimed by Sqn. Ldr. Powell-Sheddon and confirmed lost.

Four days later, three of four Hurricanes sent to Egypt were lost, but the cause is unknown. On the 17th, the Syracuse seaplane base was again raided, by four Hurricanes, Sqn. Ldr. Rabagliati and P.O. Main each claiming a Cant Z-506B destroyed, these[129] being confirmed ablaze. Also this day, a CA-312 floatplane was intercepted over the sea by three Hurricanes of

249 Squadron and jointly claimed by Sgt. Rex and P.O. Hulbert.

On the 19th August, the Macchis were back in force, for the first time that month, 12 fighters of the 10th Gruppo being met near Sicily by an equal number of 126 Squadron Hurricanes. P.O. Lardner-Burke claimed three MC200s in this engagement, Flt. Lt. Lefevre claimed one and Sgt. MacGregor a probable, but no losses were recorded by the Italians.

The last notable combat in August was on the 26th, when an afternoon raid by 15 MC200s was met by 18 Hurricanes of 126 and 185 Squadrons. Sqn. Ldr. Rabagliati, P.O. Lardner-Burke, P.O. Dickinson and Sgt. MacGregor claimed an MC200 each, while Sgt. Greenhalgh claimed a probable. On this occasion, one MC200 was actually lost, but a Hurricane of 126 Squadron was also shot down, killing Sgt. Maltby.

On the morning of the 4th September, 19 MC200s[130] were engaged by 21 Hurricanes of 126 and 185 Squadrons near Malta, Sqn. Ldr. Rabagliati, F.O. Carpenter, P.O. Lardner-Burke, Flt. Lt. Lefevre, Sgt. Simpson, Sgt. MacGregor and Sgt. Russell of the former unit each claiming an MC200, while P.O. Blackburn claimed a probable, as did Flt. Lt. Jeffries of 185 Squadron. Only two MC200s were actually lost in this engagement. That afternoon, a Cant Z-506B[131] was despatched to search for the pilots of the downed Macchis, escorted by 30 more MC200s.[132] These were engaged by eight Hurricanes of 249 Squadron, Sgts Owen and Carter of this unit each claiming one of the escorts, while Sqn. Ldr. Barton claimed a probable. One MC200 of the 10th Gruppo was lost, but two Hurricanes[133] were shot down by the MC200s, P.O.s Smith and Kimberley both being killed.

On the night of the 4th/5th September, three Cant Z-1007 bis of 9th Stormo attacked Hal Far, being engaged by two Hurricanes of the MNFU. P.O. Barnwell and Flt. Lt. Stones jointly claimed one of the bombers, which was confirmed. Four nights later, another raid by five Stukas, nine Cant Z-1007 bis and one BR-20M was also intercepted by two Hurricanes of the MNFU, one of the Z-1007 bis being claimed by P.O. Barnwell and confirmed.

On the 14th September, an engagement was reported in which a Macchi was shot down by P.O. Tedford of 126 Squadron and later the same day, another combat reportedly resulted in two Italian bombers and three fighters being claimed for the loss of two Hurricanes, one flown by P.O. Coffin, but there are no records of these engagements.

On the last afternoon of September, 11 Hurricanes of 185 Squadron attacked Comiso, but were intercepted by three MC202s,[134] which had recently arrived on Sicily, P.O. Lintern being shot down[135] and killed. Five Hurricanes of the same squadron returned later, escorting a SAR Fulmar and looking for the downed pilot, Flt. Lt. Jeffries claiming an MC202 probable as the Hurricanes were attacked by more of these potent fighters.

The MC202s ventured over Malta for the first time on the 1st October, seven of the fighters meeting eight Hurricanes of 185 Squadron north-east of Malta, late in the morning. One of the Hurricanes was shot down, killing Squadron Leader Mould, but one of the MC202s, claimed as damaged by Sgt. Knight, force-landed on Sicily.

Hurricanes on Malta.

Three days later, eight Hurricanes of 185 Squadron were scrambled to intercept six enemy aircraft and although no engagement was reported, one of the Hurricanes[136] was lost, possibly a victim of the MC202s, P.O. Veitch being killed. On the afternoon of the 5th October, a Hurricane was claimed by an MC200,[137] but there is no record of such a loss. Early on the morning of the 14th October, six MC202s attacked Luqa and were intercepted by 11 Hurricanes of 185 and 249 Squadrons and the MNFU, one of the latter unit's aircraft[138] being shot down, killing P.O. Barnwell. Before his demise, Barnwell claimed an MC202, but none were lost.

On the 19th October, two Hurricanes of 249 Squadron were on patrol south of Lampedusa when they encountered an SM.81, which was jointly claimed by Sqn. Ldr. Barton and P.O. Palliser. Next morning, six more SM.81s were intercepted at a similar location by two Hurricanes of 185 Squadron, one of the bomber-transports being claimed by Sgt. Lillywhite.

On the afternoon of the 22nd, Luqa was again the target for 14 MC202s of the 9th Gruppo, these being engaged by nine Hurricanes of 249 Squadron, one of which was shot down, but Sgt. Owen escaped unhurt. Three days later, four Cant Z-1007 bis of the 9th Stormo, escorted by more than 20 MC202s of the 9th Gruppo and the 54th Stormo, attacked at noon and were intercepted by eight Hurricanes of 185 Squadron. One of the Cants was claimed as a BR-20 probable[139] and actually crash-landed on Sicily. One of the Macchis was also claimed as a probable by Sgt. Hunton and in fact an aircraft of the 4th Stormo was lost by the Italians.

On the last night of October, four BR-20Ms of 116th Gruppo raided Malta and were engaged by two MNFU Hurricanes, one of the bombers being shot down by Sgt. Mackie. October 1941 had been a relatively quiet month, with only two SM.81s, two MC202s and a BR-20[140] claimed,[141] but four Hurricanes were lost in combat to the MC 202s.

Early in November, 34 more Hurricanes arrived on Malta from H.M.S. *Argus*, these being aircraft of 242 and 605 Squadrons.[142] The seaplane base at Syracuse was again the target for two Hurricanes of 126 Squadron on the 4th November, four Cant Z-506Bs being claimed damaged or destroyed by P.O.s Anderson and Coffin. Only one of the seaplanes was actually lost. Four days later, around 18 MC200s and MC202s of the 4th Stormo escorted four Cant Z-1007 bis bombers to Malta at noon and were engaged by four Hurricanes of 126 Squadron. Flt. Lt. Carpenter and P.O. Lardner-Burke both claimed MC202s, whereas Sgt. Haley[143] collided with another, both aircraft being destroyed and Haley being wounded. Apart from this aircraft, only one other MC202 was lost.

Next day, one of two Hurricanes of 185 Squadron patrolling over the force 'K' naval force was lost, probably shot down by an MC202 of 4th Stormo, F.O. Bailey being killed. Three days later, four Hurricanes of 249 Squadron were sent to attack Gela airfield on Sicily. Wg. Cdr. Rabagliati claiming a JU-87 in the air and a CR.42 destroyed on the ground. Unfortunately, one Hurricane was shot down by flak, killing Wg. Cdr. Brown.

Later that day, 21 Hurricanes of 126 and 249 Squadrons attacked Comiso, Sgt. Simpson of the former unit being shot down[144] by an MC202 of 9th Gruppo. One MC202 was claimed by Flt. Lt. Carpenter, also of 126 Squadron, but there were no Italian losses.

On the morning of the 21st November, Wg. Cdr. Downland of 185 Squadron flew a recce sortie over Sicily and was also shot down[145] by an MC202 of 9th Gruppo.

That afternoon, 18 MC202s of 9th Gruppo approached Malta on a strafing mission and were intercepted by four Hurricanes of 185 Squadron, one of which was shot down, killing Sgt. Cousens. Next day, an afternoon raid by 10 JU-87s of 101st Gruppo, escorted by MC202s from 9th Gruppo, was intercepted by 21 Hurricanes of 126 and 249 Squadrons. Two MC202 probables were claimed by P.O. Main of 126 Squadron, whereas 249 Squadron pilots claimed three – one each to Sqn. Ldr. Barton and F.O. Crossey, with a third claimed by an unknown pilot, as was another probable. On the 24th November, five Hurricanes of 126 Squadron attacked Comiso airfield on Sicily, one aircraft[146] being shot down by flak and Sgt. Greenhalgh becoming a PoW. In November, six MC202s[147] were claimed by the Hurricane squadrons[148] and a JU-87 was also claimed by 249 Squadron. In return, at least four Hurricanes were lost to MC202s of a total of seven lost to all causes in the month.

On the 2nd December, the MNFU was re-named 1435 (Night Fighter) Flight.

Faced with increasing North African convoy losses, Fliegerkorps II was ordered to Sicily on the same day, equipped with JU-88s and BF109s. There were no combats involving Hurricanes in December until the

18th. That day, three SM.84s[149] were misidentified by four Hurricanes of 185 Squadron as BR-20s, but engaged as they patrolled over a convoy. One SM.84 was jointly claimed by P.O.s Allardice and Oliver and confirmed lost. Next day, German units returned to the attack on Malta, four Hurricanes of 126 Squadron intercepting three JU-88s, one being claimed by Sqn. Ldr. Norris.

Later the same day, a raid of 13 bombers with fighter escort was again engaged by 126 Squadron, who lost P.O. Steele, shot down and killed by return fire from a JU-88, which he was believed to have also shot down. Only one JU-88[150] was actually lost this day.

On the 20th December, a raid of around 40 JU-88s, MC-202s and BF109Fs[151] attacked mid-morning and were engaged by 12 Hurricanes of 249 Squadron.

P.O. Palliser of this unit claimed a JU-88, but Sgt. Moren was killed in a collision with a JU-88, probably Palliser's victim. Two MC202 probables were also credited to unknown pilots, but another Hurricane of 249 Squadron was shot down by a BF109, F.O. Cavan also being killed. Some Hurricanes may have been destroyed on the ground this day. Late morning the next day, a raid of four bombers with 20 fighter escorts was engaged by 18 Hurricanes of 185 and 249 Squadrons, Wg. Cdr. Rabagliati claiming an MC202 shot down, another being claimed as a probable by an unknown pilot. A Hurricane of 185 Squadron[152] was shot down, killing Sgt. Hayes, as was an aircraft of 249 Squadron, P.O. Leggett being slightly wounded.

On the 22nd December, P.O. Matthews of 249 Squadron was shot down and killed by BF109s, which were attacking fishing boats near Grand Harbour. Two days later, four JU-88s of II/KG77 attacked early in the morning and were engaged by 17 Hurricanes of 126 and 185 Squadrons. One JU-88 was jointly claimed by Sqn. Ldr. Mortimer-Rose, F.O. Crossey and F.O. Palliser of 249 Squadron, while another was shared between Sgt. Etchells of that unit and two other pilots, one believed to be P.O. Coffin of 126 Squadron. Two JU-88s were indeed lost in this engagement; however, a Hurricane of 126 Squadron was also shot down, Flt. Sgt. Emery being killed.

On the 26th December, a Hurricane of 249 Squadron crash-landed after combat at Luqa, Sqn. Ldr. Mortimer-Rose being wounded. A reconnaissance Hurricane[153] of 69 Squadron (PRU) was also destroyed on the ground at Luqa. Two Hurricanes were claimed shot down by German fighters this day, but there is no record of any such losses.

Next morning, three JU-88s of Stab II/KG77 escorted by 20 BF109Fs were intercepted east of Kalafrana by Hurricanes of 126 Squadron, one of the bombers being claimed by Flt. Lt. Carpenter and confirmed lost. A BF109 was also claimed by P.O. Main, but no BF109s were lost. However, a Hurricane of 126 Squadron was shot down, Sgt. Copp being slightly wounded. That night, a JU-88 was engaged by P.O. Winton of 1435 Flt and destroyed.

Early on the afternoon of the 28th December, a Hurricane of 249 Squadron was shot down, Flt. Sgt. Owen of 249 Squadron being wounded. Next morning, a raid comprising of 36 enemy aircraft was engaged by 16 Hurricanes, two aircraft of 242 Squadron colliding, with P.O. Blanchard being killed and P.O. MacNamara unhurt. Flt. Lt. Thompson of 185 Squadron claimed a BF109 probable in this combat. Early the same afternoon, a raid numbering 24 enemy aircraft was intercepted by Hurricanes of 185 Squadron, a BF109 being claimed by F.O. Lloyd, but Sgt. Forth[154] was killed, being presumed shot down. Another afternoon attack by five BF109s was met by Hurricanes of 249 Squadron, for whom P.O. Stuart claimed a probable, but both Flt. Lt. Brandt and Sgt. Lawson of this squadron were shot down and killed. One BF109 of Stab/JG53 was confirmed lost this day.

On the penultimate day of 1941, five JU-88s of KGr 806 attacked the airfields and dockyard around noon and were engaged by 10 Hurricanes of 126 and 249 Squadrons. Wg. Cdr. Satchell claimed a JU-88, while another was jointly claimed by F.O. Barnes and P.O. Anderson of 126 Squadron, one bomber being confirmed lost. Unknown Hurricane pilots claimed another JU-88 as a probable.

Between the 19th December and the end of the month, nine JU-88s[155] and two BF109s[156] were claimed by the Hurricane squadrons,[157] but 16 Hurricanes were lost in the month,[158] a severe blow to the defenders. An

MC202[159] and an SM.84 were also claimed in December, but only the SM.84 was confirmed.

The first action for the Hurricanes in 1942 occurred on the morning of the 3rd January, when 22 Hurricanes of 126, 185 and 249 Squadrons engaged two or three JU-88s with BF109 escort. P.O.s Russell and Streets of 126 Squadron shot down a JU-88 of KGr 806, but a Hurricane of that Squadron was shot down by the BF109s and crash-landed, wounding P.O. Coffin. A JU-88 probable was also claimed by P.O. Hulbert of 249 Squadron, but another Hurricane[160] of 185 Squadron was also lost to the escort, Sgt. Westcott also being wounded after bailing out.

On the 13th January, an aircraft[161] of 185 Squadron was destroyed on the ground in a raid on Hal Far. Six days later, three Hurricanes of 249 Squadron and one of 126 Squadron attacked Comiso airfield, two JU-88 probables being claimed on the ground, but one of 249 Squadron aircraft[162] was hit by flak and crash-landed at Luqa.[163] An afternoon raid was intercepted by 126, 242 and 249 Squadrons, F.O. Kay and P.O. Main of 126 Squadron claiming a JU-88 probable, which was confirmed. Sqn. Ldr. Norris of this unit force-landed unhurt at Takali with a dead engine. A Hurricane was also destroyed on the ground at Takali.

On the 21st January, three more Hurricanes were badly damaged in a raid on Hal Far. Next day, a morning raid was met by 16 Hurricanes of 126, 242 and 249 Squadrons, Flt. Lt. Kemp of 242 Squadron claiming an MC202 probable, although it is likely this was a BF109. Three JU-88s were claimed as damaged by Sgt. Gardiner of 242 Squadron, P.O. Main of 126 Squadron and P.O. Crichton of 126 Squadron/Flt. Lt. Davis and P.O. Tedford of 249 Squadron, one JU-88 of I/KG54 actually being lost.

An afternoon raid was engaged by 13 Hurricanes of the same three squadrons, Sgt. Boyd of 242 Squadron claiming a JU-88 probable. Unfortunately, an aircraft[164] of 242 Squadron was shot down by British flak gunners, Sgt. Neale being killed. A Hurricane was also badly damaged on the ground at Hal Far.

On the 24th January, an afternoon raid was intercepted by 23 Hurricanes of 126, 185, 242 and 249 Squadrons, three JU-88s of III/KG77 being escorted by eight BF109s. Sgt. Horricks of 185 Squadron claimed a JU-88 probable, but a Hurricane was destroyed on the ground at Luqa and two others were badly damaged at Hal Far. That night, on an intruder mission over Sicily by five Hurricanes of 1435 Flt, a JU-88 was claimed by F.O. Palmer of that unit. Next day, 15 Hurricanes of 126, 185, 242 and 249 Squadrons were tasked with providing cover for a departing ship convoy. They were 'bounced' by BF109s of Stab/JG53, which shot down three Hurricanes[165] of 126 squadron and one[166] of 249 Squadron. P.O. Russell of 126 Squadron was killed and P.O. Blackburn of the same squadron was wounded.

In addition, an aircraft of 185 Squadron and two of 242 Squadron were forced to crash-land by the BF109s, Flt. Lt. Thomson of the former unit also being wounded. A Hurricane was destroyed on the ground at Hal Far and another[167] was badly damaged.

On the 27th of the month, a Hurricane[168] of 1435 Flt on a training flight was shot down by rampaging BF109s, P.O. Mackie being killed. Later that evening, seven Hurricanes of 1435 Flt again flew to Sicily, a JU-88 being claimed by Sgt. Wood,[169] while a biplane was claimed by P.O. Grant. Next day, a Hurricane[170] was destroyed on the ground in a raid on Hal Far and a photo-recce aircraft[171] of 69 Squadron was shot down by flak over southern Italy, Sgt. Ballantine being taken prisoner. During January 1942, three JU-88s were destroyed by Malta's Hurricanes, for the loss of eight Hurricanes in combat, two by flak, one by accident and five destroyed on the ground.

At the start of February, there were 28 Hurricanes serviceable. On the 2nd February, a Hurricane[172] of 605 Squadron was destroyed on the ground at Hal Far. That night, on an intruder mission over Sicily, F.O. Thompson of 1435 Flt claimed a Cant Z-506B. Next day, an aircraft[173] of that unit crashed on landing at Takali, the pilot being unhurt.

On the afternoon of the 4th February, 11 Hurricanes of 126, 242 and 249 Squadrons scrambled against a raid on Takali, but were 'bounced' by BF109s, Z4016 and Z4003 of 249 Squadron and BV167 of 126 Squadron being shot down. Both Sgt. McDowall and P.O. Hulbert of the former unit and P.O. Main of the latter unit were killed.

On the 8th February, Sqn. Ldr. Norris of 126 Squadron crash-landed unhurt at Luqa, having been hit by return fire from a JU-88 which he engaged. Next day, an aircraft[174] of 249 Squadron was lost accidentally, resulting in the death of P.O. Stuart.

On the 11th February, Hurricanes from 126, 242, 249 and 605 Squadrons provided cover for a naval force approaching Malta. A formation of six JU-88s and four BF109s were spotted and engaged, a JU-88 probable being claimed by Wg. Cdr Rabagliati and P.O. Coffin of 126 Squadron.[175] A BF109 probable was also claimed by Flt. Lt. Lloyd of 185 Squadron, this also being confirmed.

Next day, 12 Hurricanes of 185 and 605 Squadrons scrambled before midday, meeting a JU-88, DO-24T and BF109 escorts. The JU-88 was jointly claimed by P.O.s Wigley, McKay and Ormrod of 185 Squadron, but Flt. Lt. Allen[176] of 605 Squadron was shot down by the BF109s, his fate being unknown. On the 15th February, Hurricanes of 242 Squadron and 1435 Flt engaged three JU-88s and five BF109s heading for Sicily, Wg. Cdr. Satchell claiming a BF109 and Wg. Cdr. Rabagliati another. One aircraft of II/JG53 was believed lost in this combat.

In an evening mission by 12 Hurricanes of 605 Squadron and 1435 Flt to escort a returning recce Maryland was 'bounced' by BF109s, P.O. Lowe of 605 Squadron being shot down[177] and killed.

On the 18th February, a recce aircraft was claimed as a probable by Sgt. Ellis and Sgt. Hunton of 185 Squadron. Two days later, P.O. Wigley of 185 Squadron claimed a JU-88 probable and another JU-88 probable was claimed by P.O.s Noble and McKay of 605 Squadron, one of these aircraft being confirmed lost. Next day, a Hurricane[178] was destroyed on the ground at Luqa.

On the 22nd February, seven Hurricanes of 185 Squadron were scrambled early afternoon and engaged JU-88s escorted by BF109s, one BF109 being claimed by Sgt. Sutherland of that Squadron,[179] but a Hurricane[180] of 185 Squadron was shot down by the BF109s, Sqn. Ldr. Chaffe being killed.

The following morning, Hurricanes of 185 Squadron engaged a formation of JU-88s and BF109s, a BF109 probable being claimed by Sgt. Horricks and a JU-88 probable by Flt. Lt. Lloyd. A later raid was intercepted by 242 Squadron, for whom Sgt. Boyd claimed a BF109 destroyed, this being confirmed as an aircraft of 10/JG53. A Hurricane[181] was damaged beyond repair at Takali in one of the raids this day.

On the 24th February, eight Hurricanes of 249 Squadron scrambled mid-afternoon, but were 'bounced' by BF109s, BG771 being shot down and Z3580 crash-landing. P.O. Tedford was killed in the former and Sqn. Ldr. Turner was wounded in the latter.

On the penultimate day of the month, Hurricanes of 126, 185 and 605 Squadrons met two JU-88s and three BF109s in the afternoon, one JU-88 being claimed by P.O. Ormrod of 185 Squadron and confirmed lost. During February, Hurricanes accounted for seven enemy aircraft, while losing nine of their number in air combat and three destroyed on the ground.

On the 1st March, 13 Hurricanes of 185, 242 and 605 Squadrons were scrambled at noon to intercept three JU-88s with BF109 escort. Flt. Lt. Stones and Flt. Sgt. Howe of 605 Squadron both claimed JU-88s and these were confirmed as aircraft from 8/KG77. Flt. Sgt. Howe was hit by return fire and he bailed out[182] wounded. One of the BF109s[183] was force-landed by P.O. Lester, also of 605 Squadron, but two Hurricanes[184] of 242 Squadron were shot down by the BF109s, both P.O. Tew and Sgt. Harvey being killed. Three days later, around 12 Hurricanes of 185, 242 and 605 Squadrons were scrambled in the afternoon to intercept five JU-88s with their BF109 escort.

P.O. Ormrod of 185/605 Squadrons claimed a BF109 and two others were claimed damaged by P.O. Kidson of 242 Squadron and Sgt. Wilson of 185 Squadron, two being confirmed lost. That night, a JU-88 of 2/KuFlGr 606 was shot down by Sgt. Wood of 1435 Flt.

Next day, before noon, six Hurricanes of 242 Squadron engaged five JU-88s, escorted by 10 BF109s, but one of the Hurricanes[185] was shot down by the escort, P.O. Kidson being killed. On the 6th March, eight Hurricanes of 185 Squadron were scrambled mid-afternoon to meet BF109s, one of which was claimed by Flt. Lt. Stones. The loss of four Hurricanes shot down in the first five days of March resulted in 21 remaining serviceable on the 6th March. That day, a Hurricane[186] of 185 Squadron was destroyed on the ground at Hal Far.

The first Spitfires arrived on Malta on the 7th March, 249 and

126 Squadrons now re-equipping with these aircraft.

On the 9th March, 19 Hurricanes of 185, 242 and 605 Squadrons scrambled mid-morning to intercept three JU-88s with nine BF109s as escort. A BF109 probable was claimed by Wg. Cdr. Rabagliati. Shortly after noon, 21 Hurricanes were scrambled to meet a formation of 18 JU-88s and 26 BF109s.

Sgt. Tweedale and F.O. Anderson of 126 Squadron both claimed JU-88s and P.O. Steele of the same squadron claimed a BF109, with P.O. Hallet,[187] claiming a BF109 probable. A Hurricane of 126 Squadron crash-landed after combat with the BF109s and was written off, slightly wounding P.O. Coffin. One JU-88 of I/KG54 and a BF109 of 2/JG53 were actually lost by the Germans.

The next day, 12 Hurricanes of 126 and 185 Squadrons were scrambled mid-morning with Spitfires for the first time, again meeting JU-88s with BF109 escort. Sgt. Mayall of 126 Squadron was shot down[188] and killed and F.O. West of 185 Squadron crash-landed unhurt.

An afternoon raid was engaged by 11 Hurricanes of 185 and 242 Squadrons,[189] one JU-88 being jointly claimed by Flt. Lt. Kee, P.O. Morrison-Jones and Sgt. Boyd of 242 Squadron, but no losses were sustained by the Germans. On the 13th March, a Hurricane was destroyed on the ground at Takali and next day, another was destroyed at Hal Far. On the 15th March, a late afternoon raid by three JU-88s with six BF109s as escort was intercepted by eight Hurricanes of 126 and 185 Squadrons, plus Spitfires, Wg. Cdr. Satchell claiming a BF109. Three days later, 242 and 605 Squadrons disbanded, their pilots being absorbed into 126 and 185 Squadrons respectively.

An evening raid by 24 JU-88s with BF109 escort was engaged by 11 Hurricanes of 126 and 185 Squadrons,[190] two Hurricanes[191] of the latter unit being shot down, with Sgt. Mulloy killed and P.O. Lester severely wounded. Two more Hurricanes were also destroyed on the ground at Takali this day.

On Saturday, the 21st March, a large morning raid by over 200 aircraft was followed by a sweep of eight BF110s escorted by 35 BF109s which was engaged by six Hurricanes of 185 Squadron.

Sqn. Ldr. Mortimer-Rose claimed two of the Zerstorers, while another was jointly claimed by P.O.s Allardice and Beckitt and a fourth by P.O.s Ormrod and Wigley, although the Germans only admitted a single loss. However, four Hurricanes were destroyed on the ground at Takali during the raids this day. Next day, seven Hurricanes of 185 Squadron intercepted a morning raid by six JU-88s with 20 BF109s as escort. One Hurricane[192] of this Squadron was shot down by the JU-88s, killing P.O. Allardice. On the 23rd March, a Hurricane of 185 Squadron engaged one of four BF109 fighter-bombers on a shipping strike, Sgt. Horricks shooting down one of the BF109s. Later the same day, two more Hurricanes of 185 Squadron engaged what was reportedly an He 111,[193] both Flt. Lt. Lawrence and Sgt. Broad jointly claiming it shot down.

Next day, four Hurricanes of 185 Squadron were scrambled to intercept a late afternoon raid by eight JU-88s, three of which were claimed damaged.[194] An aircraft of 9/KG77 failed to return. To meet a mid-afternoon raid by 30 JU-88s, 25 JU-87s and 13 BF109s on the 25th March, eight Hurricanes of 185 Squadron accompanied Spitfires to intercept. A Stuka was claimed shared by P.O. Ormrod and P.O. Wigley, while a probable was also shared by Sgt. Eastman, Sgt. Wilson and Sgt. Robb, with another probable claimed by Sgt. Horricks. One JU-87 was actually lost in this raid.

On the 26th March, six Hurricanes accompanied Spitfires against a late afternoon raid by 24 JU-88s, 18 JU-87s and at least six BF109s, P.O. Steele of 185 Squadron claiming a JU-88 and an aircraft of I/KG54 was indeed lost. Next day, 10 canon-armed Hurricane IICs of 229 Squadron arrived on Malta as reinforcements.

On the last day of March, small raids by JU-88s and BF109s were made over a period of several hours, one Hurricane[195] of 185 Squadron being shot down by BF109s in one of these raids, killing P.O. Steele. A night raid the same day by six bombers was met by four Hurricanes of 185 Squadron, Sgt. Horricks claiming a JU-88 probable. Thirteen enemy aircraft were confirmed to the Hurricanes in March, for the loss of 11 Hurricanes in combat and eight more destroyed on the ground.

On the afternoon of the 1st April 1942, six Hurricanes of 185 Squadron scrambled with Spitfires to meet a raid by 15 JU-88s of I and II/KG77, with their escort. P.O.s McKay and Beckitt jointly claimed a JU-88 in this engagement and Sgt. Fletcher claimed a probable, but none were confirmed. A later raid of around 54 JU-87s plus JU-88s and escorts was met by seven Hurricanes of 185 and 229 Squadrons, Sgt. Fletcher claiming a JU-87 and a probable, while Sgt. Boyd claimed a JU-87 probable. Sgt. Pauley of 229 Squadron also claimed a JU-87 probable. Spitfires and AA gunners also submitted Stuka claims, but only two were actually lost. Next day, an afternoon raid by 26 Stukas and 29 JU-88s was intercepted by seven Hurricanes of 185 Squadron, together with Spitfires. P.O. Milburn of 185 Squadron claimed a JU-88 probable. A raid that night destroyed a Hurricane at Hal Far. The following day, another Hurricane was destroyed around noon on the same airfield.

On the 5th April, 40 JU-88s[196] and 15 JU-87s of III/StG3, plus escort, attacked early in the afternoon, four Hurricanes[197] and four Spitfires being scrambled to intercept them. One of the JU-88s was jointly claimed by P.O. Noble, P.O. McKay and Sgt. Boyd of 185 Squadron and although a JU-88 crash-landed on return to Sicily, it was believed to have been hit by AA fire. Next day, a large raid destroyed five Hurricanes[198] at Luqa. Nine more Hurricanes of 229 Squadron arrived on the 6th April.

On the 8th April, an early afternoon raid by 12 JU-88s with 21 BF109s as escort was intercepted over Kalafrana by seven Hurricanes of 185 and 229 Squadrons, plus three Spitfires. One of the bombers was claimed by both Sgt. Boyd of 185 Squadron and a Spitfire pilot, one JU-88 of KuFlGr 606 being lost.

Boyd also claimed a probable in this raid. Late next afternoon, a Hurricane was destroyed on the ground at Takali by JU-88s, 10 Hurricanes and two Spitfires scrambling to intercept this raid of 60 plus JU-88s and 12 Stukas. A JU-88 probable was claimed by the prolific Sgt. Boyd, but Sgt. Pauley of 229 Squadron was shot down[199] and wounded.

Another late afternoon raid on the 10th April by around 85 JU-87s and JU-88s, plus escort, was engaged by 12 Hurricanes of 185 and 229 Squadrons, with four Spitfires. Sgt. Horricks of the former unit claimed a BF109 shot down, an aircraft of III/JG53 being lost by the Germans, but a BF109 claim was also submitted by a Spitfire pilot. Two Hurricanes[200] were shot down, P.O. Broad being wounded and P.O. Wigley unhurt. In addition, three more Hurricanes[201] crash-landed after combat with the BF109s, P.O. Ormrod being wounded, while Sgts. Vidler and Pendlebury were unhurt. Next day, afternoon and evening raids destroyed a Hurricane on the ground at Luqa and another four at Hal Far.[202] The following day, another Hurricane[203] was destroyed at Hal Far.

Late afternoon on the 14th April, two Hurricanes of 185 Squadron were scrambled to protect a returning force of Beauforts which was under attack from BF109s. Sgt. Yarra was forced to crash-land at Hal Far after this combat. Four days later, four raids were made against Malta's airfields, no fighters being available to engage them and two more Hurricanes were destroyed at Hal Far. A similar situation prevailed the following day, when another Hurricane was burnt out on the same airfield.

A further seven Hurricanes of 229 Squadron arrived on the 19th April, and on the 20th April, another batch of 46 Spitfires arrived on Malta. That morning, a Hurricane[204] of 229 Squadron was destroyed in a raid on Hal Far. As soon as it was known by the axis that the Spitfires had arrived, raids came in thick and fast.

Five Hurricanes of 185 and 229 Squadrons scrambled against one of these, early evening, Sgt. Tweedale of the former unit claiming two JU-88 probables. Sgt. Yarra was again forced to crash-land at Hal Far after this combat.

Next morning, the first raid of 37 JU-88s, escorted by 34 BF109s approached at 0730 hrs and was intercepted by five Hurricanes of 185 and 229 Squadrons, also with 10 Spitfires. P.O. Horricks of 185 Squadron claimed a JU-88 probable, but Sgt. Fullalove of 229 Squadron was shot down[205] and killed.

On the 22nd April, a late afternoon raid of 50 JU-88s, 20 JU-87s and BF109 escort was engaged by two Hurricanes of 185 Squadron and six Spitfires. P.O. Wigley claimed a BF109 probable, but P.O. Ormrod[206] was shot down by both flak and a BF109 and killed. Next day, a mid-morning raid by 42 JU-88s, 15 JU-87s and BF109 escort destroyed a Hurricane on the ground at Takali and another at Hal Far. Six Hurricanes and six

Spitfires intercepted the raid, a Stuka being claimed by Sgt. Tweedale of 185 Squadron.

This was confirmed as an aircraft of III/StG 3. On the morning of the 24th April, a raid by 30 JU-88s with 20 BF109s as escort, hit Luqa and destroyed two Hurricanes on the ground.

Just after noon the following day, 80 JU-88s and JU-87s attacked and were intercepted by six Hurricanes of 185 and 229 Squadrons, plus seven Spitfires. Sgt. Dodd of 185 Squadron claimed a Stuka probable, while Sgt. Tweedale of the same Squadron claimed a BF109. However, Flt. Sgt. Corfe of 229 Squadron[207] was shot down by a combination of BF109s and AA fire and killed.

An evening raid of 57 JU-88s and 24 JU-87s attacked the airfields and was met by seven Hurricanes of 185 and 229 Squadrons, with four Spitfires. P.O. Noble of 185 Squadron claimed a BF109 and P.O. Fletcher of the same Squadron, a JU-88, which was confirmed as an aircraft of KGr 806 or 5/LG1, both of which lost bombers this day.

Sgt. Brooks of 229 Squadron is thought to have destroyed a JU-87 before he was himself shot down[208] by BF109s and killed. On the afternoon of the 26th April, 55 JU-88s, 15 JU-87s and their BF109 escort mounted a raid on Kalafrana and Valetta, being met by four Hurricanes of 185 and 229 Squadrons and six Spitfires. Sqn. Ldr. Dafforn of 229 Squadron[209] was hit and crash-landed at Hal Far, being wounded.

That night, a Hurricane[210] of 1435 Flt on an intruder mission over Sicily, was shot down by flak, killing Sgt. Wood. Two days later, an early morning raid by approximately 43 JU-88s, 20 JU-87s and BF109 escort was engaged by four Hurricanes of 185 Squadron plus three Spitfires as the raid reached Malta. A Hurricane[211] flown by P.O. Fletcher was shot down by a BF109, Fletcher being killed.

The two Hurricane Squadrons claimed four JU-88s,[212] three JU-87s[213] and two BF109s[214] in April.[215] Fourteen Hurricanes were shot down in the month, mostly by BF109s and a further 22 were destroyed on the ground. On the 20th April, a further 46 Spitfires had arrived on Malta, but such was the intensity of the attacks that within three days, the survivors had all been grounded. In March, the Spitfire units had claimed 16 enemy aircraft[216] and in April, this increased to 48.[217] Spitfire losses had been four in the air, plus two on the ground in March and 17 in the air, plus 22 on the ground in April.

On the 1st May, night raiders were intercepted by three Hurricanes of 185 Squadron, Sgt. Yarra of that Squadron claiming a JU-88 probable, but there is no confirmation of this loss. Three days later, a late afternoon raid by 12 JU-88s destroyed two Hurricanes on the ground at Hal Far. A further five replacement Hurricanes arrived for 229 Squadron on the 4th May and another on the 5th. On the morning of the 6th May, four Hurricanes of 229 Squadron, with four Spitfires, scrambled to engage a raid of 10 JU-88s and 10 BF109s. A Hurricane[218] was hit by fire from one of the bombers and crash-landed at Hal Far, Sgt. Roy being wounded.

Another aircraft of the same squadron[219] was also lost in this combat, killing Sgt. Lees. Next day, the Italians despatched five Cants and 15 MC202s early in the evening, as 20 plus BF109s patrolled the coast. Eight Hurricanes and six Spitfires intercepted, Sgt. Tweedale of 185 Squadron claiming a BF109, but no confirmation is possible.

On the 9th May, a morning raid of six JU-88s, 15 JU-87s and 14 MC202s as escort was engaged by 11 Hurricanes of 185 and 229 Squadrons, with four Spitfires.

Sgt. Boyd of 185 Squadron claimed a JU-88, Sgt. Tweedale a BF109, plus a probable and a JU-88 probable and Sgt. Dodd an MC202 probable. A JU-88 of KGr 806 was actually lost by the Germans. However, a Hurricane[220] of 185 Squadron was hit and belly-landed at Takali.

A Stuka attack on the 13th May destroyed a Hurricane[221] at Hal Far. Five days later, in the morning, four Hurricanes of 229 Squadron accompanied two Spitfires to protect an air-sea rescue launch, Sgt. Pendlebury being shot down[222] by BF109s and killed. On the 27th May, 12 Hurricanes of 229 Squadron departed for the Middle East, sufficient Spitfires now being available on Malta. Sgt. Wilcox[223] was shot down by an MC202 but was unhurt, while two others[224] failed to arrive, Sgt. Ganes and P.O. Lee being taken prisoner.

May 1942 was the last month of significant Hurricane operations over Malta, although Hurricanes continued to operate from the island. Three Hurricanes were destroyed on the ground in May, five were shot down and another two failed to return. One JU-88,[225] two BF109s[226] and an MC202 probable were the only Hurricane claims this month.

On the 13th July, a late morning raid on Luqa destroyed a Hurricane on the ground.

From March to November (7th) 1942 inclusive, although 513 claims were made in air combat by Spitfire units operating from Malta, only 205 of these can be confirmed, for the loss of 166 Spitfires in the air and 34 on the ground. Hurricane squadrons claimed approximately 227 enemy aircraft over Malta,[227] of which 126 can be confirmed for 120 Hurricanes[228] lost in air combat, five to flak, 20 accidentally plus 49 destroyed on the ground.[229]

Victory-to-loss ratios in air combat were thus very similar if confirmed, rather than claimed victories are compared – 1.05 for the Hurricane Squadrons and 1.23 for Spitfire units. Of course, the Hurricanes fought for 20 months before the Spitfires arrived and were often only available in small numbers to meet the German and Italian attackers. The top scoring Hurricane pilot of the Malta campaign was Wg. Cdr. A.C. 'Sandy' Rabagliati DFC, with nine kills, plus one half share, one quarter share and two probables.

References
1   Of the 259th Squadriglia, 109th Gruppo, 36th Stormo.
2   Of the 9th Gruppo.
3   Of the 233rd Squadriglia, 59th Gruppo, 40th Stormo.
4   Of the 195th Squadriglia.
5   An aircraft of the 192nd Squadriglia which was claimed as a probable, but upgraded to confirmed.
6   P2623.
7   Of the 259th Squadriglia, 109th Gruppo, 36th Stormo.
8   N2716.
9   Of the 192nd and 193rd Squadriglias, 87th Gruppo, 30th Stormo.
10 Of the 236th and 237th Squadriglias.
11 Of the 237th Squadriglia.
12 Of the 70th Squadriglia.
13 Of the 71st and 72nd Squadriglias.

14 Of the 80th Squadriglia, 17th Gruppo, 1st Stormo.
15 From the 72nd Squadriglia.
16 Of the 75th Squadriglia, 23rd Gruppo.
17 In N2701.
18 Of the 193rd Squadriglia, 87th Gruppo, 30th Stormo.
19 N2622.
20 Plus two probables.
21 Of LG1.
22 Of I/StG1.
23 Of 7/LG1.
24 Of the 6th Gruppo.
25 Two of I/StG1 and one of II/StG2.
26 Of 8/LG1.
27 P2629.
28 From 6/LG1.
29 One other was claimed by a Fulmar pilot.
30 Of 5/KG26.
31 Of II/LG1.
32 N2715 and P3733.
33 Well above 20,000 ft.
34 In V7731.
35 Extracts from Flt. Lt. Teddy Peacock-Edwards Flying Log, courtesy of his son, Rick Peacock-Edwards.
36 Of 1/NJG3.
37 BF109s of 7/JG26, MC200s of the 6th Gruppo and CR.42s of the 156th Gruppo.
38 Including V7121 and V7474.
39 McDougal's Hurricane was V7102.
40 Of 4/LG1.
41 Of StG1.
42 In P2645.
43 Possibly of the 23rd Gruppo.
44 'A' Flight of 274 Squadron.
45 P2653, V7493, V7799, V7358 and V7672.

46 Of JG26 and possibly also JG3.
47 Of III/StG1.
48 Of the 6th Gruppo.
49 In V7495.
50 Of the 184th Squadriglia.
51 In V7340.
52 Or the 3rd April?
53 Of the 17th Gruppo.
54 Of the 23rd Gruppo.
55 Of 7/JG26.
56 In Z3036 and Z2904.
57 In P3978.
58 In V7116.
59 In V7418.
60 Of 2(F)/123.
61 Of 9/StG1.
62 In Z2838.
63 In V7472.
64 In Z2032.
65 Of LG1.
66 Of 9/LG1.
67 Z2900 and Z3061.
68 In Z3054.
69 Of 9/KG30.
70 Of II/KG26.
71 Of 7/JG26 and III/JG27.
72 Z3057, Z3059 and Z3060.
73 Of 8/KG30.
74 Of 4/KG26.
75 V7365 and V7548.
76 By II and III/StG1.
77 Of 9/StG1.
78 Of III/JG27.
79 In Z2837.

80   V7115.
81   Of III/JG27.
82   Z2901.
83   Z3035.
84   Again of III/JG27.
85   Of the 10th and 30th Stormos.
86   N2673.
87   Of the 56th Squadriglia, 30th Gruppo, 10th Stormo.
88   Of the 99th Gruppo.
89   Of the 193rd Squadriglia.
90   Of the 7th Gruppo.
91   Z2480.
92   Of the 67th Squadriglia, 32nd Gruppo.
93   Of the 7th Squadriglia, 17th Gruppo.
94   Of the 612th Squadriglia.
95   Of the 23rd Gruppo.
96   Of the 74th Squadriglia.
97   Of the 23rd Gruppo.
98   Of the 7th and 17th Gruppos.
99   Of the 16th Gruppo.
100 Z4058.
101 Of the 32nd Gruppo, 58th Stormo.
102 Of the 10th and 16th Gruppos.
103 One each.
104 Of the 16th Gruppo.
105 Of the 193rd Squadriglia.
106 Of the 7th, 10th and 16th Gruppos.
107 Of the 90th Squadriglia, 10th Gruppo.
108 Of the 7th Gruppo.
109 Of 5-RST.
110 Of the 43rd Stormo.
111 Of the 10th Stormo.
112 Of the Ricognizione Marittima.
113 Of the 612th Squadriglia.

114 Of the 54th Stormo.
115 Of the 7th, 10th and 16th Gruppos.
116 Of the 10th Gruppo.
117 Of the 10th Gruppo, 54th Stormo.
118 Of the 98th Squadriglia, 7th Gruppo.
119 Of the 7th Gruppo.
120 Of the 98th and 76th Squadriglias.
121 Of the 56th Squadriglia, 30th Gruppo, 10th Stormo.
122 Ten confirmed.
123 Z3055.
124 MNFU.
125 Of the 43rd Stormo.
126 Including one from 99th Gruppo.
127 Of the 43rd Stormo.
128 Of the 10th and 30th Stormos.
129 Both of the 612th Squadriglia.
130 Of the 10th Gruppo.
131 Of the 612th Squadriglia.
132 Of the 10th Gruppo and 54th Stormo.
133 Z3056 and Z3521.
134 Of the 9th Gruppo, 4th Stormo.
135 In Z5265.
136 Z2518.
137 Of the 75th Squadriglia, 23rd Gruppo.
138 Z3512.
139 By unknown pilots.
140 Plus one probable.
141 Two SM.81s, one MC202 and one BR.20M confirmed.
142 Forty-nine more had arrived in September.
143 In Z3033.
144 In Z3158.
145 In Z3053.
146 Z2491.
147 Plus three probables.

148 Two confirmed.
149 Of the 259th Squadriglia, 109th Gruppo, 36th Stormo.
150 Of 1/NJG2.
151 Of I/JG53.
152 Z2823.
153 Z2332.
154 In Z4943.
155 Plus one probable.
156 Plus two probables.
157 Six JU-88s and one BF109 were actually lost.
158 Three in collisions and one on the ground.
159 Plus three probables.
160 Z5155.
161 Z2592.
162 BV174.
163 Sqn. Ldr. Beazley was unhurt.
164 BE346.
165 BG765, BD828 and Z2827.
166 Z5147.
167 Z4315.
168 Z3571.
169 And confirmed.
170 BG752.
171 Z3173.
172 Z2509.
173 Z3570.
174 Z5326
175 And confirmed.
176 In Z2527.
177 In BG755.
178 BG744.
179 And confirmed.
180 Z3452.
181 BG754.

182 Of Z3756.
183 Of II and III/JG53.
184 Z2824 and Z4002.
185 Z2402.
186 Z2819.
187 Also of 126 Squadron.
188 In Z5140.
189 Plus four Spitfires.
190 Also Spitfires.
191 Z2840 and Z5213.
192 BG711.
193 This was probably a JU-88 of KuFlGr 606.
194 By P.O. Beckitt, Sgt. Broad and P.O. Noble / Flt. Sgt. Fletcher jointly.
195 Z5302.
196 Some of KGr 806.
197 Of 185 and 229 Squadrons.
198 Z3757, BE349, BE351, BG698 and BG 7640.
199 In Z3505.
200 Including Z3766.
201 BG756, BN122 and BN 142.
202 Including BN122 and BN142.
203 BE562.
204 BE710.
205 In BN278.
206 In Z4011.
207 In BE708.
208 In BN182.
209 In BV163.
210 BE347.
211 Z2698.
212 Plus six probables.
213 Plus four probables.
214 Plus one probable.
215 Two JU-88s and a JU-87 confirmed.

216 Nine confirmed.
217 Fourteen confirmed.
218 BM964.
219 BN181.
220 BD789.
221 BE716.
222 In BN362.
223 In Z4005.
224 Z2982 and BE642.
225 Plus two probables.
226 Plus a probable.
227 Plus 78 probables.
228 Possibly 122?
229 It is believed that 311 Hurricanes arrived on Malta in the various delivery flights. Fifty-four more are known to have been lost while being delivered.

Chapter Twelve
Channel Front – Post Battle of Britain

Although the Battle of Britain officially drew to its completion at the end of October 1940, there was much air combat over the English Channel and its environs for the remainder of that year. Hurricane squadrons claimed 78½ enemy aircraft[1] in November 1940 and 10[2] in December 1940.

Included in these totals were a 'Stuka Party' over the Thames Estuary on the 8th November, during which 15 JU-87s and six probables were claimed by 17 Squadron, although only three were actually lost by the Germans. P.O. Leary claimed two, one shared and a probable, Wg Cdr Farquhar, two, Sgt. Hogg, one and one shared and Sgt. Griffiths, two and one shared.

Also, on the 11th November came the only major daylight bomber raid against Britain by the Italian Air Force, which was beaten-off with heavy losses to the attackers. Nine BR.20 bombers and four CR-42 biplane fighters were claimed off Harwich by 46 and 257 Squadrons, three of each type actually being lost to Hurricanes.[3] 17 Squadron also claimed three JU-87s and four probables, two BF109s and a probable this day. Sgt. Bartlett claimed one of the JU-87s and a probable.

In an engagement on the 17th November off Harwich, four BF110s were claimed by 17 Squadron and two BF109s and a probable by 257 Squadron. However, one Hurricane of each squadron[4] was shot down by Obst. Lt. Adolf Galland of JG26 in a BF109. F.O. Czernin of 17 Squadron bailed out safely, but Sgt. Henson of 257 Squadron was killed.

Flt. Lt. Teddy Peacock-Edwards of 253 Squadron reported on the 22nd November,

> *'Patrol. Hastings – Beachy Head. 1 DO-17Z attacked and damaged.'*

He had better luck on the 3rd December,

> 'Interception – 1 DO-17Z badly damaged. Attacked with Cooper and Edgley – then chased bandit out over channel and set it on fire – confirmed.'[5]

Interestingly, the 253 Squadron ORB for that day describes this combat in detail, but records a different result;

> 'Three Hurricanes of 253 Squadron Blue Section left Kenley at 1350 hrs with orders to scramble base at 10,000 ft and were subsequently vectored onto an enemy raid over the I.A.Z.[6] No bandit was seen and after orbiting the I.A.Z. for some minutes, the section was vectored onto a second enemy raid, south-west of London.
> When over Weybridge District at 12,000 ft a bandit was sighted about seven miles distant, 2,000 ft lower down. F.O. Edwards, Blue Leader, fired a five second burst from quarter rear position and return fire from the rear gunner's position ceased almost immediately.
> F.O. Edwards continued to chase the enemy aircraft, which was heading for France, skimming the surface of the cloud at about 7,000 ft. He caught enemy aircraft as they reached the coast and fired the remainder of his ammunition from dead astern at 75–100 yards range. He saw white smoke coming from the enemy aircraft and pieces falling off wings and fuselage as it went into cloud in a shallow dive – 1 DO-17Z damaged.'

Squadron Leader Tuck of 257 Squadron claimed DO-17s destroyed on the 9th and 29th December and a BF109 on the 12th of that month.

Sixty-two Hurricanes were lost in November 1940, of which 37 were in air combat. A further 26 Hurricanes were lost in December 1940, including seven in air combat and at least 16 in accidents.

By the beginning of 1941, there were 39 Hurricane Squadrons and 19 Spitfire squadrons in Fighter Command, but by June 1941, only 26 Hurricane Squadrons remained in the command, as against 23 of Spitfires. Replacement of Hurricanes by Spitfires had commenced, as other Hurricane Squadrons were also posted to the Middle East.

Nevertheless, Hurricanes were extensively used in both defensive and offensive operations on this front during 1941, resulting in 181½ enemy aircraft being claimed by Hurricane Squadrons, for the loss of 239 Hurricanes, including at least 78 in air combat.

Hurricane Mk. II.

The first three months of 1941 were relatively quiet for the Hurricane squadrons, with claims for 29 enemy aircraft in combat, for the loss of 60 Hurricanes.[7] These claims were mostly for bombers, including five He 111s, six DO-17s, two DO-215s and eight JU-88s. Six BF109s and two BF110s were also claimed. 85 Squadron scored its first night victory on the 25th February.[8] Night claims by Hurricane squadrons increased over the following three months.

Although offensive operations, known as 'Circuses', had commenced as early as January 1941, they did not continue in great regularity until after the German attack on Russia, on the 22nd June 1941. It was soon realised after this date that defence of the West by the Germans then rested with only two fighter-wings, JG2 and JG26, and pressure was increased on this relatively small force by Fighter Command.

Hurricanes participated in these and other offensive operations, although Spitfire units predominated. This resulted in increased air combat claims for the two BF109-equipped Jagdgerschwadern.

Following claims by Hurricane Squadrons for 21½ enemy aircraft in April 1941 and 44 in May, although only 34 were claimed in June, 26 of these were BF109s.[9] Eight of these claims[10] were by 1 Squadron. Hurricane losses were 31 in April,[11] 36 in May[12] and 24 in June.[13]

The pace of offensive operations continued in July 1941, Hurricane-equipped units submitting claims for 23 enemy aircraft, of which 16 were BF109s. Only 14 Hurricanes were lost this month, including at least three in air combat. The pace eased in August, 13 enemy aircraft being claimed by Hurricane Squadrons, five of which were BF109s, for the loss of 22 Hurricanes, although only five of these were in air combat. September 1941 brought only five enemy aircraft claimed by Hurricane pilots and 13 Hurricanes lost, of which at least three were probably shot down by BF109s.

The rate that Hurricane Squadrons replaced their aircraft with Spitfires increased in October 1941, four Squadrons[14] exchanging their Hurricanes for the Supermarine fighter. This, and the continuing move of Hurricane squadrons overseas, contributed to the reduced number of enemy aircraft claimed by Hurricane Squadrons in the last quarter of 1941.

Only 11 enemy aircraft were claimed from October to December, inclusive, seven of which were JU-88s and only one BF109. Thirty-nine Hurricanes were lost, but only five of these are known to have been in air combat, whereas at least 13 were shot down by flak.

Pilot Officer Richard Stevens of 151 Squadron claimed 14½ enemy bombers at night, during 1941, before he was lost in December.

By the end of January 1942, only 13 Hurricane squadrons remained in

Fighter Command and only four of these were in 11 Group, which still bore the brunt of operations. In fact, during the whole of 1942, only 52 enemy aircraft[15] were claimed by Hurricane squadrons on the Channel Front.[16]

The top scoring Hurricane Squadron on the Channel Front in 1942 was 1 Squadron, which claimed 22 enemy aircraft on intruder missions, from the 1st April to the 1st July. Of these, 15 bombers were claimed by Flight Lieutenant Kuttelwascher, a Czech, to add to the three BF109s he claimed in 1941. 3 Squadron claimed 15 kills, plus one shared and five probables during the year.

A total of 78 Hurricanes were lost during the year, only approximately 10 of these in air combat. Twenty-one of the Hurricanes lost were during the Dieppe Operation of the 19th August, 15 being lost to flak.

No further air combat claims were made by Hurricane Squadrons on this front, but 16 Hurricanes were lost on operations in 1943, at least one of these in air combat. Three more Hurricanes were lost to flak in January and February 1944, before the type was withdrawn from combat operations in this theatre.

Hurricane Mk.IIC fitted with two 90 gallon ferry tanks.

Hurricane fighter bomber.

Hurricane IIs.

Hawker Hurricane – defender of the skies

Hurricane Mk.IIC.

Hurricane Mk.IIB.

Hurricane Mk.IID.

Hurricane of the Eagle Squadron preparing for take-off.

References

1. Thirty-four confirmed.
2. Four confirmed.
3. Flt. Lt. Gaunce of 46 Squadron claimed two CR-42s, a share in another and a probable and P.O. Mrazek of the same squadron claimed two destroyed. Flt. Lt. Blatchford and P.O. Pniak of 257 Squadron both claimed a BR.20 and shared another between them, Pniak also sharing another.
4. V7500 of 17 Squadron and N2342 of 257 Squadron.
5. Extract from Flying Log of Flt. Lt. Teddy Peacock-Edwards.
6. Inner Air Defence Zone.
7. Twenty-one in air combat.
8. A DO-17.
9. Only four BF109s were claimed in April and 12 in May.
10. Plus three probables.
11. Ten in air combat.
12. Eighteen in air combat.
13. Thirteen in air combat.
14. 303, 316, 317 and 504 Squadrons.
15. And 11 probables.
16. Included in this total were 16 JU-88s; 14 DO-217s; 12 He 111s and only three BF109s.

CHAPTER THIRTEEN

Battle of Greece

Italy attacked Greece on the 28th October 1940 and although RAF units had been assisting the Greeks from early in the campaign, the first six Hurricanes for 80 Squadron did not arrive until the 17th February 1941. These were closely followed on the 19th February by the 17 Hurricanes of 33 Squadron. In their first operation on the 20th February, four G.50s were claimed by 80 Squadron,[1] without loss to themselves, two G.50s actually being lost by the Italians.

On the 27th February, a patrol of nine Hurricanes[2] intercepted a formation of CR-42s over Valona and although nine CR-42s were claimed,[3] individually only four-and-a-half were claimed by 80 Squadron and one by 33 Squadron in official records.[4] Again, no Hurricanes were lost, but only two CR-42s were actually lost by the Italians.

Next day, claims were even greater, when a combined patrol of 33 Squadron,[5] 80 Squadron[6] and 112 Squadron Hurricanes and Gladiators engaged large numbers of Italian fighters and bombers between Tepelene and the coast. Flt. Lt. Pattle claimed two BR-20s and two CR-42s,[7] with F.O.s Ackworth and Wanklyn Flower claiming one BR-20 each and F.O. Cullen claiming two SM-79s and two CR-42s. Actual losses by the Italians were three BR-20s[8] and two CR-42s to the Hurricanes and Gladiators. 33 Squadron could only claim two Cant Z.1007s damaged in this combat.

On the 1st March, three CR-42s were claimed by Sgt. Ted Hewett of 80 Squadron,[9] while on the 3rd, five unescorted Cant Z.1007s and one S.81 were claimed near Corfu, also by 80 Squadron,[10] two of the Cants actually being lost.

Next day, during a combined patrol by 10 Hurricanes,[11] five G.50s and three CR-42s[12] were claimed by 80 Squadron near Valona, Flt. Lt. Pattle claiming three G.50s and a CR-42 probable, Sgt. Hewett, three CR-42s

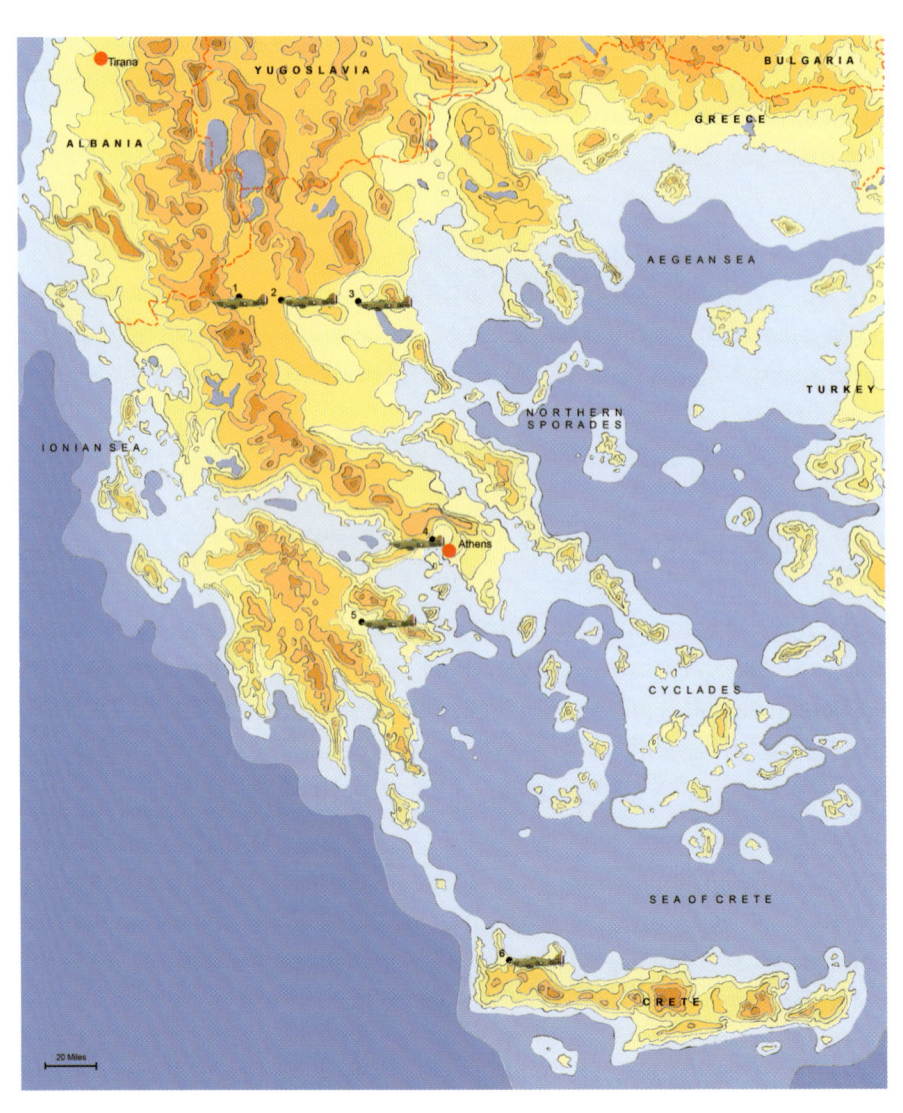

1 Yannina 3 Larissa 5 Argos
2 Trikkala 4 Eleusis 6 Maleme

and a G.50 and P.O Vale another G.50. However, W.O. Goodchild of 33 Squadron[13] and F.O. Cullen of 80 Squadron[14] were both killed. Only two CR-42s were lost by the Italians this day.

The next series of combats involving Hurricanes were on the 13th and 14th March. On the 13th March another combined patrol of six Hurricanes of 33 Squadron and 14 Gladiators of 112 Squadron again claimed heavily, in the Kelcyre area. Three CR-42s[15] and a G.50 probable were claimed by 33 Squadron, two of the CR-42s being admitted by the Italians.

In a large battle next day, in the same area, F.O. Holman of 33 Squadron claimed a monoplane, while Flt. Sgt. Cottingham and P.O. Starett of the same squadron each claimed a monoplane and a probable. In return, F.O. Holman was shot down, but bailed out unhurt. Two MC200s were admitted lost by the Italians this day.

In a strafing attack on Fieri airfield on the 23rd March, Sqn. Ldr. Pattle,[16] F.O. Holman and F.O. Woodward each claimed a G.50 in air combat, while F.O. Newton claimed a probable. Pattle also claimed three G.50s on the ground. The Italians only admitted to one G.50 destroyed on the ground and none in air combat. One Hurricane[17] was shot down by a G.50 in an earlier attack on Berat, F.O. Dyson being wounded.

On the 2nd April, 33 Squadron intercepted a raid on Volos and claimed five Cant Z.1007 bis and a probable, three and a probable to F.O. Woodward and single claims to Flt. Lt. Littler and F.O. Kirkpatrick. Two Cants were actually lost by the Italians.

The Hurricanes of 33 Squadron returned to strafe again on the 5th April, claiming another two G.50s in the air and two on the ground. Earlier in the day a Hurricane of 33 Squadron was shot down by flak, F.O. Dyson bailing out uninjured.

On the 6th April, Germany entered the Balkan campaign by attacking Greece and Yugoslavia. The Hurricanes had a great start against the Luftwaffe, as 33 Squadron encountered 20 BF109s of III/JG 27 over Bulgaria this day and claimed five for no loss. Squadron Leader Pattle claimed two, Flt. Sgt. Cottingham claimed one and shared another with P.O. Winsland and F.O. Wickham claimed the fifth. Three BF109s were actually lost and another crash-landed. A JU-88D was also claimed[18] this day as it approached Athens, by F.O. Dowding of 80 Squadron.

On the 7th April, a DO-215 was claimed by Sqn. Ldr. Pattle over Yugoslavia, but this aircraft was only damaged. On the 8th, several enemy aircraft were claimed destroyed on Petrich airfield in Bulgaria by 33 Squadron, including two by Sqn. Ldr. Pattle. Next day, Pattle claimed a JU-88 damaged near Larissa, although this may have been a DO-17 that was lost by the Germans and actually on the 10th April. He also claimed a BF110 and a BF109 over Macedonia, but these claims were unconfirmed. A Hurricane of 80 Squadron was shot down south of Bitolj by flak on the 10th, but Flt. Lt. Woods managed to belly-land uninjured.

On the 11th, a JU-88 and an He 111 were claimed near Volos by Pattle, although these were in fact both JU-88s and on the 12th, a DO-215 and an SM-79 were claimed by him east of Salonika, with another SM.79 shared by F.O.s Holman and Starett, also of 33 Squadron.

A BF109 was claimed by F.O. Woodward and a BF110 by F.O. Wickham of 33 Squadron over Mount Olympus on the 13th, the BF110 being confirmed. Also, this day, a JU-88 was lost, probably also to 33 Squadron,[19] although it wasn't claimed.

The next day, 33 Squadron claimed even more heavily – three JU-87s,[20] one HS126,[21] one BF109, two JU-88s, one BF110 and an SM-79[22] being claimed, but only two JU-88s and several JU-87s were actually lost by the Germans. One JU-87 was also claimed near Servia by P.O. Vale of 80 Squadron. A Hurricane of this Squadron was hit and force-landed.

On the 15th April, however, three of 33 Squadron's Hurricanes were 'bounced' on take-off from Larissa by BF109s and two were shot down, Flt. Lt. Mackie and P.O. Chetham being killed, although Mackie had managed to shoot down one of the BF109s first and another BF109 was force-landed by Sgt. Genders. Another Hurricane was destroyed on the ground.[23] Six JU-88s[24] were also claimed over Athens and a BF109 further north by 80 Squadron, but only two of the JU-88s crash-landed, in reality. P.O. Vale claimed two of the bombers, Sgt. Hewett one and a probable, with one each to P.O. Still, P.O. Dahl and Flt. Sgt. Rivalant. F.O. Coke claimed the BF109.

By the end of the day, the RAF in Greece had 18 Hurricanes left on its strength – 11 with 80 Squadron, five with 33 Squadron and two reconnaissance machines with 208 Squadron.

On the 16th April, a JU-88 was claimed north-east of Poltika by F.O. Graham of 80 Squadron and confirmed. An HS126 was also claimed by Flt. Sgt. Cottingham of 33 Squadron, but was, in fact, only damaged. Later the same day, three more JU-88s were claimed near Eleusis by 80 Squadron,[25] three DO-17s actually being lost. Next day, a BF109 was claimed near Katerine by Sgt. Barker of 80 Squadron and confirmed by Australian troops.[26]

On the 18th April, five replacement Hurricanes arrived to reinforce 33 Squadron. Early on the 19th, two JU-88s[27] were claimed near Athens by Sqn. Ldr. Pattle of 33 Squadron, but not confirmed in German records. A Stuka attack was then intercepted near Pmokos by 80 Squadron, four JU-87s[28] and an escorting BF109 (by F.O. Trollip) being claimed, but only two JU-87s were actually lost.

On subsequent patrols, 33 Squadron claimed an HS126[29] and five BF109s, plus a probable[30] in the Lamia area and a JU-88[31] over Khalkis harbour, although two Hurricanes of 33 Squadron were force-landed by BF109s.[32] The HS126, JU-88 and one BF109 were confirmed as lost and another BF109 force-landed.

The RAF units had now withdrawn south to the Athens area and on the 20th April, the air battle over Greece reached its climax.

On the morning of the 20th, a Hurricane of 80 Squadron[33] was shot down near Tanagra by BF109s, P.O. Still being killed and one of 33 Squadron[34] was force-landed, also killing F.O. Holman. In return, a DO-17 was shared by several pilots of 33 Squadron and confirmed. Early in the afternoon, Sqn. Ldr. Pattle claimed two BF109s of JG77 over Eleusis and Tanagra airfields, which were confirmed.

Less than two hours later, in a raid on Eleusis, two of 33 Squadron's Hurricanes were destroyed on the ground. Pattle also claimed a JU-88 around this time.

There were now 15 serviceable Hurricanes[35] and in the late afternoon on the 20th, all 15 engaged a large raid on Piraeus. 33 Squadron claimants in this battle were Flt. Sgt. Cottingham,[36] F.O. Woodward,[37] Flt. Lt. Kettlewell[38] and credited to Sqn. Ldr. Pattle, one JU-88 or BF110.

The victorious 80 Squadron pilots were Sgt. Casbolt,[39] Sgt. Hewett,[40] F.O. Newton,[41] F.O. Wickham,[42] Flt. Sgt. Wintersdorff[43] and Flt. Lt. Woods.[44] In total, five JU-88s, eight BF110s, one FW187, one DO-17 and five BF109s were claimed. In addition, seven twin-engined types and a BF109 were listed as 'probables'.

Although the detailed 33 and 80 Squadron records were destroyed in Greece, the 80 Squadron Operational Record states that:

> 'In the afternoon, the greatest combat in the epic battle for Athens when 15 Hurricanes took on 90 German fighters and bombers; was fought with great determination; shown always by pilots of the Royal Air Force. In spite of the fact that the enemy were superior in numbers, the 15 Hurricanes destroyed no less than 15 of the enemy.'

The price of victories was very high, however. 33 Squadron lost Sqn. Ldr. Pattle[45] and F.O. Starrett[46] was killed and Flt. Sgt. Cottingham[47] wounded. Flt. Lt. Woods of 80 Squadron[48] was also killed, whereas Flt. Lt. Kettlewell[49] and Flt. Sgt. Wintersdorff[50] were wounded.

Sqn. Ldr. Pattle had possibly accounted for his 50th victory, before he was killed, making him the top-scoring RAF fighter pilot of the war, the majority of his victories coming on Hurricanes. Actual Luftwaffe combat losses this day were four DO-17s, two JU-88s, three BF110s and four BF109s.

Next day, two more Hurricanes were destroyed in a Stuka raid on Eleusis. The remaining 18 Hurricanes of 33, 80, and 208 Squadrons withdrew to Argos on the 22nd April and in the late morning of the 23rd, a JU-88 was claimed by F.O. Newton of 33 Squadron, the bomber crash-landing near Almyros.

Three JU-87s attacking Piraeus were also claimed by Sgt. Genders of 33 Squadron, but it is possible that this engagement took place on the 24th April, when three Stukas were reported missing. A BF109 was also claimed by Genders. However, following earlier raids on the 23rd, a devastating

Battle of Greece

raid by I/ZG 26 BF110s on Argos airfield in the afternoon destroyed 13 of the Hurricanes on the ground. A Hurricane of 80 Squadron[51] was also shot down on take-off by the BF110s, wounding Sgt. Barker.

Next day, the seven remaining serviceable Hurricanes[52] withdrew to Crete.

References

1. Sgt. Casbolt claimed two and Flt. Lts. Pattle and Woods one each.
2. Five of 80 Squadron, four of 33 Squadron.
3. Including two in a collision.
4. Flt. Lt. Pattle and F.O. Cullen, Sgt. Hewett (two), F.O. Ackworth and F.O. Wanklyn Flower (reportedly shared with F.O. Starett of 33 Squadron) of 80 Squadron and Flt. Sgt. Cottingham of 33 Squadron are known to have claimed.
5. Including five Hurricanes.
6. Four Hurricanes.
7. Plus a probable.
8. Plus another force-landed.
9. There is no Italian record of this action.
10. Four Cants to F.O. Cullen and one to F.O. Ackworth, with the S.81 claimed by P.O. Vale.
11. Four of 80 Squadron and six of 33 Squadron.
12. Plus one probable.
13. In V7801.
14. In V7288.
15. Plus two probables.
16. He had been promoted to command 33 Squadron.
17. V7415.
18. And confirmed.
19. Pattle.
20. Two by F.O. Woodward and one by F.O. Dean near Servia.
21. By P.O. Winsland.
22. All by Sqn. Ldr. Pattle.
23. One source stated that 14 Hurricanes were destroyed on the ground at

	Larissa this day, although the German claim was for four Hurricanes destroyed on the ground, plus several unidentified types.
24	Plus one probable.
25	P.O. Vale, P.O. Still and Sgt. Hewett claimed one each.
26	But not admitted by the Germans!
27	Plus one probable.
28	Two by P.O. Vale, one by F.O. Dowding and one by Flt. Sgt. Rivalant.
29	Shared by Sqn. Ldr. Pattle, F.O. Woodward and Flt. Lt. Littler.
30	Three and a probable by Pattle, one by Woodward and one by F.O. Moir.
31	Also by Pattle.
32	F.O. Moir in P2643 at Amphiklia and Flt. Lt. Mitchell at Eleusis.
33	V7748.
34	V7860.
35	Nine of 80 Squadron, six of 33 Squadron.
36	Three BF110s.
37	One BF110 and one JU-88 probable.
38	One BF110.
39	Three BF109s.
40	Two BF109s.
41	Two JU-88s.
42	One JU-88.
43	One FW187.
44	Two BF110 probables.
45	In AS988.
46	In V7804.
47	In V7765.
48	In V7852.
49	In V7807.
50	In V7718.
51	V7773.
52	Five replacements had arrived on the 23rd April.

Chapter Fourteen

Crete

On the 24th April 1941, the remaining eight Hurricanes of 33 and 80 Squadrons[1] were evacuated from Greece to Maleme in Crete (all of 208 Squadron's Hurricanes were lost in Greece). These were formed into a composite unit called 'The Hurricane Unit, Crete' and its first victory came on the 28th April when a reconnaissance JU-88 was shot down by F.O. Kirkpatrick of 33 Squadron. Next day, the same pilot claimed an HS126 or Italian RO-44, but no confirmation was available.

Also on the 29th April, a raid of 20 JU-88s attacked Suda Bay and was intercepted by the Hurricanes, two of the raiders being claimed shot down by F.O. Vale of 80 Squadron. Another JU-88 was claimed by Vale on the 30th, although no German losses were recorded over Crete on this date.

> *'From the beginning of May until 12th May a normal routine was maintained, consisting of protective patrols over ships evacuating troops from Greece until about 4th May, followed by standing patrols over Suda Bay and a number of "scrambles" during the following week. Two of these "scrambles" were successful in intercepting the enemy.'*[2]
>
> *'In the first of these*[3] *F/O Woods and Sgt. Genders encountered about 24 JU-88's, F/O Woods shooting down one confirmed and damaging a second, while Sgt. Genders damaged four.'*

In fact, two JU-88s were lost by the Germans.

The next day,

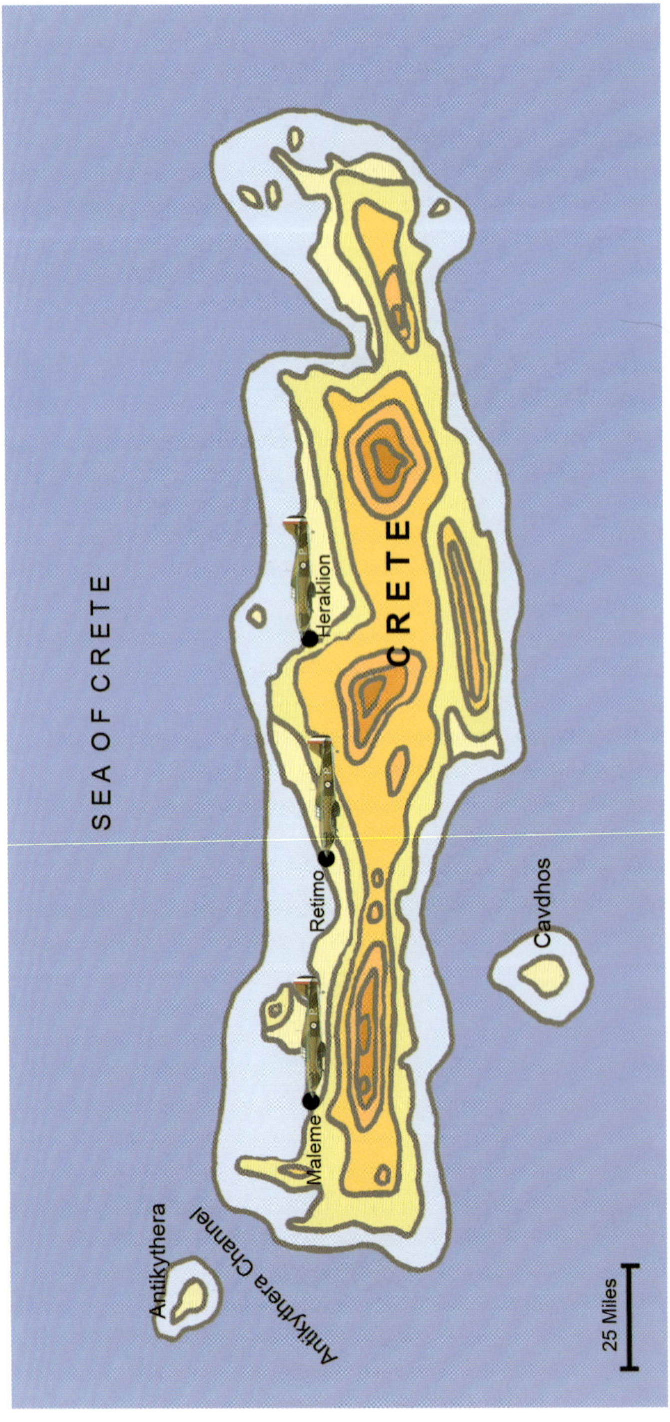
SEA OF CRETE
CRETE
Heraklion
Retimo
Maleme
Cavdhos
Antikythera
Antikythera Channel
25 Miles

> *'in the second engagement, F/O Woods and F/O Noel-Johnson encountered 12 more JU-88s, each pilot damaging at least two enemy aircraft.'* [2]

A further JU-88 claim on the 5th May by F.O. Vale of 80 Squadron was unconfirmed (no loss was recorded this day by the Germans).

By the 6th May, the Hurricane unit was down to six serviceable aircraft.[2] On the evening of the 12th May, Squadron Leader Howell arrived from Egypt and took charge of the unit. He was accompanied by six other relief pilots who replaced six pilots who had been in Crete since the Greek evacuation.

During flying practice on the 13th May, F.O. Dunscombe overshot the aerodrome and crashed.[4] The same day, two replacement Hurricanes were flown into Crete as reinforcements and a JU-52 was claimed by F.O. Vale.

Next day, serious attacks were made on Suda Bay and Maleme airfield:

> *'09.00 HRS. A large number of M.E. 109s strafed the aerodrome for half an hour. Three Hurricanes took off to intercept, Sgt. Ripscher and Sgt. Reynish getting off before the strafing had developed. In the third machine, S/Ldr Howell took off as the aerodrome was being strafed.*
>
> *'He passed 20 yards to the rear of one enemy aircraft and across the path of another, and keeping very low until he reached the hills, he was then able to climb safely. A few minutes later he shot down one M.E. 109 confirmed, one M.E. 109 damaged.*
>
> *'Meanwhile, Sgt. Reynish was in combat with three E/A, one of which was seen to dive steeply into the hills after the Hurricane had made a stern attack. At the same time, Sgt. Ripscher sighted six E/A out to sea and attacked. One E/A was seen to dive steeply towards the sea. Sgt. Ripscher was also attacked and apparently damaged and was killed whilst making his approach to the aerodrome. Sgt. Reynish was shot down and bailed out over the sea, and succeeded in swimming*

> *a distance of two miles back to safety. In the first raid, one Hurricane was burnt out on the ground, while in the evening raid a second was also destroyed.'*[2]

Two BF109s were actually claimed by Sqn. Ldr. Howell and Sgt. Reynish (and confirmed) but four Hurricanes were lost – Reynish[5] was shot down by the BF109s, Sgt. Ripsher[6] was shot down accidentally by Flak and another two Hurricanes were destroyed on the ground.

On the 15th May, a Hurricane was shot up on take-off by BF109s, although Flt. Lt. Woodward escaped unhurt and a further four replacement Hurricanes arrived, two each for 33 and 112 Squadrons.

On the 16th May, at 1700 hrs,

> *'a number of J.U.87s and 88s escorted by M.E. 109s attacked Suda Bay and were intercepted by S/Ldr Howell, who shot down one M.E. 109 confirmed and one J.U.87 'probably'. Two further M.E. 109s were shot down by others, the enemy aircraft crashing on Maleme beach and their pilots taken prisoner.'*[2]

Three BF109s,[7] a JU-52,[8] a JU-87 and a BF110[8] were claimed by the Hurricane pilots, but three Hurricanes were shot down and another force-landed. F.O. Vale of 80 Squadron claimed one of the BF109s and the JU-87, Lt. Ramsay[9] claimed two BF109s, Squadron Leader Howell of 33 Squadron claimed the JU-52 and the BF110 was claimed by Flt. Lt. Fry of 112 Squadron. Two of 805 Squadron pilots[10] were killed and Flt. Lt. Fry[11] was wounded as he bailed out.

On the 18th May, a replacement Hurricane was shot down by BF109s as it was attempting to land, Sgt. Vernon Hill being killed. Another Hurricane[12] was destroyed on the ground during a raid, only one serviceable Hurricane then remaining at Maleme. Two other Hurricanes from Heraklion diverted to Retimo, whilst the other Hurricane at Heraklion was unserviceable. These two Hurricanes were then ordered to evacuate to Egypt. On the 19th May, the last serviceable Hurricane at Maleme followed them to Egypt.[13]

Crete

Thus, prior to the actual invasion of Crete, 16 enemy aircraft and a probable were claimed[14] by the composite Hurricane unit for the loss of nine Hurricanes in the air, three on the ground, plus two unserviceable machines left at the airfields. The invasion of Crete commenced on the 20th May.

On the 23rd May, 73 Squadron was ordered to despatch six Hurricanes to Heraklion, to operate against the invasion forces. Five of the Hurricanes returned, after encountering the British Naval Flak barrage, but one aircraft[15] landed at Heraklion and was destroyed by strafing BF110s. Later in the day, another six Hurricanes of 73 Squadron arrived at Heraklion. They returned to Egypt next morning, but encountered strong headwinds, two Hurricanes[16] being lost without trace and two others[17] force-landing. F.O. Donati and P.O. Moss were unharmed in the latter two aircraft.

274 Squadron at Gerawla had now received four Hurricanes with long-range tanks fitted, but with reduced ammunition and the seat-back armour plating removed to balance the increased weight. As a result, these aircraft were also slower and less manoeuvrable.

Early on the 25th May, three Hurricanes of 274 Squadron left Egypt for Crete. A JU-88 was claimed shot down by P.O. Hamilton of that unit, but on landing at Heraklion, his Hurricane was severely damaged. Later in the day, another two Hurricanes of 274 Squadron attacked Maleme. A JU-52 and an SM-79 were claimed by Flt. Lt. Honor, but both were probably JU-52s. However, the two Hurricanes[18] were both shot down, at least one by BF109s. Flt. Lt. Honor was injured after bailing out, but Flt. Lt. Down in the other Hurricane failed to return. 274 Squadron now received another six long-range Hurricanes.

Next day, 274 Squadron was ordered to send six Hurricanes against the transport aircraft flying into Maleme.

> *'All our long-range Hurricanes took off to attack at 15 minute intervals every aircraft over and around Maleme. Quite a number of aircraft were seen and P.O. Tracey destroyed one J.U.52 and one M.E.109. F/Sgt. Le Bois also destroyed one J.U.52 whilst F/O Peronne severely damaged a J.U.52.*

P/O Tracey's aircraft was badly damaged whilst in combat and he was forced to land at Sidi Barani where he will remain the night. F/Lt. Jacquier, Sgt. Glover and Sgt. Kerr have not yet returned from these operations.'[19]

A total of six JU-52s and a BF109 were claimed by 274 Squadron, of which three JU-52s were confirmed. Flt. Lt. Jacquier[20] claimed three of the JU-52s, a JU-52 and the BF109 were claimed by F.O. Tracey and Sgt. Kerr and F. Sgt. Lebois[20] claimed one JU-52 each. However, F.O. Tracey[21] force-landed back at Sidi Barrani, Sgt. Kerr[22] was shot down by a BF109[23] and Flt. Lt. Jacquier[24] was also hit and captured after crash-landing on Crete.

On the afternoon of the 27th May, two Hurricanes of 274 Squadron claimed two JU-88s near to the Cretan coast. F.O. Weller claimed one and Sgt. Nicolson the other, but only one JU-88 was actually lost.

The 28th May saw no conclusive encounters, but next day,

'eighteen Hurricanes carried out protective patrols over H.M. Ships between Alexandria and Crete from dawn until dusk. Whilst on patrol, P/O Tracey with a Maryland intercepted a J.U.88 and after a short combat shot it down into the sea. P/O Summer also had a combat with a D.O.17 and damaged same.'[19]

The JU-88 was confirmed lost, although a Hurricane[25] of 274 Squadron was shot down by a BF109, Sgt. Nicolson being lost.

On the 30th May,

'during this morning patrol, F/O Peronne intercepted three H.E.111Ks and after a short combat shot one down into the sea. This afternoon, P/O Tovey in company with a Maryland intercepted another H.E.111K and after doing some attacks the enemy aircraft dived into the sea.'[19]

In fact, two He 111s and a JU-88 were claimed by 274 Squadron this day and although all three bombers were confirmed, one was actually a DO-17. F.O. Peronne claimed one He 111,[26] P.O. Tovey claimed the other He 111 and P.O. Sumner claimed the JU-88, although this may have been shared with a Beaufighter.

The 31st May was the penultimate day of the evacuation from Crete.

> *'This morning, P/O Summer encountered a J.U.88 and shot same down into the sea, whilst Captain Driver had a similar success a little later and about midday, F/O Littolf*[20] *shot another down whilst on patrol. This afternoon, Lt. Talbot very severely damaged two aircraft and shortly afterwards P/O Talbot identified a CANT 1007 on recce and after a short combat, shot down same into the sea. Sgt. Guillou has not yet returned from this morning's operations.'*[19]

Three JU-88s were claimed by 274 Squadron this day, one of which was shared with a Maryland.[27] A Hurricane[28] failed to return, having probably been shot down.

Since the invasion of Crete began, 18½ enemy aircraft had been claimed by 274 Squadron for the loss of seven of that Squadron's Hurricanes. In addition, 73 Squadron lost three aircraft. Eight-and-a-half of 274 Squadron's claims can be confirmed. A total of 34½ enemy aircraft were claimed during the Crete campaign by Hurricane pilots, of which 17½ can be confirmed. At least 24 Hurricanes[29] are believed to have been lost, 13 in air combat.

In July 1943, a large-scale air strike was made on Crete in reprisal for the death of a 100 Cretans who had been executed after a commando raid on the island. On the 23rd of that month, a force of 93 Hurricanes from 12 Squadrons[30] of 212 and 219 Groups, Air Defence, Eastern Mediterranean, set out in three formations to attack Crete in an operation called 'Thesis'. Anti-aircraft defences were very effective and 13 of the Hurricanes were lost.[31]

References

1. 33 Squadron had four Hurricanes and eight pilots, while 80 Squadron had four Hurricanes and three pilots. Pilots of 112 and 805 (Naval) Squadrons also fought with the Hurricane Unit.
2. 33 Squadron ORB.
3. On the 3rd May – 33 Squadron ORB.
4. In V7800 – 33 Squadron ORB.
5. In V7714.
6. In W9297.
7. Two confirmed.
8. Confirmed.
9. An 805 Squadron pilot.
10. Lt. Ash and Lt. Richardson.
11. In V7857.
12. N2610 of 33 Squadron.
13. 33 Squadron ORB for the 19th May reports that He 112s were being used as well as M.E. 109s for repeated strafing raids. Sgt. Bennett flew the remaining Hurricane to Egypt.
14. Nine confirmed.
15. V7424.
16. V7736 and V7764 with P.O.s Goord and Likeman both failing to return.
17. V7802 and V7879.
18. W9266 and P3469.
19. 274 Squadron ORB.
20. Free French.
21. In Z4511.
22. In Z4312.
23. But survived.
24. In Z4632.
25. Z4634.
26. Actually the DO-17.
27. Only one confirmed.
28. W9273 piloted by Sgt. Guillou.

29   Possibly as many as 40.

30   9, 74, 94, 123, 134, 237, 238, 335, 336, 451, 7 SAAF and 41 SAAF Squadrons.

31   OPERATION 'THESIS' LOSSES:

      94 SQUADRON – KW935 – Sgt. W.G. Imrie missing.

      123 SQUADRON – KZ141; HW538; KW964 – Sqn. Ldr. K.N.T. Lee; F.O. J.D. Lemare; Flt. Sgt. F.W. Farfan all missing.

      134 SQUADRON – HW299; HW372 – F.O. W.A.P Manser; Sgt. D.A. Horsley both missing.

      41 SAAF SQUADRON – Lt. Jack Bliss? Missing.

      238 SQUADRON – KZ130; HW483 – Flt. Sgt. P.A. George; Flt. Sgt. H.D.R. Rayment both missing.

      335 SQUADRON – Flt. Sgt. Doucas; Flt. Sgt. Laitmer both missing.

      336 SQUADRON – W.O. Athanassakis; W.O. Scantzicas both missing.

Chapter Fifteen
Iraqi Campaign

On the 1st April 1941, a coup in Iraq brought to power a pro-German leader, Rashid Ali. The likelihood of this regime proving a threat to British interests in the Middle East prompted the British to inform Rashid Ali on the 16th April of their intention to send troops through Iraq to Palestine, in accordance with existing treaty rights. Not waiting for German assistance, the Iraqi army mobilised against the British airfield at Habbaniyah on the 30th April. Although this operation failed, it was obvious to the British that military assistance was required and a small force known as 'Habforce' arrived at Habbaniyah from Transjordan on the 18th May.

The first German aircraft had arrived in Iraq on the 15th May, attacking Habbaniyah on the 16th and on the 17th May, 94 Squadron, equipped with four Hurricanes and nine Gladiators, had arrived at Habbaniyah to assist 'Habforce'. A further two Hurricanes soon arrived for 94 Squadron from Egypt, equipped with long-range tanks. Five more Hurricanes, including a tactical reconnaissance version, were delivered later to 94 Squadron.

On the 20th May,

> *'Two Hurricanes sent to pursue four ME110s which had attacked West of Ramadi failed to make contact.'*[2]

Later the same day,

> *'a total of seven Hurricanes took off on alarms. Two pursued ME110s that had attacked Falluja and one got in a burst. Two sighted no enemy aircraft and two attacked and damaged two of three He 111s, silencing the rear gunner. Three Gladiators and two Hurricanes escorted bombers in a raid on Rashid and machine gunned the hangar on the east side of the aerodrome, but with no apparent damage.'*[1]

On the 22nd May,

> 'Two Hurricanes attacked dispersed aircraft at Mosul and destroyed two, probably more. A/F/Lieutenant Sir R.A. MacRobert[3] is reported 'missing' as a result of an engagement during this attack.'[1]

Three days later,

> 'Four aircraft on Mosul Aerodrome were machine gunned – one Hurricane was hit but not affected.'[1]

Later that day,

> 'Two Hurricanes machine gunned Baguba, destroying two aircraft and damaging others.'[1]

Next day,

> 'Two Hurricanes recce'd Baguba, Shahnadan, Guaragha and Raschid without result'.[1]

On the 29th May,

> a Hurricane on recce near Ramedi machine gunned three lorries and boats on Lake Habbaniya.'[1]

The following day,

> 'one Hurricane made a recce of Ruguba; no enemy aircraft seen.'[1]

Later the same day,

'One Hurricane and three Gladiators escorted bombers in a raid on Khadiman; no enemy aircraft seen.'[1]

On the last day of May, in another uneventful mission,

'Two Hurricanes escorted bombers in an attack on Washash; no enemy aircraft seen.'[1]

An armistice had been signed by this day.

References
1. 94 Squadron ORB.
2. These were the two long-range Hurricanes, fitted with extra fuel tanks.
3. In Hurricane – 2498 – believed shot down by flak.

Chapter Sixteen

Syrian Campaign

On the 8th June 1941, British, Commonwealth and Free-French forces invaded Syria to eliminate the threat posed by Vichy French Forces. Hurricane Squadrons were operated throughout the campaign, including 80, 208, 260, 450 (Australian) and 127 Squadrons.

On the first day of the campaign, a Hurricane[1] of 208 Squadron was shot down by a Dewoitine D.520 of French unit GCIII/6. The fate of the pilot is unknown but,

> *'it was learnt that F/Lt. J.R. Aldis was missing from a recce in the Damascus area.'*[2]

Next day, an enemy bomber was claimed by Flt. Lt. Lockhart of 80 Squadron,[3] while F.O. Westlake of the same Squadron claimed a D.520, a share in another D.520 with Sgt. Wallace and a Potez 63 probable. However, two Hurricanes of 80 Squadron were shot down in this encounter, P.O.s Lynch and Crowther both being killed. In addition, a Hurricane and a D.520 are believed to have been lost when they collided, but the Hurricane pilot, Sgt. Bennett, survived.

On the 11th June, P.O. Bill Vale of 80 Squadron claimed a Potez 63-11[4] and the following day, he claimed two D.520s (wrongly), but his Hurricane was wrecked in a forced landing when its engine failed, Vale being unhurt. A Hurricane of 208 Squadron was also shot down by flak and crash-landed this day.

On the 13th June,

> *'Six Hurricanes escorted a formation of Blenheims to bomb Rayak (Syria) aerodrome. Two of the Hurricane formation broke away to intercept one Potez 63.'*[5]

Hawker Hurricane – defender of the skies

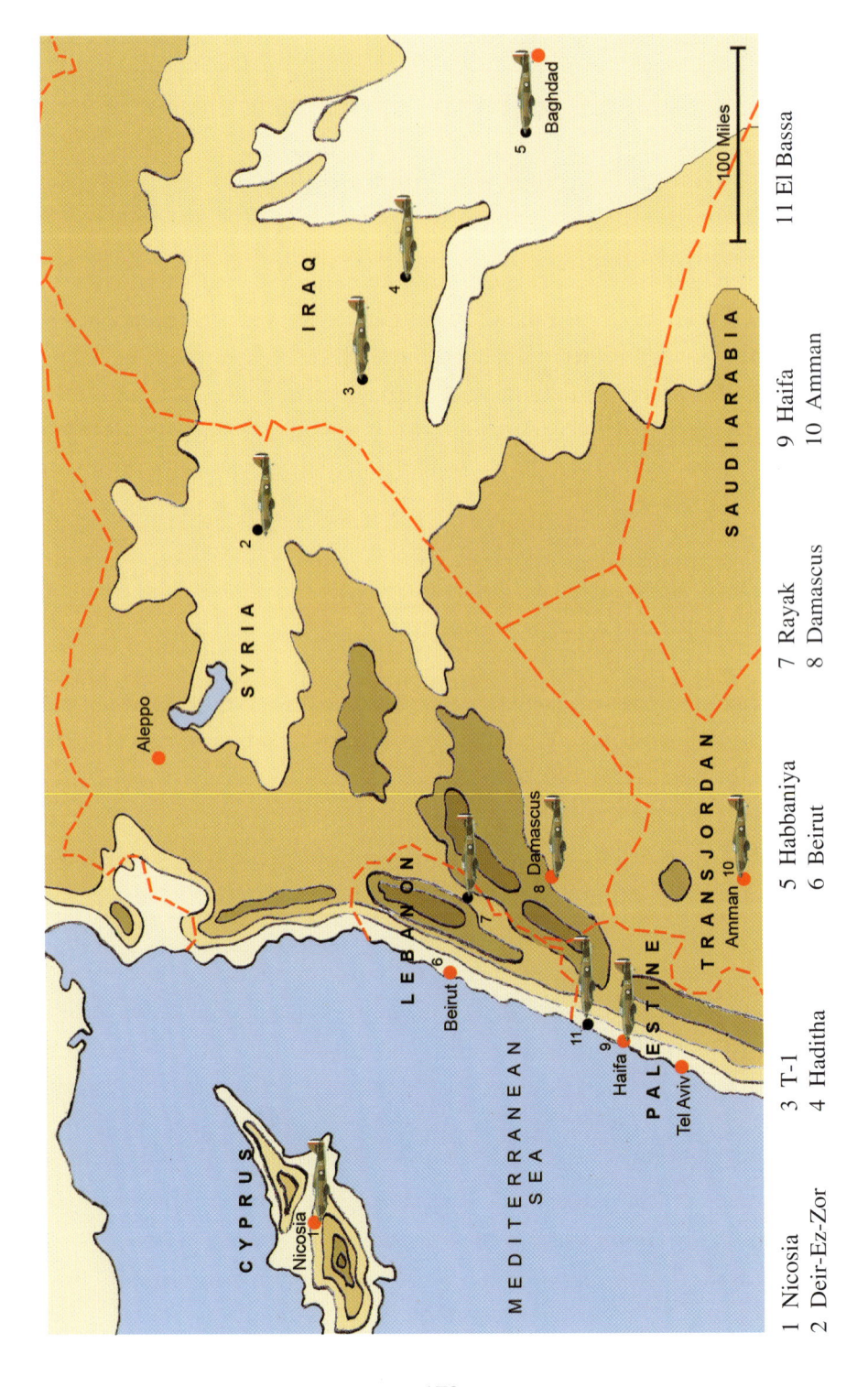

1 Nicosia
2 Deir-Ez-Zor
3 T-1
4 Haditha
5 Habbaniya
6 Beirut
7 Rayak
8 Damascus
9 Haifa
10 Amman
11 El Bassa

However, this interception was indecisive.

Next day,

> '*protective patrols were carried out during the day over the fleet. A formation of three Hurricanes chased Dewoitines, but were in turn attacked by six Dewoitines. In the ensuing combat, one confirmed and one unconfirmed victory was obtained.*'⁵

In fact, a D.520 was claimed by F.O. Dowding and a probable by F.O. Hancock. Dowding's victim was reportedly seen to crash by the Navy, but was in fact written off on landing.

On the 15th June,

> '*Six Hurricanes intercepted a formation of approximately nine JU-88s, which were attacking the fleet. One was shot down into the sea. Later it was reported by the fleet that another force-landed in Syria and one in the sea off Cyprus.*'⁵

One of the JU-88s was claimed shot down by P.O. Roald Dahl⁶ of 80 Squadron and another was claimed force-landed by the same unit. One JU-88 actually force-landed in Turkey. Two Hurricanes of 208 Squadron (including -2626), were tragically shot down by allied flak this day, both F.O. Macrostie and F.O. Holdsworth being killed.⁷

However, the decisive actions of the Syrian campaign were the strafing attacks on Vichy airfields, commencing on the 23rd June, which General Jeannequin, the enemy air commander, reported destroyed or damaged beyond repair, some 55 aircraft.

That day,

> '*a formation of six Hurricanes ground strafed Rayak and Talia Aerodromes in Syria with excellent results. At least five aircraft were left burning at Talia. Amongst those strafed were three Glen-Martins, three Potez 63 and three Dewoitines.*⁸ *The formation was protected by a flight of No. 260 Squadron Hurricanes, who were attacked by Dewoitines from Rayak. In the combat, two Hurricanes were shot down.*'⁵

In fact, three Hurricanes[9] of 260/450 Squadrons were shot down by D.520s of GC III/6. P.O. Baldwin was killed, Sgt. Black became a PoW and P.O. Livingstone was wounded.

Next day, the Baalbeck airfields were attacked by 260/450 Squadrons but no losses were recorded.

However, on the 26th,

> 'Six Hurricanes of 80 Squadron operating from the airport[10] accompanied by six Hurricanes of No. 260 Squadron operating from the Satellite, ground strafed Rayak Aerodrome. At least three Dewoitines and one Potez bomber were left in flames,[11] while at least six other Dewoitines were heavily machine gunned and left U/S. All our aircraft returned safely.'[5]

On the last day of June, 10 Hurricanes of 260/450 Squadrons attacked Madjaloun, where a Martin 167F was destroyed in flames.

On the 1st July, 127 Squadron entered the fray.

> 'Contact was made by one of our own aircraft with two Dewoitine fighters, one of which was damaged.'[12, 13]

Next day,

> 'Three fighter patrols were carried out over Deir Ez Zor. During the first patrol, five Dewoitines were encountered by one of our aircraft, which led to a dog fight without apparent damage.'[13, 14]

On the 3rd July,

> 'three fighter patrols over Deir Ez Zor. From the evening patrol two of our machines failed to return. It was later established that both had been shot down.[15] Flight Sergeant Adams was buried at Deir Ez Zor, but no trace was found of Warrant Officer Pitcher.'[13]

The D.520s of GC III/6 claimed two Hurricanes in this combat, but one of these[16] was actually lost in a collision. On an airfield south-west of Hama, also on the 3rd, two bombers were claimed set on fire and eight probably damaged by Hurricanes of 260/450 Squadrons.[17]

On the 5th July,

> *'two fighter patrols operated over Deir Ez Zor. The evening patrol encountered 10 bombers escorted by a number of fighters. In the fight which followed, two of our machines were reported missing.'*[13]

Two more Hurricanes of 127 Squadron were indeed shot down by D.520s of GC III/6 in this engagement.

Next day,

> *'Flt. Lt. Cremin (one of the missing pilots) returned to the Squadron and reported the loss of both machines.'*[13]

Also this day, the Naval D.520 squadron, 1 AC, Flotille 1F, claimed a Hurricane shot down. 450 Squadron attacked Baalbeck Aerodrome this day.[18]

On the 7th July,

> *'Squadron Leader Bodman (the other missing pilot) returned to the unit, slightly wounded.'*[13]

Two days later,

> *a formation of seven Hurricanes carried out a ground strafing sweep of Rayak Valley. A number of Glen Martins and Farman trainers were damaged.'*[5]

No more decisive actions involving Hurricanes occurred before an armistice was signed on the 12th July.

Twenty-one enemy aircraft were claimed destroyed on the ground in this campaign by Hurricane Squadrons, including at least five Potez

63-11s, two Potez 650s, three D.520s, two M.S. 406s, five Martin 167Fs and a PZ 25TOE.

As well as the enemy aircraft destroyed on the ground, 80 Squadron claimed one bomber, four D.520s, one Potez 63, plus a probable, one JU-88 and two force-landed in the air. In reality, only two MB200s, one D.520 and a force-landed JU-88 can be confirmed. P.O. Bill Vale of 80 Squadron was the top scoring Hurricane pilot of the campaign with three claimed kills.

However, at least 15 Hurricanes were lost; nine to the D.520s, plus two in collisions; three to flak and one to engine failure.

References

1 Z4364.
2 208 Squadron ORB
3 Two MB200s of EB 3/39 were actually lost.
4 Although no known French loss was recorded.
5 80 Squadron ORB.
6 He later became a famous author.
7 Holdsworth was actually killed on the ground by French colonial troops.
8 Three Martin 167Fs, 5 Potez 63-11s and a Pz 25TOE were actually destroyed in this attack.
9 Z4353, Z4537 and Z6984.
10 Haifa.
11 Although these are believed to have been destroyed earlier in the day by Tomahawks.
12 This D.520 was claimed damaged by Flt. Lt. Cremin of 127 Squadron and was probably an aircraft of GC II/3 which crash-landed this day.
13 127 Squadron ORB.
14 GC II/3 wrongly claimed a Hurricane this day, probably of 127 Squadron – Le Dewoitine D.520, Aero Journal No.8, Dec. 2004.
15 V7543 and V7654 were the aircraft lost.
16 V7654.
17 Four aircraft of GB I/25 were actually destroyed.
18 450 Squadron ORB – 4 LEOs + 1? were hit – the ORB is illegible here.

Chapter Seventeen

Cyprus

Several RAF Hurricane Squadrons were deployed to defend Cyprus during the war in the Mediterranean, but opportunities for decisive air combats were rare. However, on the 18th July 1941,

> 'Pilot Officer Westlake, attached to 80 Squadron, shot down a JU-88, the first to be destroyed over the island.'[1]

The small island of Castelrosso, to the east of Rhodes, had fallen into British hands in September 1943, along with other Eastern Mediterranean islands, but responding to strong counter-attacks from the Germans, the British soon withdrew from the area.

However,

> 'On the 18th October, six aircraft (Hurricanes) took off for a patrol over Castelrosso during the early morning (at 0750 hrs) and were heard to return just before 11 o'clock (1050 hrs.). Soon the news broke – three, probably four, JU-88s shot down over Castelrosso out of a total of 12 encountered – passed the 200 mark.'[1]

Individual claims were:
Flight Lieutenant R.R. Rowlands – 1 JU-88 destroyed.
Pilot Officer A. Jackson – 1 JU-88 destroyed.
Warrant Officer Pilot Officer Haslam – 1 JU-88 destroyed.
Warrant Officer T.A. Jowett – Results not verified, claimed as a possible.

References
1 213 Squadron ORB. The claims of the 18th October included 200th claimed victory of the war for the Squadron.

Chapter Eighteen

West African Campaign

After the fall of France in 1940, the British Territories of the Gambia and Sierra Leone were surrounded by potentially hostile Vichy French colonies. Martin 167F bombers, from Dakar in Senegal, flown by French Navy airmen, were able to reconnoitre the anchorage at Freetown, the capital of Sierra Leone, and it was thought that this information was being relayed to the Germans.

In June 1941, the Freetown Defence Flight was formed at Hastings with Hurricanes to protect Sierra Leone. On the 22nd August, a Martin 167F bomber was claimed shot down by Sgt. Arthur Todd of this unit near Hastings.

The flight was re-named as 128 Squadron on the 7th October and Squadron Leader Billy Drake assumed command a week later. The Squadron flew sector patrols called 'Jim Crows'[1] and had detachments at Jeswang and Port Locco. The Hurricanes carried the code letters 'WG' and some had red, white and blue propeller spinners.

On Sunday the 13th December 1941,

> '*a plot was received from the A.D.O.R. Squadron Leader Drake and Sergeant Todd took off to locate enemy aircraft. After a long chase, Squadron Leader Drake shot down the Martin in the Port Locco District.*[2] *Sergeant Todd pursued another enemy aircraft, but was unable to contact.*'[3]

Squadron Leader John Kilmartin, a Battle of Britain ace, took command of the Squadron in March 1942 and remained C.O. until August of that year. At this time, Squadron Leader H.A.B. Russell assumed command.

On the 11th October 1942,

'Two Hurricanes of 128 Squadron shot up a Glen Martin which attempted a recce over the Freetown area. Pilots – Flt. Lt. R.N.G. Allen and F/O Woodgate. Rear gunner of Glen Martin believed killed.'[3]

This was the last action of the campaign.

Towards the end of 1942, a detachment was sent to the Gambia and remained there until the new year. 128 Squadron disbanded on the 8th March 1943, after the Vichy surrender.

References
1   This was a slang term for coastal patrols.
2   This was Drake's fourth confirmed victory.
3   128 Squadron ORB.

Chapter Nineteen

Iranian Campaign

On the 12th July 1941, 127 Squadron was formed into a new 261 Squadron and moved to Shaibah in Iraq ready for Operation 'Y', a joint British-Russian advance into Iran,[1] following Hitler's invasion of Russia on the 22nd June 1941, after demands for the expulsion of German nationals had been refused.

Air operations in this brief campaign commenced on the 25th August.[2] 'Three low-flying machine-gun attacks were made on Ahwaz Aerodrome, during which three Audaxes were 'heavily machine-gunned.'[3]

Next day, there were 11 more low flying attacks on Ahwaz[4]. The only air combat of the campaign also occurred on the 26th August,

> '*at 0830 hrs a Pegasus-Engined Audax which had taken off from Ahwaz Aerodrome was attacked and shot down by Squadron Leader Mason*[5] *and Sergeant Hitching.*'[3]

Later the same day it was reported that,

> '*unfortunately, in the afternoon, a Vincent of No. 244 Squadron was shot down in error over our front-line troops by a Hurricane piloted by Pilot Officer Marshall. The pilot of the Vincent was wounded in the leg and the aircraft written-off.*'[3]

All fighting ceased on the 28th August.[6] As well as the airfield attacks, standing patrols over the oil ports of Abadan and Khorramshar had been flown by 261 Squadron. British and Russian troops entered the capital, Tehran, on the 17th September. This secured a vital supply route to Russia, through which vast amounts of military hardware were to pass.

References

1   Or Persia, as it was previously known.
2   Fifty-five sorties were flown up to 1800 hrs, involving 102 hours of flying. 261 Squadron ORB.
3   261 Squadron ORB.
4   Thirty-nine sorties were flown involving 71 hours, 40 minutes flying, actually from 1800 hrs on the 25th to 1800 hrs on the 26th. 261 Squadron ORB.
5   This was Squadron Leader 'Imshi' Mason's 17th and last victory.
6   On the 27th August, 10 sorties were flown, of 17 hours, 45 minutes total flying time, actually from 1800 hrs on the 26th to 1800 hrs on the 27th. No ammunition was expended. Twenty-four sorties were flown on the 28th August, involving 47 hours, 15 minutes flying and again, no ammunition was expended – actually from 1800 hrs on the 27th to 1800 hrs on the 28th. 261 Squadron ORB.

Chapter Twenty

Russia

In order to introduce Russian pilots to the Hurricanes that Churchill had promised them and to protect the ports of Murmansk and Archangel, which were vital for unloading arctic convoys, No.151 Wing, comprising nos. 81 and 134 Squadrons, was formed on the 12th August 1941.

Twenty-four Hurricanes from both squadrons were flown off the carrier H.M.S. *Argus* on the 7th September[1] and landed at Vaenga. Their primary roles were to defend Murmansk from air attack and to escort Russian bombers.

The first patrols were flown by both squadrons on the 11th September, but the first decisive encounter with the Luftwaffe occurred next day. Five Hurricanes of 81 Squadron engaged the same number of BF109Es of I/JG77, which were escorting an HS126 of 1.[H]/132. Three BF109s were claimed and the HS126 was claimed as damaged, for the loss of one of the Hurricanes.[2] Two of the BF109s were subsequently confirmed as destroyed.

On the 17th September in two engagements near Balucha, three BF109s and a BF110 were claimed by 81 Squadron, one BF109 actually being confirmed. In the next clash, on the 26th September, six Hurricanes of 81 Squadron encountered three BF109s, claiming two and a probable.[3]

Next day, 12 Hurricanes of 81 Squadron met at least four BF109s around midday, claiming one destroyed.[4] A Hurricane of 134 Squadron was lost in an accident this day.[5] On the 28th September, in another combat with BF109s, 81 Squadron claimed one destroyed.[6]

The last decisive air battle of this short campaign was on the 6th October, when 14 JU-88s of I/KG30, escorted by six BF109s of I/JG77, attacked Vaenga mid-afternoon. Two JU-88s, a probable and two damaged were claimed by 134 Squadron and one BF109, one JU-88,[7] three probables and two damaged by 81 Squadron.[8]

81 Squadron claimed a total of 12½ enemy aircraft, three probables

and three damaged in this campaign, for the loss of one Hurricane. 134 Squadron claimed two enemy aircraft, one shared, a probable and two damaged.[9] Of the 11 BF109s claimed by 81 Squadron, only three can be confirmed. Flight Sergeant Charlton 'Wag' Haw was the top-scoring pilot of the campaign, with three kills. No Russian bomber escorted by No. 151 Wing Hurricanes was lost to enemy fighters.

By the 22nd October, all of No. 151 Wing's Hurricanes had been handed over to the Russians.

References

1 Sixteen others were crated and shipped to Archangel.
2 Sergeant Norman Smith was killed in Z3746.
3 None of these can be confirmed.
4 Unconfirmed.
5 BD825 – two airman on tail on take-off killed.
6 Unconfirmed.
7 Shared with 134 Squadron.
8 Three of the JU-88s were lost, but one was probably destroyed by flak.
9 All on the 6th October.

CHAPTER TWENTY-ONE

Singapore

Fifty-one crated Hurricanes arrived by sea at Singapore on the 13th January 1942. There was much local optimism that the Hurricanes would sweep the Japanese from the skies, but they were old Mark Is or early II A series Is and were fitted with desert air filters, as they had been destined for the Middle East, until the Japanese attacks in the Far East had forced a change of plan. The Hurricanes were also fitted with 12 machine guns, instead of the more usual eight, and this added to the weight and lack of manoeuvrability of the aircraft. The Hurricanes were rapidly assembled and air-tested in time to meet the heaviest air raid yet on Singapore, which arrived on the 20th January. The Hurricanes had been organised into 'A', 'B' and 'C' flights of 232 (Provisional) Squadron, 'A' and 'B' flights being based at Seletar and 'C' flight at Kallang. Twenty-four pilots were available to fly the Hurricanes, but only one had any previous combat experience.

A large formation of approximately 80 Army and Navy bombers, escorted by Army 'Oscars' and Navy 'Zeros' attacked Singapore on the 20th and although the Hurricanes claimed eight bombers[1] and three of the escorting 'Oscars,' three Hurricanes[2] were lost, probably shot down by the 'Oscars.' Sqn. Ldr. Landels and P.O. Marchbanks[3] were killed and P.O. Williams was wounded. P.O. Parker and Sgts. Nicholls and Dovell each claimed an 'Oscar' and Flt. Lt. Murray Taylor, Sgts. Hackforth, Hardie and Leetham[4] each claimed two 'Sally' bombers. A 'Sally' probable was also claimed by each of the latter three sergeant pilots. Three 'Oscars' were confirmed as lost by the Japanese, but surviving Japanese records do not list all aircraft losses, so it is not possible to confirm all RAF claims.

Next day, in another large attack, two 'Nell' bombers and a probable were claimed by Flt. Lt. Farthing and another 'Nell' by P.O. Daniel,[5] but two Hurricanes[6] were shot down and two more[7] were crash-landed,

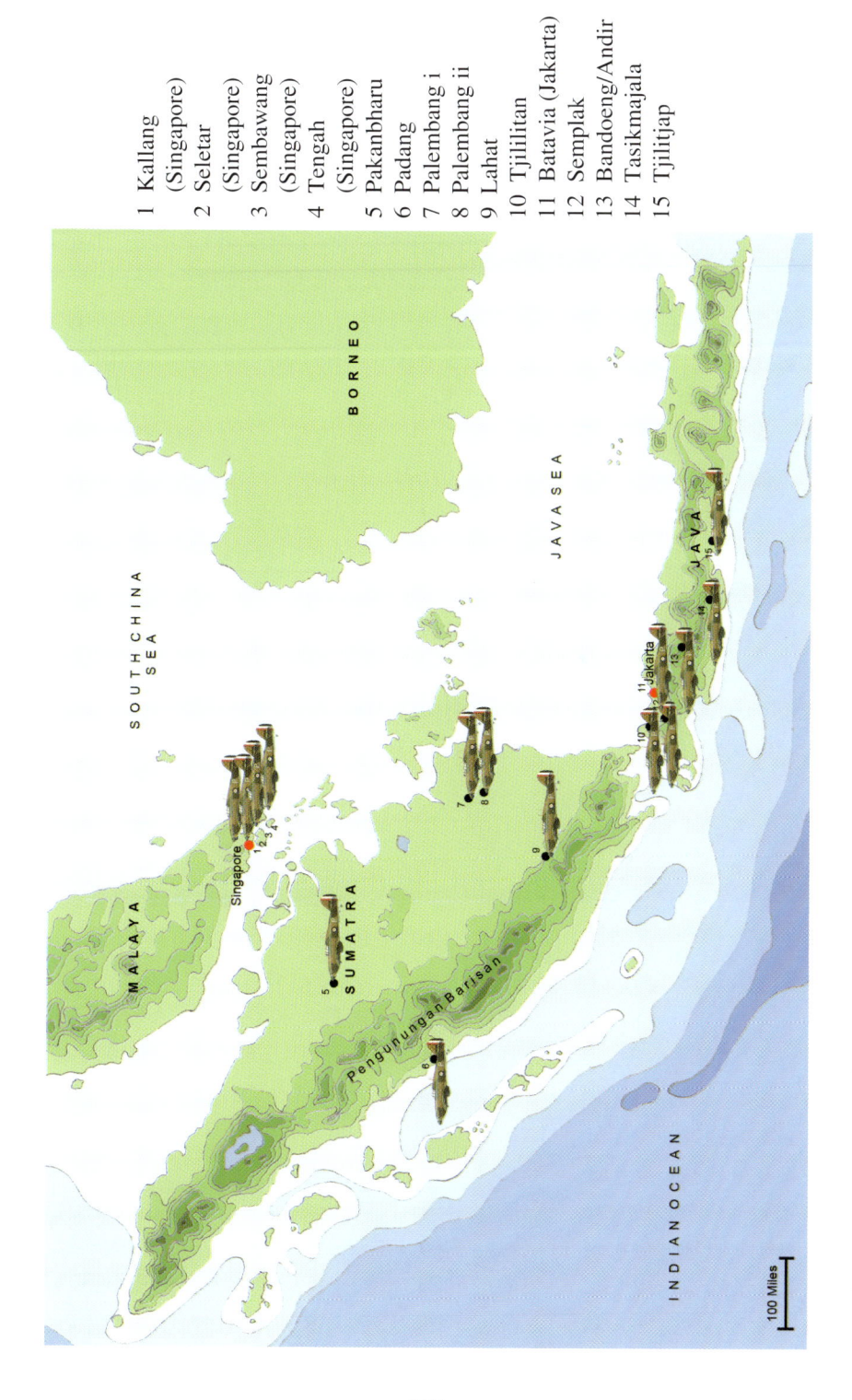

Singapore

1 Kallang (Singapore)
2 Seletar (Singapore)
3 Sembawang (Singapore)
4 Tengah (Singapore)
5 Pakanbharu
6 Padang
7 Palembang i
8 Palembang ii
9 Lahat
10 Tjililitan
11 Batavia (Jakarta)
12 Semplak
13 Bandoeng/Andir
14 Tasikmajala
15 Tjilitjap

probably again by 'Oscars.' Sgt. Lowe was killed and P.O. Gorton was wounded.

On the 22nd January, a solely Navy attack formation of 'Nell' and 'Betty' bombers, escorted by 'Zeros' was intercepted by the Hurricanes. 'Nells' were claimed by Flt. Lts. Cooper-Slipper[8] and Murray Taylor, Sgts. Hackforth[8] and Hardie,[9] while P.O.s Medizabal and Parker claimed probables. Flt. Lt. Farthing and Sgt. Nicholls each claimed a 'Zero'. Three 'Nells' and two 'Zeros' were confirmed lost by the Japanese.

However, the Hurricanes were badly bounced by the 'Zeros', five aircraft[10] being shot down. Flt. Lt. Farthing, P.O. Daniel and Sgt. Leetham[4] (RCAF) were killed and Sgts. Hardie and Hackforth were wounded. The Hurricane pilots made the mistake of dog fighting with the more manoeuvrable 'Zeros'[11] with fatal consequences.

On the 23rd January, in claiming a 'Sally' bomber (Sgt. Marsh[4]), two 'Oscars' (Sgt. Schaffer[12] and P.O. McCulloch[12]) and a probable (Sgt. Fairbairn),[12] a further two Hurricanes[13] were shot down by 'Oscars' and another[14] was lost when it force-landed out of fuel on Pulau Blakang Mati island. Sgts Schaffer and Fairbairn were both wounded.

Another Hurricane[15] was lost next day, when it was force-landed with a glycol leak (the pilot was unhurt) and on the 25th, two more[16] were lost in bad weather, killing Sgts. Marsh[4] and Coutie.[12]

The 26th January saw the Hurricanes escorting two raids on Japanese forces which were landing at Endau, further up the East Malayan coast. A total of nine 'Nates'[17] and an 'Oscar' were claimed by 232(P) Squadron, although in reality, only two 'Nates' were lost by the Japanese. Sgt. Dovell claimed four, Sgt. Nicholls two, Sqn. Ldr. Brooker and Flt. Lt. Murray Taylor one each, P.O. Parker one 'Nate' and an 'Oscar' and probables were claimed by P.O. Mendizabal and Sgt. Fleming. In return, the Hurricane[18] flown by Sgt. Fleming was lost, probably shot down by a 'Tojo' fighter, although the pilot was unhurt.

By the 27th January, of the original 51 Hurricanes that had arrived on Singapore, 19 had been lost and a further seven were under repair. 488 New Zealand Squadron had commenced its re-equipment with Hurricanes[19] on the 24th January, but before this squadron had had the chance to blood

Singapore

them in action, six[20] were destroyed at Kallang in a devastating raid this day. Two Hurricanes[21] of 232(P) Squadron were also destroyed on the ground. Earlier in the day, another Hurricane[22] had been lost in the air, killing Sgt. Christian, but the cause is unknown.

On the 29th January, a 'Nell' bomber and a probable were claimed by P.O. Mendizabal and next day a 'Nate' and a 'Sally' probable were claimed by Flt. Lt. Murray Taylor, a 'Nate' probable by Sgt. Nicholls and a 'Sally' probable by P.O. McCulloch.

Reinforcements then arrived in the shape of 232 and 258 Squadrons, the first 16 Hurricanes arriving at Seletar on the 29th January and the second batch of 16 on the 30th.

On the last day of January, both 258 and 232(P) Squadrons were scrambled to intercept a raid that was escorted by 'Oscars'. One of the fighters was claimed by each of the Hurricane squadrons,[23] together with a 'Sally' bomber by Flt. Lt. Sharp[24] of 258 Squadron. Only one 'Oscar' was actually lost by the Japanese. In return, however, a Hurricane of 258 Squadron was shot down, killing P.O. McAlister[24] and three others were force-landed, probably by the 'Oscars'.

488 Squadron was then ordered to leave Singapore and next day, the majority of 232(P) Squadron was also evacuated. During its 11 days in combat, the Squadron had claimed 32 victories for the loss of 13 Hurricanes in air combat and two destroyed on the ground. Only 12 of the claims can be confirmed from Japanese records.

The Singaporean airfields were now in range of Japanese artillery and it was decided to maintain only a small fighter force of six surviving Buffaloes and approximately eight Hurricanes on the island.

On the 1st February, eight or nine of 258 Squadron's Hurricanes also left for Palembang in Sumatra, together with the four remaining aircraft of 488 Squadron. However, on the 3rd February, a dozen of 258 Squadron's Hurricanes flew back to Tengah, but next day, all non-operationally capable but airworthy Hurricanes were ordered to fly to Palembang.

On the 5th February, two flyable Hurricanes were flown from Sembawang to Tengah, as the shelling of Sembawang had intensified. However, Tengah was now also receiving heavier shellfire and the evacuation of this airfield was also ordered, with aircraft proceeding to Kallang. Nevertheless, a dozen Hurricanes of 232 Squadron then flew back from Palembang to Tengah.

Their stay was short and the Squadron moved on to Kallang, together with two 258 Squadron Hurricanes. Five of the remaining 232(P) Squadron aircraft also left for Palembang, but 232 Squadron 'B' flight were scrambled from Kallang on the afternoon of the 5th and claimed two 'Sally' bombers (P.O. Gartrell[24] and Sgt. King). Earlier in the day an 'Oscar' probable was claimed by Flt. Lt. Julian of 'A' flight. By the evening of the 5th, only 14 serviceable Hurricanes remained at Kallang.

Next day, a 'Nate' was claimed by P.O. Fitzherbert of 232 Squadron[25] as the evacuation from Singapore continued and on the 7th February the Hurricanes were again scrambled to intercept a large raid. Unfortunately, one of the Hurricanes[26] was lost on take-off, killing Sqn. Ldr. Llewellin and another was shot down by 'Nates'[27] for a claim of one 'Nate' destroyed by Hutton. On the return flight, the Hurricanes were bounced by 'Zeros' and one aircraft[28] crash-landed.[29]

On the 8th February, another scramble resulted in a 'Sally' bomber being claimed by 2nd Lt. Stewart[30] and a probable by Sgt. Sandeman Allen, both of 232 Squadron, but the Hurricane[31] of 2nd Lt. Stewart crash-landed after combat, wounding him and three others were badly damaged by the escorting fighters.

The 9th February was a day of several scrambles and in morning combats, a 'Nell' plus a probable were each claimed by P.O. Gartrell and Flt. Lt. Julian and two 'Zero' probables were claimed by Sgt. Sandeman Allen of 232 Squadron, while another 'Nell' was claimed by Sgt. Healey of 258 Squadron.

In the afternoon, two 'Ann' light bombers were claimed by Sgt. Sandeman Allen, plus a probable by Flt. Lt. Julian and a 'Sally' probable by Sgt. Young[12], all of 232 Squadron.

However, three more Hurricanes were lost by 232 Squadron – one to flak[32] and two others[33] shot down in combat. Sgt. Moodie[24] was killed and Sgts. Margarson and Young were wounded.

232 Squadron was ordered to evacuate next day and eight Hurricanes departed for P1 airfield on Sumatra at dawn on the 10th, but one aircraft

was lost to engine failure en route.[34] On the 11th February, three more Hurricanes were made airworthy and evacuated to Sumatra, but another[35] was lost when it ran out of fuel and force-landed.

The gallant, but ultimately futile, defence of Singapore was now over. As well as the 38 air combat claims by 232(P) Squadron, 232 Squadron proper claimed a further nine enemy aircraft over Singapore and 258 Squadron claimed three. In claiming 50 enemy aircraft, 22 Hurricanes were lost in air combat, at least eight were destroyed on the ground and a further eight were lost to other causes. Only 13 of the Hurricane squadrons' claims can be confirmed in Japanese records. Sgt. Dovell claimed six[36] and Flt. Lt. Murray Taylor claimed five and a probable in this campaign.

References

1 Plus three probables.
2 BG818, BG848 and BM906.
3 US.
4 RCAF.
5 One 'Nell' was confirmed.
6 Including BE577.
7 BG864 and BE633.
8 Two.
9 Also a probable.
10 BE579, BG720, BG796, BG804 and BG810.
11 Or had no choice but to.
12 RAAF.
13 BG846 and BM848.
14 BE639.
15 BG807.
16 BE589 and BE641.
17 Plus two probables.
18 BG828.
19 From Buffaloes.
20 BE585, BE632, BE640, BG723, BG800 and BG845.
21 BE588 and BM902.

22   BE590.
23   Sgt. Dovell of 232 (P) and P.O. Campbell (US) of 258 Squadron.
24   NZ.
25   And confirmed.
26   Z5482.
27   P.O. Hutton was unhurt.
28   BE208.
29   Flt. Lt. Wright was also unhurt.
30   SAAF.
31   BE195.
32   BG797.
33   One of which was BE158.
34   The pilot, Sgt. Dunn, was unhurt.
35   BG830.
36   All fighters.

Chapter Twenty-Two

First Burma Campaign

When the war in the Far East started in December 1941, there were no Hurricanes in Burma, but 17 Squadron arrived at Mingaladon in January 1942 and commenced operations on the 23rd of that month. Single 'Sally' bombers were claimed on the 24th and 27th of January, while on the 29th, a 'Nate' fighter was claimed by Squadron Leader Carey, a 135 Squadron pilot operating with 17 Squadron and confirmed. P.O. Storey also claimed a damaged which was subsequently confirmed as destroyed.[1] 135 Squadron's first mission as a Squadron came on the 3rd February, and on the 6th February,

> '*at 0900 hrs scramble was ordered. Pilot Officers Storey, Underwood and Sgt. McRae all went up (in fact six Hurricanes took off, but two lost formation). P.O. Storey got two destroyed confirmed and two damaged. P.O. Underwood also had one destroyed confirmed. Sgt. McRae claimed one damaged. Owing to late get way, our pilots were not able to gain sufficient height to have distinct advantage which would have brought better results.*'[1]

As well as the three 'Nates' claimed by 135 Squadron two 'Nate' probables were also claimed by Flt. Lt. Sutton of 17 Squadron. In fact, only one 'Nate' was lost and another force-landed. Earlier in the day, two 'Ann' light bombers were claimed by Flt. Lt. Carvell and Sgt. Rathbone of 17 Squadron, one actually being lost by the Japanese.

Next day, three 'Nates' were claimed by Sgt. Barrick[2] and F.O. Thomas[3] of 17 Squadron and two by 136 Squadron,[4] for that Squadron's first claims in this theatre. As per the previous day, one 'Nate' was actually lost and another force-landed. The next combat was not until the 22nd February, when an 'Ida' recce aircraft was claimed damaged by Flt. Lt. Mann of

17 Squadron. This was actually a 'Babs' recce aircraft that crash-landed, badly damaged. A Hurricane of 17 Squadron was shot down by ground fire this day, P.O. Dunsford-Wood surviving unhurt.

On the 23rd February, 135 Squadron scrambled at 0930 hrs.

> *'Vectored to Kayaikto. Sighted E/A. Travelling East – pursued for 20 miles. W/Cdr Carey intercepted and destroyed one 2 seater recce. A/C (a 'Sonia'). P.O. Storey pursued one N.97 (a 'Nate') which was acting as top cover and destroyed it after 10-mile chase.'*[1]

Both the 'Sonia' and the 'Nate' were confirmed lost. Flt. Lt. Watson in BG876 of that Squadron was lost in a later dogfight with the 'Nates'.

Next day, in an attack on Moulmein, a transport and a 'Nate' were claimed in the air by Wg. Cdr. Carey of 135 Squadron and a fighter and a bomber on the ground by Sqn. Ldr. Stone of 17 Squadron. None of these were admitted by the Japanese.

On the 25th February, engaging a Japanese fighter sweep on Mingaladon, a 'Nate' was wrongly claimed by Sgt. Barrick of 17 Squadron. In a later attack on Mingaladon, a 'Lily' bomber was claimed by P.O. Hemmingway of 17 Squadron. 135 Squadron also engaged the enemy,

> *'base attacked late afternoon and in ensuing battle S/Ldr Sutton got two Japs confirmed and one probable.'*[1]

One of the claims was believed to be a 'Lily' bomber and the other, a 'Nate' fighter. 50th Sentai lost two 'Nates' this day and one may have been Sutton's claim.

On the 26th February, another strafing attack was made on Moulmein by 135 Squadron,

> *'first flight in morning strafed Moulmein. W/Cdr Carey leading with P/Os Monk and Underwood. W/Cdr Carey destroyed 3 E/A. P/O Underwood missing from this raid.'*[1]

Another 'Nate' was claimed by P.O. Underwood before he was shot down in BG821, wounded and taken prisoner. Flt. Lt. Cotton claimed another 'Nate' shot down and a probable destroyed on the ground.[5] Capt. Penton, the Army liaison officer attached to 17 Squadron, was also shot down in combat this day,[6] escaping injury. Attacking a later raid, Flt. Lt. Cotton claimed a bomber before his Hurricane[7] was damaged and subsequently written-off, Cotton being wounded.

Next day, P.O. Stout of 135 Squadron crashed on landing, wrecking his aircraft, although he was unhurt.

March 1942 started with newly-promoted Flt. Lt. Storey of 135 Squadron force-landed by flak[8] on the first of the month. Next day, on a recce sortie, Flt. Lt. Mann in a 17 Squadron Hurricane[9] was force-landed by 'Nates', slightly wounded and later in the day, another of this Squadron's aircraft crashed on landing, P.O. Earnshaw escaping injury. On the 3rd March, 17 Squadron suffered another loss when Sgt. Wisrodt failed to return from a recce sortie and was presumed to have been shot down by ground fire.

By the 4th March, it was becoming clear that Rangoon would soon fall to the Japanese and 135 Squadron was ordered to leave Mingaladon. Unserviceable Hurricanes were burned and 17 Squadron also prepared to move.

However, on the 6th, 'Nates' of the 77th Sentai flew a patrol over Mingaladon and were intercepted by 17 Squadron, F.O. Lloyd claiming one 'Nate' and a possible. In return, one or two Hurricanes were damaged beyond repair on the ground. 17 Squadron was now also ordered to leave immediately.

Next day, one of the remaining Hurricanes at Mingaladon took-off on patrol flown by Sgt. Bunting, a 136 Squadron pilot. It was damaged in combat and on landing, burned on the ground to avoid capture. On the 9th March one of two Hurricanes being evacuated to Magwe suffered an engine failure and was lost, Sgt. Fox of 135 Squadron bailing out. Rangoon had fallen the day before.

On the 11th March, the remains of 'X' wing moved to Magwe and were disbanded. In its place, Burwing was formed, including 17 Squadron's Hurricanes and this unit became operational on the 18th March.

Akwing was also established at Akyab and included 136 Squadron with Hurricanes. To face these were 260 aircraft of the reinforced JAAF 5th Air Division, whereas only 27 Hurricanes remained at Magwe and Akyab.

Reconnaissance over Rangoon on the 20th March had revealed at least 50 Japanese aircraft now at Mingaladon and these were attacked next day. A total of 14 enemy aircraft were claimed destroyed or badly damaged on the ground and three 'Nates' claimed in the air by Sgts. Barrick and Gibson and Flt. Lt. Carvell of 17 Squadron.[10] Two aircraft were actually destroyed on the ground in the raid and 11 more were badly damaged. Hurricane Z5599, flown by P.O. Earnshaw was hit by ground fire and force-landed, Earnshaw being uninjured.

In a massive retaliatory raid on Magwe on the afternoon of the 21st March, six Hurricanes of 17 Squadron were damaged beyond repair on the ground and two others were shot down, P.O.s Hemingway and Brooks escaping unhurt. Three 'Nates' and a probable were claimed by 17 squadron in return.[11] A 'Zero' was also claimed by P.O. Everard, but this was in fact a Hurricane[12] of 3 PRU that belly-landed and was badly damaged. The pilot, F.O. Ken Perkin, was only slightly injured.

Next day, Magwe was attacked in force again. After an intercept mission, a Hurricane of 17 Squadron crashed on landing and was written-off, Sgt. Macdonald being unhurt. The decision was then taken to evacuate Magwe, nine Hurricanes departing for Akyab, but one was lost to engine failure en route, Sgt. Barrick bailing out unhurt.

However, Akyab was attacked on the 23rd March and although two 'Sally' bombers[13] and an 'Oscar' fighter[14] were claimed by 136 Squadron Hurricanes, no aircraft were actually lost by the Japanese, but a 136 Squadron Hurricane[15] was shot down by an 'Oscar' and another crash-landed after an engine malfunction. P.O. Brown was wounded in the former and Sgt. Bunting was unhurt in the latter.

The eight remaining Hurricanes of 'B' flight 17 Squadron were now handed over to 136 Squadron. Akyab was attacked again on the 24th and two 'Sally' probables were claimed by P.O. Kitley and Sgt. Viens of 136 Squadron, while an 'Oscar' and a probable were claimed by Sgt. Wilding of that Squadron. Two Hurricanes[16] were shot down and

First Burma Campaign

another crash-landed. Sgt. Payne was killed and Sgts. Butler and Fortune were slightly wounded.

On the 26th March, six flyable, but non-combat-worthy, Hurricanes were evacuated to Chittagong, across the border in India. Next day, Akyab was attacked for the last time and seven Hurricanes were destroyed on the ground. One of two 136 Squadron Hurricanes that succeeded in getting airborne was also shot down, wounding P.O. LeCraw.

At the end of March, Burwing was established at Lashio and included 17 Squadron, which was awaiting aircraft. On the 5th April, an unserviceable Hurricane was destroyed on the ground at Akyab and eight Hurricanes arrived at Lashio for 17 Squadron.

On the 9th April, a raid on Loiwing was intercepted by 17 Squadron, but on return to the airfield, one of the Hurricanes crash-landed and two others force-landed and were lost.[17] P.O.s Chadwick and Everard and Sgt. MacDonald were all unhurt.

Next day, while intercepting a further attack on Loiwing, two 'Oscars' were claimed by 17 Squadron Hurricanes[18] for the loss of a Hurricane[19] shot down and another[20] force-landed. 2nd Lt. Peter was wounded in the former and Sgt. Barrick in the latter. Most 17 Squadron pilots were evacuated after the middle of April.

According to Air Vice-Marshal Stevenson, the RAF in Burma claimed 54 enemy aircraft during the campaign. Of these, 42 were claimed by the Hurricane Squadrons[21] for the loss of 14 Hurricanes in air combat. At least three more Hurricanes were lost to flak, possibly four, nine in operational accidents and at least 15 were destroyed on the ground in air raids.

Others were burned on the ground to avoid capture.

17 Squadron was the top-scoring Hurricane Squadron of this campaign, with 21 claims, 135 Squadron claimed 15 and 136 Squadron, six. Wing Commander Frank Carey was the top Hurricane ace of the campaign with six kills.

References

1. 135 Squadron ORB.
2. Two.
3. One.
4. One each to P.O. Brown and Sgt. Bunting.
5. Wg Cdr Carey claimed three of the 'Nates' and P.O. Underwood and Flt. Lt. Cotton claimed one each. Cotton also claimed the ground claim, which was confirmed.
6. In BE171.
7. BD963.
8. In BG843.
9. Z5473.
10. One each.
11. One each by Brooks, Sgt. MacDonald and P.O. Everard and the probable by Hemingway.
12. Z4949.
13. One by Sgt. Wetherall and the other jointly by Sgts Butler and Pickard.
14. By Flt. Lt. Marsland.
15. Z4650.
16. Including BG858.
17. Including BM909.
18. One by Sgt. Barrick and one by P.O. Earnshaw.
19. BH121.
20. BG824.
21. Eleven confirmed – eight 'Nates', one 'Ann', one 'Babs' and one 'Sonia'.

Chapter Twenty-Three

Sumatra

Although Japanese air attacks on Sumatra had occurred as early as December 1941, the first RAF Hurricanes did not arrive on the island until the 29th January 1942. These were flown from the carrier H.M.S. *Indomitable*, firstly, to Batavia on Java. A total of 48 Hurricanes of 232 and 258 Squadrons were flown to Java and 23 of these were subsequently flown on to Singapore via Sumatra. Four damaged Hurricanes remained on Java, the remaining 21 then flying to Sumatra.

By the 5th February, following the arrival of survivors from Singapore, there were 33 Hurricanes available to 258 and 232 Squadrons. Next day, the Japanese attacked P.1 Airfield and for only one claim by P.O. Bainbridge of 232 Squadron, two Hurricanes of 258 Squadron failed to return.[1] Another Hurricane crash-landed and was written-off.[2]

A further attack on the 7th resulted in three Hurricanes being destroyed on the ground and 11 damaged. In intercepting the raid, three Hurricanes of 258 Squadron failed to return[3] and two others crash-landed after combat.[4] Two enemy fighters were claimed by 258 Squadron[5] and two 'Nates' were claimed damaged. Two losses were admitted by the Japanese, including one 'Oscar'.

For the third day running on the 8th February, the Japanese attacked P.1 and although two 'Oscars' were probably despatched,[6] the two intercepting Hurricanes[7] of that unit were shot down, both Flt. Lt. Taylor and Sgt. Hackforth being killed. On the 10th February, a further seven Hurricanes of 232 Squadron arrived from Singapore, but on the 12th, a Hurricane of 232 Squadron[8] crash-landed in the jungle due to bad weather, injuring P.O. McKechnie.

On the 13th February, seven reinforcement Hurricanes from Tjililitan arrived over P.1, just as another Japanese air raid struck. Two of the Hurricanes were shot down by 'Oscars',[9] but in return, two 'Zeros' were claimed[10] – one 'Oscar' was actually lost. Meanwhile, several Hurricanes of 232 and 258 Squadrons had managed to get airborne, Sgt. Allen claiming two 'Zeros' and a bomber probable and Squadron Leader Brooker, one bomber for one Hurricane[11] shot down[12] and one written-off on landing.[13] That evening, a patrol of 14 Hurricanes lost two in crash-landings, due to bad weather.[14]

As part of the Japanese invasion of Sumatra, a parachute assault was made on P.1 on 14th February. The attack formation was engaged by 232 and 258 Squadrons, a bomber[15] and a fighter[16] being claimed for one Hurricane of 258 Squadron crash-landed by 'Oscars'.[17]

Subsequently, a formation of replacement Hurricanes from Batavia approached P.1 and was engaged by 'Oscars', five being forced to crash-land in the jungle.[18] The remainder managed to escape to P.2 Airfield where two were damaged on landing. As P.1 was abandoned, the unserviceable Hurricanes were destroyed.

The last 15 Hurricanes were evacuated to Java on the 15th February, but not before two 'Nates' had been claimed over P.1[19] and two 'Zeros'[20] were claimed destroyed on the ground by 232 Squadron.[21] The two 'Nates' actually crash-landed.

A total of 13 enemy aircraft were claimed in this short campaign, plus three probables, for the loss of 26 Hurricanes,[22] up to 20 of the Hurricanes being lost in air combat. Eight aircraft can be confirmed lost by the Japanese, including five 'Oscars' and two 'Nates'.

References

1   P.O. Cardell was killed and P.O. Campbell-White was unhurt.
2   Sgt. Nelson Scott was unhurt.
3   Sgt. Glynn was killed. P.O. Nicholls was wounded and P.O. McCulloch was unhurt.
4   Sgt. Keedwell was killed and P.O. Nash was unhurt.
5   A 'Zero' by P.O. Campbell – actually an 'Oscar' which was confirmed – and another fighter by P.O. Milnes.
6   One each to Flt. Lt. Taylor and Sgt. Hackforth.
7   BE115 and BE219.

8   BG768.
9   Sgt. Scott was wounded and Sgt. Nicholls was unhurt.
10 By Wg Cdr Maguire and Sgt. Nicholls.
11 BG693.
12 P.O. Emmerton was killed.
13 In fact, two 'Oscars' were actually lost by the Japanese.
14 2nd Lt. Dummett was wounded and Sgt. Bidewell was unhurt.
15 By P.O. Lockwood.
16 By Sgt. Kelly.
17 F.O. Macnamara was unhurt.
18 P.O. McCulloch was wounded, but the other four pilots were unhurt.
19 By P.O.s Watson and Bainbridge.
20 Probably 'Petes'.
21 One by Flt. Lt. Julian.
22 Excluding those destroyed to avoid capture.

Chapter Twenty-Four

Java

Following the RAF withdrawal from Sumatra, a re-organisation of the remaining fighter forces on Java now ensued. 232, 258 and 488 Squadrons were disbanded and 242 and 605 Squadrons were re-formed. Java now stood as the last of the Dutch East Indian islands, as yet unconquered by the Japanese. The Dutch air units on the island had been decimated by the overwhelmingly superior Japanese air flotillas, which had attacked from Southern Borneo and Celebes. With the fall of Sumatra, nearer air bases were now available to them for attacks on Western Java.

The two RAF Hurricane squadrons had 25 aircraft available, sufficient for only one squadron, so the plan was to alternate the operation of the aircraft between 242 and 605 Squadrons. In addition, 12 of the Hurricanes that had been delivered on the 4th February 1942 had been handed to the Dutch and these were operated by their 2-VIG-IV unit. The RAF Hurricanes were based at Tjililitan and the Dutch Hurricanes moved up to Kalidjati on the 16th February.

Following a dawn scramble on the 20th February, 242 Squadron engaged Japanese aircraft and claimed two 'Nates' destroyed.[1] Later in the day, a 'Floatplane' was claimed by Sgt. Young of 242 Squadron over Batavia harbour.

During the morning of the 24th February, a large raid was intercepted over Western Java, an 'Oscar' being claimed by P.O. Campbell of 605 Squadron. That afternoon, an attack on Tjililitan resulted in two more 'Oscars'[2] and three bombers[3] being claimed by 605 Squadron, but in return, a Hurricane[4] was shot down[5] and another lost in a collision.[6] Two Dutch Hurricanes had also crash-landed after intercepting the morning attack.

Next day, 605 Squadron 'A' flight engaged a morning raid on Western Java, P.O. Campbell claiming a 'Zero', but two Hurricanes[7] were lost in the process.[8] Yet again, dog fighting with the 'Zeros' had proved a fatal mistake.

Sgt. Allen of 242 Squadron also claimed a 'Zero' in this engagement, but this was probably a 'Babs' reconnaissance aircraft.

On the 26th February, the Dutch moved most of their remaining fighters to strengthen the East of Java, including six Hurricanes of 2-VIG-IV to Blimbing airfield, Ngoro. On the 27th February, a 'Zero' possible was claimed by Flt. Lt. Hutton of 605 Squadron.

Japanese forces launched their invasion of Java with landings on the 1st March and in attacks on the invasion forces, a Hurricane of each of the RAF fighter squadrons was shot down by flak. F.O. Sharp of 605 Squadron was killed, while Sgt. Young of 242 Squadron was unhurt.

In the early afternoon of the 1st, two flying boats were claimed destroyed on the water by P.O. Fitzherbert of 242 Squadron, one 'Pete' actually being burned. A 'Floatplane' was also claimed shot down by Sgt. Kuhn of 605 Squadron, but this claim was in error.

605 Squadron was now ordered to stand-down and its remaining Hurricanes were handed over to 242 Squadron. Two Dutch Hurricanes were hit by flak while attacking the Japanese invasion forces and force-landed, while another was lost as the Japanese reached Kalidjati airfield.

In a strafing attack by 'Zeros' on Blimbing, early in the morning, two more were damaged beyond repair and single Hurricanes were also destroyed at Maospati and Bedjonegare to avoid capture.

On the 2nd March, 242 Squadron was ordered to strafe Kalidjati, where Japanese aircraft had already arrived. Three aircraft were set on fire on the airfield, but a Hurricane was shot down by 'Nates', Sgt. Fleming being wounded and captured. In a later attack on enemy troop concentrations, another of 242 Squadron's Hurricanes was shot down by flak and crash-landed, injuring P.O. Watson. Later still, in a fighter attack on Tjililitan, an enemy fighter was claimed shot down by Sgt. King.

Next day, Kalidjati was attacked again, seven Hurricanes participating, and although one of the several aircraft strafed was seen to catch fire, one of the Hurricanes was shot down by fighters, P.O. Mendizabal being unhurt. In return, three enemy aircraft were claimed in combat by P.O.s Gartrell and Fitzherbert and Sgt. King of 242 Squadron. One of the two surviving Dutch Hurricanes of 2 VIG-IV was also force-landed and wrecked this day.

On the morning of the 4th March, 10 Hurricanes were despatched to attack Kalidjati again, on their way back to Andir, which was to be their new base. The Hurricanes fought a fierce battle with Japanese Navy 'Zeros' over Kalidjati, claiming 7 and a probable, for the loss of 1 Hurricane.[9] Two of the 'Zeros' and a probable were claimed by Sgt. Allen, two by Sgt. King and one each by Sqn. Ldr. Brooker, Flt. Lt. Julian and P.O. Fitzherbert.

Late in the afternoon, another Hurricane was badly damaged on landing after a reconnaissance sortie.

On the 5th March, a bomber claimed shot down by Flt. Lt. Parker of 242 Squadron was the only decisive air combat on this day.

On the 6th, it was planned to use the six remaining Hurricanes as decoys, whilst the remaining Dutch Brewster fighters were evacuated to Australia. One of the Hurricanes force-landed in a swamp, almost immediately, having suffered an engine failure, but Sgt. King was unhurt. The remaining Hurricanes engaged Japanese bombers and claimed four plus a probable, for one of the Hurricanes damaged and force-landed at Tasikmalaja. Claims were made by Flt. Lt. Parker, P.O. Lockwood, Sqn. Ldr. Julian[10] and P.O. Gartrell, who also claimed a probable.

As it happened, the Dutch Brewster evacuation never occurred. Later that day, another of the Hurricanes was damaged by a fighter and landed at Pameungpeuk airfield.

At dawn on the 7th March, the last five serviceable Hurricanes flew to Tasikmalaja. However, this airfield was attacked soon after the arrival of the Hurricanes. One of the Hurricanes was destroyed and another damaged.

Next day, following a final reconnaissance sortie, the last two serviceable Hurricanes were destroyed on the ground at Tasikmalaja, to avoid them being captured. The damaged Hurricane at Pameungpeuk took-off for Tasikmalaja but crashed on take-off, although Flt. Lt. Parker was unhurt.

During the brief but valiant defence of Java, 605 Squadron claimed eight enemy aircraft for three Hurricanes lost in air combat, whereas 242 Squadron claimed 20 in the air and two probables, also for three Hurricanes lost in the air. Although these claims were undoubtedly optimistic, this was a very creditable exchange ratio by the Hurricane units. Top scorer of the campaign was Sgt. Jimmy King with five-and-a-half victories.

References

1. One by Flt. Lt. Julian and one shared by P.O. Watson and Sgt. King.
2. One each to F.O. Sharp and Sgt. Kuhn.
3. One each to Flt. Lt. Hutton and Sgt. King with the third shared between P.O. Watson and 2nd Lt. Anderson.
4. BG876?
5. F.O. Sharp was unhurt.
6. Sgt. Lambert was also unhurt.
7. BE332 and BG821?
8. Flt. Lt. Dobyn was killed and P.O. Campbell was wounded.
9. 2nd Lt. Anderson became a PoW but died in captivity.
10. Recently promoted.

Chapter Twenty-Five
Ceylon

A large Japanese Naval task force, commanded by Vice-Admiral Nagumo, entered the Indian Ocean in April 1942 to strike at Ceylon. Five of the six aircraft carriers that had attacked Pearl Harbour were included in the force and facing them on Ceylon were the three Hurricane squadrons; 30, 258 and 261. Twenty-two Hurricanes of 30 Squadron had flown in from the carrier HMS *Indomitable* on the 6th March and 19 more of 261 Squadron followed them next day from the same carrier. Fourteen more Hurricanes were flown in from India on the 22nd March and became a revived 258 Squadron on the 30th.

The first of two attacks by the Japanese was on Easter Sunday, the 5th April, and although not unexpected, the early warning radar posts were unmanned (incredibly) and the defending fighters were taken by surprise – it has been suggested that the range of the 'Zero' escort fighter had been underestimated, so a strike on the 6th April was considered more likely.

The raiding force on Colombo comprised 38 'Val' dive-bombers, 53 'Kate' torpedo bombers, and 36 'Zero' fighters. Ratmalana airport, where 30 Squadron was based, was already under attack as 30 Squadrons' 21 Hurricanes were scrambled. The Hurricane pilots had no time to form up and had no choice but to dogfight with the more agile 'Zeros'. Eight Hurricanes of 30 Squadron were shot down or crash-landed and four pilots killed, for 14 of the enemy claimed destroyed.[1] P.O. Jimmy Whalen claimed three of the 'Vals,' P.O. Alan Wagner claimed two and Flt. Lt. Bob Davidson claimed a 'Val' and a 'Zero'.

258 Squadron was based on the racecourse airfield, which was unknown to the Japanese, and managed to take off without interference. However, 258 Squadron fared no better than 30 Squadron, seven Hurricanes being lost, two damaged and five pilots killed, for a claim of four 'Vals' destroyed, a 'Zero' probable and four damaged.

> 'The 9 Hurricane II's scrambled as a Squadron and the 5 Hurricane I's as an independent flight. One or Two enemy A/C were encountered overhead, but the main body, approximately 75 E/AC were then concentrated over the Harbour, with approx. 35 NAVY 'O's a few thousand feet above, acting as cover. As 258 Squadron approached the Harbour the enemy bombers were preparing to attack. When the Squadron arrived at the harbour it was on a level with the enemy bombers and below the NAVY 'O's. S/LDR Fletcher attacked the enemy bombers with Hurricane II's. He continued to attack for as long a period as possible.'[2]

Five of the nine Hurricane IIs were lost and two of the five Hurricane Is, with two more of the Hurricane Is damaged.

Flt. Lt. Teddy Peacock-Edwards claimed one of the 'Vals' and the 'Zero' probable. He recorded in his log book,

> 'Scramble – intercepted Navy '96s' and Navy 'O' – shot down Navy '96' + probable Navy 'O' + shot down by 6 Navy 'O's. Award DFC. R.I.P "B" for Bertie.'

The Japanese admitted the loss of only five aircraft over Colombo, though conceding that several others failed to make it back to the carriers. Eyewitnesses reported seeing five Japanese aircraft crash although only three wrecks were found around Colombo.[3]

The second attack, on the 9th April, was against Trimcomalee, which was defended by 261 Squadron. The attacking force comprised 91 'Kates' and 41 'Zeros' and although the 16 Hurricanes of 261 Squadron[4] had adequate warning from radar, they were severely outnumbered and lost eight of their number,[5] although only one pilot was killed.[6]

Four 'Zeros', three probables and one damaged and four 'Kates', one probable and five damaged were claimed by 261 Squadron.[7] Only three 'Zeros' and one 'Kate' were reported lost by the Japanese, while another 'Kate' force-landed.

No further Japanese air attacks were made on Ceylon after this date.

Hurricane losses / casualties:

5th April

30 Squadron:

BG795 Plt. Off. Caswell killed.
BM910 Flg. Off. Allison wounded.
Z5447 Sgt. Browne killed.
BE352 Plt. Off. Geffere killed.
       Flt. Sgt. Overs killed.
       Flt. Sgt. Paxton wounded.
       Plt. Off. Cartwright wounded.
       Plt. Off. Macdonald crash-landed unhurt.

258 Squadron:

Z5680 Sqn. Ldr. Fletcher wounded.
Z5461 Flt. Lt. Peacock-Edwards wounded.
BD701 Flt. Lt. Lockhart killed.
Z5665 Flt. Lt. McFadden killed.
Z4227 Plt. Off. Tremlett killed.
Z7711 Plt. Off. Neill (RAAF) killed.
Z5385 Sgt. Thain killed.
Z4372 (damaged) Plt. Off. Milne unhurt.
Z4983 (damaged) Sgt. Gavin (RNZAF) unhurt.

9th April

261 Squadron:

Z4961 Sqn. Ldr. Lewis wounded.
BG786 Sgt. Rawnsley (RAAF) wounded.
BE227 Sgt. Lockwood unhurt.
BE241 Flg. Off. Counter unhurt.
BG676 Sgt. Bowie wounded.

Z5533   Sgt. Pearce killed.
BG909   Sgt. Mann unhurt.
Z2573   Flt. Sgt. Gauthier wounded.

References

1 Including at least nine 'Vals' and three 'Zeros,' plus six probables and five damaged.
2 258 Squadron ORB.
3 Other (Japanese) sources list the loss as six 'Vals' and one 'Zero' with 15 other Japanese aircraft damaged.
4 Three other Hurricanes were previously written off in accidents.
5 Plus a Hurricane destroyed on the ground.
6 Sergeant Pearce.
7 Sgt. L.T. Rawnsley, RAAF, claimed one 'Zero' and a probable while Flt. Sgt. C.J. Gauthier claimed two 'Kates,' which collided after one had been hit by him.

Chapter Twenty-Six
Second Burma Campaign

Following the Japanese attack in the Far East, the last British forces had retreated from Burma into India in May 1942. The Hurricanes of 146, 607 and 615 Squadrons arrived in India during that month, to join 17, 67, 135 and 136 Squadrons, which had fought during the first Burma campaign. There was no air combat from May to the beginning of December 1942, but some 24 Hurricanes were lost in accidents before 135 Squadron moved up to Chittagong in East Bengal at the end of November 1942, to join 136 Squadron.

Hurricane IIB HL660 of Far East Air Force.

The first Japanese air raids after the monsoon had started in October 1942, but the raid of the 10th December on Chittagong saw decisive results for both sides. Some 30 'Oscars' of the 50th and 64th Sentais escorted a formation of 'Lily' bombers and were intercepted by six Hurricanes of 135 Squadron and six of 136 Squadron. Four pilots of 135 Squadron[1] claimed three

Second Burma Campaign

1 Dalbhumgarh
2 Alipore
3 Red Road (Calcutta)
4 Dum Dum
5 Jessore
6 Fenny
7 Comilla
8 Agartala
9 Silchar West
10 Dimapur
11 Kohima
12 Imphal
13 Tulihal
14 Palel
15 Tamu
16 Yazagyo
17 Kalewa
18 Kalemyo
19 Kan
20 Monywa
21 Ye-U
22 Lashio
23 Onbauk
24 Thazi
25 Heho
26 Meiktila
27 Magwe 'Maida Vale'
28 Akyab
29 Ramu I, II, III
30 Cox's Bazaar
31 Chiringa
32 Chittagong
33 Nazir

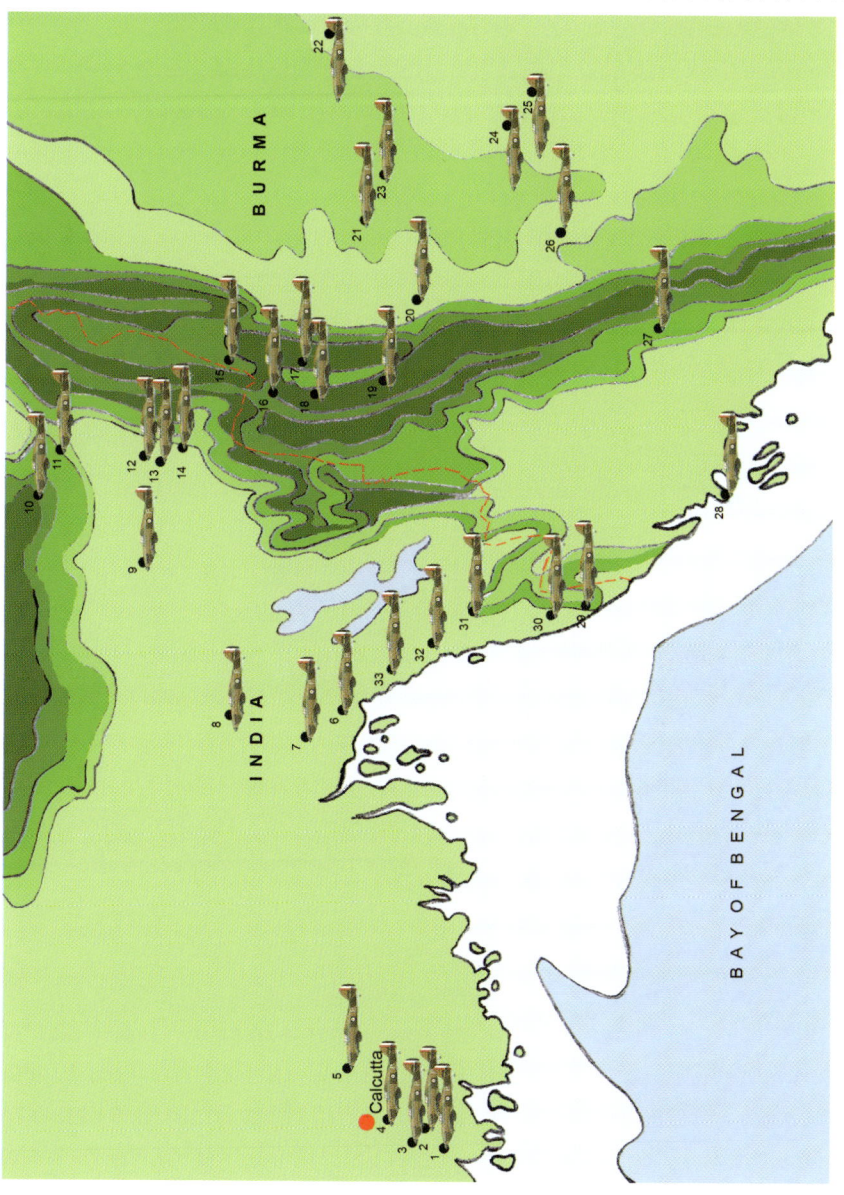

'Oscar' probables between them (one confirmed), but two Hurricanes[2] of 135 Squadron failed to return and a Hurricane[3] of 136 Squadron was shot down. F.O. Monk and Sgt. Goldney of 135 Squadron were both killed, but Flt. Sgt. Davis of 136 Squadron was unhurt. Thus started the first 'Arakan' campaign with a three-to-one victory by the 'Oscars' over the Hurricanes, a trend that was set to continue.

On the 14th December, 79 Squadron moved to Chittagong to relieve 136 Squadron and next day, Chittagong was attacked again by 40 'Lily' bombers with 'Oscars' as escorts, 10 Hurricanes of 79 Squadron countering the raid. Five 'Lilys' and an 'Oscar' damaged were claimed, although subsequently, the claims were upgraded.[4]

One of the 'Lilys' was lost and another force-landed. In addition, Sgt. North claimed an 'Oscar' and one damaged, while P.O. Gray also claimed an 'Oscar', one 'Oscar' actually being lost. Returning from an attack on Gangaw the same day, a Hurricane of 607 Squadron was hit by groundfire and lost, without injury to the pilot, F.O. Halbeard.

17, 607 and 615 Squadrons had also now moved up, and over the following nine days there were a series of combats. On the 16th December, 'Oscars' of the 50th and 64th Sentais escorted 'Lilys' in another raid on Chittagong. This was intercepted by 28 Hurricanes of 79, 135, 607 and 615 Squadrons, a 'Sally' bomber being claimed by W.O. McIvor of 135 Squadron.[5] Flt. Lt. Hedderwick of 607 Squadron claimed one of the escorting 'Oscars,' but was then himself shot down[6] and slightly wounded. P.O. James[6a] was also shot down by the 'Oscars' and severely burned. A Hurricane of 615 Squadron also force-landed, without injury to Flt. Sgt. Oldham.

On Sunday, the 20th December, in a raid on Magwe airfield, one of three 'Oscars' which attempted to intercept was claimed by Sgt. Goold of 607 Squadron,[6b] but no losses were reported by the Japanese.

Next day, another 607 Squadron Hurricane[6c] was force-landed by flak while strafing Akyab Island, Flt. Sgt. Richardson being taken prisoner. On the night of the 22nd/23rd December, three 'Sallys' raided Calcutta and were intercepted by six Hurricanes of 17 Squadron. P.O. Gibson was credited with bringing down one of the 'Sallys', the first RAF night victory in this theatre. In fact, one of the 'Sallys' force-landed and another crash-landed. During daylight on the 23rd, an attack on Feni by 'Lilys', escorted by 'Oscars' of the 50th Sentai, was engaged by Hurricanes, Flt. Sgt. Gill of 607 Squadron claiming a 'Zero'.[6d]

On Christmas Eve 1942, Magwe was again the target for 607 and 615 Squadrons. Eight Hurricanes met six 'Oscars', but Flt. Sgt. Yates of 607 Squadron claimed a 'Zero' and a probable, shared with Flt. Sgt. Clarke, plus one damaged each.[7]

An 'Oscar' was also claimed destroyed on the ground by Flt. Sgt. Oldham of 615 Squadron and confirmed. However, Sgt. Kostromin of 615 Squadron[8] and F.O. Ferguson of 607 Squadron[6e] both failed to return, the former being killed and the latter becoming a prisoner.

That night, a bomber was claimed over Calcutta, by Wg. Cdr. O'Neill of 293 Wing.[9] On the 28th December, in yet another raid on Magwe, two Hurricanes of 615 Squadron were shot down by flak. Sqn. Ldr. Duckenfield was taken prisoner, but Flt. Sgt. Pavely was killed. Next day, Sqn. Ldr. Riddler of 136 Squadron accidentally flew into the sea and was injured.[10]

An army reconnaissance aircraft was claimed destroyed on the ground by 615 Squadron on the 2nd January 1943, in another raid on Magwe. However, P.O. Finn, who had been seen hitting this machine, was shot down and killed. In the next decisive air combat on the 17th January, a 'Zero' was wrongly claimed by F.O. Doudy of 607 Squadron, for the loss of a Hurricane of 607 Squadron and its pilot, Flt. Sgt. Gill, who was killed. This engagement was actually against 'Oscars' of the 50th Sentai. A Hurricane[11] of 28 Squadron was shot down near Kyaukpadan by an 'Oscar' on the 23rd January, killing Flt. Sgt. Hilton and one 'Oscar' and a probable were claimed by Flt. Sgt. Cross of 136 Squadron the same day,[12] for the loss of one of that squadron's Hurricanes, probably shot down by an 'Oscar'. Sqn. Ldr. Giddings was found dead in this aircraft next day.

In February 1943, two enemy aircraft were claimed destroyed on the ground at Akyat on the 9th, by 607 Squadron and two 'Oscars' were confirmed to W.O. Mann of 261 Squadron on the 13th, but Sgt. Gee of this Squadron was shot down by an 'Oscar'[13] and killed. One 'Oscar' was also claimed this day by Sgt. Windle of 'A' Flight, 135 Squadron,

Sgt. Robertson of the same squadron claiming a probable. Sgt. Evans of 79 Squadron also claimed an 'Oscar' probable, but Sgt. North[14] was force-landed in this engagement, though not injured. On the 20th February, five Hurricanes of 135 Squadron intercepted 'Oscars' of the 64th Sentai in the Akyab area, but were 'bounced' and lost two aircraft,[15] with Lt. Boysoon (SAAF) killed and P.O. Fox wounded.

The last day of February saw 136 Squadron clashing with the 50th Sentai and again the 'Oscars' triumphed. Although P.O. Cuthbert claimed an 'Oscar', two Hurricanes were shot down[10a] and another[10b] was force-landed. All three pilots escaped unhurt.

It was 615 Squadron's turn to engage the 'Oscars' on the 1st March and although a probable was claimed by P.O. Aurisch, F.O. Astley was shot down,[8a] bailing out unhurt. Next day, an aircraft[16] of 146 Squadron was shot down by flak and its pilot, W.O. Cochrane killed.

The most successful day during this period for the RAF, in terms of claims, was on the 5th March. 607 Squadron escorted bombers attacking Abiyat, P.O. Fraser claiming an 'Enemy Fighter', while probables were claimed by Sqn. Ldr. Holland and P.O. Clarke. In return, a Hurricane crash-landed after combat, wounding Sgt. Longley. 79 Squadron also escorted bombers, but the target was Kalachaung, F.O. Bowes claiming an 'Oscar' but Sgt. Delemere failed to return.[14a] However, it was 135 Squadron which claimed the heaviest this day in two engagements. An 0915 scramble resulted in combat over Akyab, Flt. Lt. Storey and W.O. Dean both claiming 'Oscars', with probables claimed by F.O. Hawkins, P.O. Armstrong and Flt. Sgt. Crawford. Soon after midday, in the same area, Storey claimed another two 'Oscars', Sgt. Brown claimed one and Sgt. Crawford a probable. It is highly likely that the two 'Oscars' actually lost were those claimed by Storey.

A Hurricane of 607 Squadron[6f] was lost to flak on the 11th March, killing F.O. Macdonald and one of 17 Squadron's aircraft met a similar fate on the 13th, Flt. Sgt. Cropper becoming a PoW. Next day, eight Hurricanes of 135 Squadron escorted Blenheims to Donbaik, but were intercepted by the 64th Sentai around 1245hrs. Two Hurricanes[15b] were shot down by the 'Oscars', P.O. Morrison and Flt. Sgt. Robertson both being killed. Sgt. Windle also force-landed[15c] unhurt with combat damage.

Flt. Lt. Perkin claimed an 'Oscar' probable and a damaged in return, with Sgt. Picton claiming another damaged. Two of the 'Oscars' actually force-landed but were repairable.

Next day, four Hurricanes of 136 Squadron and eight of 607 Squadron met 14 'Oscars' over Rathedaung, while escorting Blenheims. Sqn. Ldr. Bayne and Flt. Sgt. Carpenter of 136 Squadron both claimed 'Oscars', but two Hurricanes of that Squadron[10c] were shot down, both F.O. Pickard and W.O. de Cruyenaere being killed.

An 'Oscar' and three damaged[6g] were also claimed by 607 Squadron, who lost F.O. Gibbs[6h] and P.O. Main,[6i] both also being killed. In addition, W.O. Blythe force-landed[6j] but was unhurt. No 'Oscars' were lost by the Japanese.

A Japanese raid on Cox's Bazaar was launched on the 17th March and intercepted by 79 Squadron. F.O. Bowes claimed an 'Oscar' and one damaged, but Sgt. Elder was killed[14b] and Flt. Sgt. Simpson crash-landed unhurt.[14c] Overall, from the 1st to the 17th March, 11 'Oscars' were claimed by 79, 135, 136, 607 and 615 Squadrons in air combat,[17] for the loss of 13 Hurricanes as the fight for air superiority over Burma was vigorously contested. However, only two 'Oscars' were confirmed lost by the Japanese this month.[18]

In a further combat over Maungdaw on the 18th March, Sgt. Edge of 135 Squadron was force-landed[15d] by 'Oscars' of the 64th Sentai, but not hurt. An 'Ida' reconnaissance aircraft was claimed by Flt. Lt. Perkin and F.O. Graham, also of 135 Squadron and confirmed on the 21st March. 67 Squadron moved up to Chittagong on the 24th March to replace 607 Squadron, but then came another period of intense air activity in support of heavy ground fighting around Donbaik.

On the 26th March, 'Oscars' of the 50th Sentai were intercepted by 67 and 135 Squadrons over the front. A Hurricane[19] of 67 Squadron was lost, with F.O. Sadler reported missing, but F.O Hawkins of 135 Squadron claimed a 'Zero'.[20] Two Hurricanes[10d] of 136 Squadron force-landed, but both pilots were safe.

In one of the best days of the campaign for the RAF, next day, an unescorted formation of an estimated 15 to 18 'Lily' bombers, targeting the Cox's Bazaar area, were engaged by four Hurricanes of 79 Squadron and seven of 135 Squadron. Eight of the bombers[21] were claimed shot down, plus five probables.[14d, 15e] In fact, between six and eight were lost to the Hurricanes. They had failed to rendezvous with their escort from the 50th Sentai.

On the 29th March, 10 'Oscars' of the 50th Sentai encountered six Hurricanes of 79 Squadron in the Maungdaw area and caused HV647 to crash-land, without injury to Flt. Sgt. Simpson. Next morning, in the same area, six Hurricanes of 79 Squadron intercepted the 50th Sentai 'Oscars', escorting 'Lily' bombers, P.O. Boughton claiming an 'Oscar' probable and F.O. May, a 'Lily' probable. Four Hurricanes of 135 Squadron then joined the engagement and three more 'Oscars' were claimed as probables.[15f] However, no Japanese aircraft were reported lost in these combats. On the last day of March, eight 'Oscars' of the 50th Sentai were engaged early in the morning by 10 Hurricanes of 135 Squadron, east of Buthidaung. Three of the Hurricanes[15g] were shot down by the 'Oscars', P.O. Dean and Sgt. Edge both being killed, while Sgt. Benson bailed out wounded. P.O. Armstrong claimed an 'Oscar' and Sgt. Peabody a probable for 135 Squadron, but no 'Oscars' were lost.

A combat report by P.O. Armstrong of 135 Squadron dated 1st April 1943, regarding the engagement the previous day, reported:[15a]

> 'We were scrambled from Hove at 0700hrs. We climbed to the North to 17,000ft and proceeded South. Red 1, White 2 and myself as Yellow 1, climbed into sun to about 21,000ft and sighted E/A above and to East of us and several about 2,000ft below us.
>
> 'Red 1 and myself dived to attack E/A below us. I made a starboard quarter attack on E/A which was turning slightly to starboard of about four seconds' burst closing in to about 50 yards.
>
> 'White smoke started coming from E/A and I pulled up in a steep climbing turn to starboard. E/A followed me up but was left behind. E/A levelled out and I stall turned on him

giving him a two- or three-seconds' burst from astern and above. White and black smoke poured out of him and he went down in a very flat spin. I climbed back to 22,000 but could see no aircraft so I returned to base. I claim this Army 01 as destroyed.'

'Oscars' of 50th and the 64th Sentais escorted 'Sally' bombers attacking Feni on the 1st April, encountering 11 Hurricanes of 615 Squadron and six of 67 Squadron. The former unit claimed three 'Sallys'[8b] and two probables[8c] but F.O. Ortmans of 615 Squadron was shot down[8d] and killed. Three of the 'Sallys' were indeed lost and another crash-landed on return.

Next day, Hurricanes of 67 Squadron were engaged by 'Oscars' as they escorted Blenheims, BN968 force-landing, reportedly through engine trouble, with F.O. Worsley unhurt. A Hurricane of 28 Squadron was also lost to engine failure, but F.O. Humphries was killed.

On the 4th April, seven 'Oscars' of the 64th Sentai met Hurricanes of 136 Squadron north-east of Chittagong, four 'Oscar' probables being claimed by Sqn. Ldr. Bayne, Flt. Sgt. Fortune, P.O. Goddard and Flt. Sgt. Rudling. One Hurricane[10e] was shot down in this combat, killing Flt. Sgt. Carpenter. 135 Squadron also engaged the 'Oscars', resulting in Flt. Lt. Perkin crash-landing wounded.[15h] The following morning, Hurricanes of 79, 135 and 607 Squadrons escorted Blenheims attacking Meiktila and encountered an 'Oscar' of the 50th Sentai which was claimed by F.O. Bowes of 79 Squadron.[22] That afternoon, nine Hurricanes of 136 Squadron engaged a sweep by 12 'Oscars' of the 64th Sentai against Chittagong, Flt. Sgt. Cross claiming an 'Oscar' probable, but none was lost.

On the 9th April, a further sweep by 16 'Oscars' of the 64th Sentai 'bounced' nine Hurricanes of 67 Squadron, shooting-down HV976 and BN476 and killing F.O. Christiansen (RNZAF) and Sqn. Ldr. Bachmann. On the 26th of the month, a 28 Squadron Hurricane was lost to flak, wounding P.O. Carmichael.

The first air combats of May 1943 involving Hurricanes occurred on the 2nd of the month, with five aircraft of 146 Squadron and four of 136 Squadron clashing with 20 'Oscars' of the 50th Sentai, escorting

'Lilys' attacking Dohazari. One aircraft[16a] of 146 Squadron was shot down, killing F.O. Henderson, while Flt. Sgt. Cross claimed a 'Lily' and an 'Oscar' damaged, one 'Oscar' actually crash-landing.

Two days later, an afternoon engagement between 13 'Oscars' of the 50th Sentai attacking Cox's Bazaar and eight Hurricanes of 135 Squadron, resulted in one of the Hurricanes belly-landing at base, having been shot up, although Sgt. Picton was unhurt. Next day, six Hurricanes of 135 Squadron attacked Kyauksadaung, Flt. Lt. Storey claiming an '01', which was subsequently confirmed.

On the 15th May, eight Hurricanes of 67 Squadron attacked Kangaung airfield where P.O. Williams and Sgt. Elliott jointly shot down an 'Oscar' which scrambled to intercept. Three more 'Oscars' were claimed destroyed on the ground. On the 21st May, 17 'Oscars' of the 64th Sentai met Hurricanes of 79 Squadron near Cox's Bazaar, shooting down BN880 and one other aircraft,[14e] for one 'Oscar' probable claimed by P.O. McClure. No 'Oscars' were lost by the Japanese.

Next morning, a formation of 'Lilys' raided Chittagong, escorted by 'Oscars' of the 50th and 64th Sentais. Eleven Hurricanes of 67 Squadron and nine of 136 Squadron intercepted the raid, but one of the former Squadron's aircraft[10f] was shot down, wounding Sgt. Rainger. A 'Lily' was claimed by Flt. Sgt. Muggleton of the same squadron.

Soon after this combat, eight Hurricanes of 136 Squadron also engaged 'Lilys' and 'Oscars' over Chittagong, three of the bombers being claimed[10g] plus a probable.[10h] 'Oscars' were also claimed by P.O. Conway[10i] and Flt. Sgt. Fortune of this Squadron. However, a single 'Lily' bomber was the only Japanese loss in these engagements. A Hurricane of 136 Squadron was shot down, wounding Flt. Sgt. Rudling and another of the Squadron's aircraft was destroyed on the ground at Chittagong.

On the 28th May, HV606 force-landed in enemy territory, P.O. Drake becoming a PoW. Next morning, nine Hurricanes of 136 Squadron and 12 of 67 Squadron intercepted a formation of 'Lily' bombers escorted by 'Oscars', three 'Oscars' being claimed by F.O. Conway, F.O. Gillies and Flt. Sgt. Rudling of 136 Squadron, together with a 'Lily' each by F.O. Gillies and Sgt. Kearson. An 'Oscar' probable was also claimed by

Flt. Sgt. Muggleton of 67 Squadron. One 'Oscar' was actually lost by the Japanese. On the last day of May, HV702 was hit by flak and force-landed, wounding Flt. Sgt. Buckley.

This ended the first Arakan campaign. 135 Squadron was the most successful Hurricane squadron of this campaign, in terms of claims, with 14 and two-thirds victories, followed by 136 Squadron (14), 79 Squadron (11 and a third), 607 Squadron (seven), 615 Squadron (three), 67 Squadron (two), 261 Squadron (two), 17 Squadron and 293 Wing one each. Fifty-six victories were thus claimed for the loss of 50 Hurricanes in air combat.[23] Top scorer of this campaign was F.O. Bowes of 79 Squadron, with five and a third victories.

At least 28 'Oscars' are included in the claims, a further 21 probables and 41 damaged also being claimed. Eighteen 'Lilys' were also included in the claim, as were six 'Sallys' and five 'Zeros', although the latter were probably 'Oscars', the 'Zero' being a Navy, rather than an Army, fighter and rarely used in this theatre. In reality, only 13 'Oscars' and nine 'Lilys' are known to have been lost in air combat by the Japanese to Hurricanes, plus six 'Sallys', one 'IDA' and another unidentified bomber, a total of 30 enemy aircraft. The 'Oscar' was proving a deadly adversary, being more manoeuvrable than the Hurricane and although believed less able to sustain damage, the number of 'Oscars' claimed as probable or damaged, most of which appear to have survived, casts considerable doubt on this belief. Fighter versus fighter combat had resulted in a near four-to-one victory ratio for the Japanese.

During the period June to September inclusive, at least 11 Hurricanes were lost in this theatre of operations, none in air combat.

615 Squadron now moved to Alipore and 135 Squadron to Madras, the monsoon now reducing air activity until October 1943. However, a 'Sally' bomber was intercepted by four Hurricanes of 261 Squadron on the 5th September and shot down by F.O. Brain over Middle Baronga Island. On the 4th October, two Hurricanes of 136 Squadron encountered a 'Dinah' reconnaissance aircraft over Baigachi, Flt. Sgt. Davis claiming this as a probable.

In October 1943, 136, 607 and 615 Squadrons converted to Spitfires, but Hurricanes were still operated as fighters in this theatre of operations. On the 20th October, Chittagong was attacked by 'Sallys' escorted by around 19 'Oscars', Hurricanes of 146, 258 and 261 Squadrons intercepting. 'Sally' probables were claimed by Flt. Lt. McDonald and W.O. Walker of 261 Squadron, but three of that squadron's Hurricanes[13a] were shot down by 'Oscars', Flt. Lt. Osmond and Sgt. Cowley both being killed and F.O. Greenwood being slightly wounded. W.O. Blackmore of 146 Squadron claimed a 'Sally' probable and an 'Oscar' probable, but there were no Japanese losses.

On the 27th October, an 'Oscar' was claimed destroyed on the ground by 67 Squadron Hurricanes at Auzdaing airfield. On the 9th November, 34 Squadron Hurricanes claimed an 'Oscar' probable, which was in fact an RAF Mohawk that was forced to land at Palel. Two Hurricanes of 28 Squadron were destroyed on the ground in an air attack this day.

On the 28th November, Feni was attacked by bombers escorted by 'Oscars', 67, 258 and 261 Squadrons scrambling to intercept. F.O. Bargh of 67 Squadron claimed an 'Oscar,' but a Hurricane[19b] of that unit was shot down, Sgt. Harris being killed.

The last major air combat of 1943 in this theatre involving Hurricanes was on the 5th December, when a joint Japanese Army and Navy formation attacked Calcutta. This formation included 101 'Oscars' of the 33rd, 50th, 64th and 204th Sentais and 27 'Zeros' of the 331st Kokutai, escorting 'Sally' and 'Betty' bombers.

Twenty-eight Hurricanes of 60, 258 and 261 Squadrons were scrambled initially, alongside 37 Spitfires, to intercept. A 'Sally' was claimed by W.O. Hickes of 258 Squadron and confirmed, but a Hurricane[24] of that squadron was shot down by 'Oscars', Flt. Lt. Brown being killed. Twenty-one Hurricanes of 67 and 146 Squadrons were also scrambled, F.O. Williams of the former unit claiming an 'Oscar', but W.O. Bond of this squadron was shot down[19c] and killed, two other Hurricanes[19d] force-landing, although both Sgt. Corston and P.O. Wilson were unhurt.

An 'Oscar' probable was claimed by Sgt. Dawber of 146 Squadron, but a Hurricane[16b] of this squadron was shot down and another[16c] crash-landed, Flt. Sgt. Evans bailing out safely from the former and W.O. Horne being unhurt in the latter.

Five of 176 Squadron were also scrambled but were 'bounced' by the Navy 'Zeros', three[25] being shot down, Flt. Lt. Halbeard and F.O. Pring being killed, although P.O. Whyte was unhurt. Finally, this day, six Hurricanes of 261 Squadron attacked Akyab, hoping to catch the enemy formation refuelling, but meeting 'Oscars' of the 204th Sentai. An 'Oscar' probable was claimed by F.O. Gibson of this squadron. The net result of this day was nine Hurricanes lost or force-landed after air combat for only one 'Sally' bomber confirmed shot down.

On the 9th January 1944, Hurricanes of 258 Squadron strafed Dadaing Strip on Akyab Island and claimed a twin-engined aircraft probably destroyed on the ground. On the 15th of the month, an aircraft of 6 IAF Squadron was reported damaged in combat and force-landed, without injury to F.O. Bhullar. Then on the 27th January, three Hurricanes of 6 IAF Squadron[26] were lost to fighters,[27] F.O. Bhullar being reported missing, but the fates of F.O.s Mukerji and Varma is unknown.

On the 4th February, 'Oscars' of the 50th, 64th and 204th Sentais on a sweep over the Taung Bazaar area caught a Hurricane[26a] of 6 IAF Squadron on a reconnaissance mission and shot it down, P.O. Gracious being reported missing.

Next day, another sweep by 'Oscars' was intercepted by Spitfires and 12 Hurricanes of 11 Squadron also scrambled, losing two aircraft[28] which were assumed shot down, F.O. Blight being killed, while Sgt. Corbett was taken prisoner. On the 8th February, two more Hurricanes[26b] of 6 IAF Squadron failed to return and were assumed to have been shot down by another 'Oscar' sweep, F.O.s Delima and Reddy both being reported missing. Twelve Hurricanes of 134 Squadron reported meeting six 'Oscars' this day, probables being claimed by F.O. Knapton and P.O. Walker, but two of the Hurricanes crash-landed, F.O. Prendergast being wounded and Flt. Sgt. Phillips unhurt. Next day, 261 Squadron Hurricanes engaged another sweep by 'Oscars' over Seinnyinbya, one being claimed by F.O. Atkins, which was confirmed.

On the 11th February, another Hurricane[26c] of 6 IAF Squadron on a tactical reconnaissance mission was shot up and force-landed near

Buthidaung, F.O. Singh escaping unhurt. Four days later, another 6 IAF Squadron aircraft was shot down, P.O. Murlidhar being killed, but an 'Oscar' was claimed by F.O. Varma of this squadron, this being the only IAF victory claim of the war.

On the 18th February, 'Oscars' of the 64th Sentai escorted 'Sonia' tactical reconnaissance aircraft to Myohong and 'bounced' two Hurricanes[29] of 20 Squadron. Both Flt. Lt. Thomson and Flt. Sgt. Pirani were reported missing.

On the 20th of the month, 20 Squadron Hurricanes attacked a 'Sally' in the Myohong area, reporting it had belly-landed on the airfield. Next day, the same Squadron returned and the 'Sally' was claimed destroyed on the ground by F.O. Hulme. Hurricanes of 134 Squadron also strafed this aircraft.

On the 12th March, 60 'Oscars' escorted 'Lily' bombers attacking Silchar, the 'Oscars' sighting a pair of 28 Squadron Hurricanes and shooting one down,[11a] although W.O. Walker was unhurt. Two of the 'Oscars' were wrongly claimed to have collided in this combat.

On the 12th April, a Hurricane[30] of 123 Squadron failed to return, F.O. Stewart being killed. He may have been the victim of a the 64th Sentai 'Oscar'. On the 24th April, another Hurricane[30a] of 123 Squadron failed to return, Flt. Lt. Davies being killed and he was probably another victim of 'Oscars' of the 50th, 64th or 204th Sentais. On the 26th April, 'Oscars' of the 64th and 204th Sentais escorted 'Lilys' to the Imphal Valley and were engaged by Hurricanes of 5 and 11 Squadrons, an 'Oscar' probable being claimed by F.O. Mann of 5 Squadron. A Hurricane of 11 Squadron crash-landed after combat, but Flt. Lt. Ditmas was unhurt.

On the 20th May, 22 'Oscars' and 'Tojos' of the 50th, 64th and 87th Sentais swept over Imphal and caught two Hurricanes of 5 Squadron just after take-off, shooting down and killing Flt. Lt. Thornton and Flt. Sgt. Bibeau. Next day, 20 'Oscars' of the 50th and 64th Sentais escorted 'Sallys' raiding the Bishenpur area, the 'Oscars' shooting down a Hurricane of 1 IAF Squadron, P.O. Masih being reported missing, believed killed. On the 23rd May, around 35 'Oscars' of the 50th, 64th and 204th Sentais met a Hurricane[28a] of 11 Squadron, which was shot down, killing W.O. Bowden, but one 'Oscar' belly-landed after combat and may have been shot down by Bowden, before his demise.

On the 8th June, 15 'Oscars' of the 50th and 204th Sentais engaged a 28 Squadron Hurricane[11b] over Imphal and forced it to crash-land, wounding F.O. Muff. On the 13th September, a 'Sally' bomber was claimed destroyed on the ground at Taukkyan Airstrip by Hurricanes of 1 IAF Squadron.

On the 19th February 1945, a 28 Squadron Hurricane crash-landed, Flt. Lt. Hunter being reported missing and he may have been the last Hurricane air combat victim of the 'Oscars'.

In total, 62.99 enemy aircraft were claimed by Hurricanes in air combat in this theatre of operations, of which 31 are confirmed by the Japanese, for the loss of 77 Hurricanes shot down or force-landed in air combat, 114 more lost on operations (mostly to flak or unknown causes) and at least 72 in accidents.

Spitfire squadrons claimed 106 enemy aircraft in air combat in this theatre of operations, of which 60 can be confirmed, for the loss of up to 18 Spitfires in air combat. Of course, Hurricanes fought in this theatre for 10 months before any Spitfire fighters[31] arrived and were the primary interceptors during the critical first Arakan campaign. The highest scoring Hurricane pilot against the Japanese was P.O. W.J. (Jack) Storey (RAAF) who claimed eight plus two probables.

References

1 Sqn. Ldr. Giddings, W.O. Fox, Flt. Sgt. Hinton and Flt. Sgt. Arrowsmith.
2 BG863 and BG991.
3 BH142.
4 Squadron Leader Jones claimed one and one damaged, F.O. Bowes claimed one and Sgt. May claimed one, a probable and one damaged. In addition, Sgt. North claimed an 'Oscar' and one damaged, while P.O. Gray also claimed an 'Oscar,' one 'Oscar' actually being lost.
5 The claim was later reduced to damaged.
6 In 'T'.
6a In 'O'.
6b Escorting Bisleys and Blenheims.

6c	HL786.
6d	Probably an 'Oscar' – 607 Squadron ORB?
6e	In HM127.
6f	HV781.
6g	P.O. Fraser claimed the kill.
6h	In HW270.
6i	In HV788.
6j	In BG955.
7	These were actually 'Oscars', but none were lost – 607 Squadron ORB?
8	In BN989.
8a	In HV799.
8b	W.O. Chandler, Flt. Sgt. Andrews and Sgt. Dickson.
8c	Sgt. Dickson and Sgt. Fox.
8d	In HV771.
9	And confirmed.
10	In Hurricane 'S' – 136 Squadron ORB?
10a	BN976 and BM929.
10b	BN168.
10c	BN388 and BM936.
10d	HV635 and HV661 – 136 Squadron ORB?
10e	HV726.
10f	HV640.
10g	By Flt. Lt. Brown, F.O. Adamson and F.O. Stout.
10h	By F.O. Jacobs.
10i	Who also claimed a probable.
11	JS223.
11a	HV475.
11b	LD336.
12	One being confirmed.
13	In BH135 – 261 Squadron ORB?
13a	AP896, AP936 and HV788.
14	In HV405.
14a	In BN902.

14b	In HV903.
14c	In HV658 which was written-off.
14d	For 79 Squadron, F.O. Bowes claimed one and a third, W.O. Sergeant one and a probable, Sgt. Peabody one, Sgt. Simpson two probables and Sgt. Grapes a probable.
14e	Flt. Lt. Bowes and Sgt. Burchard were killed.
15	HM137 and HV772.
15a	135 Squadron ORB.
15b	HV773 and HV783.
15c	In HV791.
15d	In BG905.
15e	For 135 Squadron, F.O. Hawkins claimed one and a probable, P.O. Armstrong one and a half, plus a third share, Flt. Sgt. Crawford a half plus a third share and P.O. Fox one.
15f	By Flt. Lt. Perkin, P.O. McIvor and Flt. Sgt. Arrowsmith.
15g	BG994, HW273 and BM935.
15h	In HV416.
16	BN132.
16a	HV418.
16b	HV983.
16c	HL802.
17	A further eight probables and 10 damaged were also claimed.
18	On the 5th March.
19	BN972.
19a	HV640.
19b	HW499.
19c	In LB569
19d	KZ888 and LB608.
20	Actually an 'Oscar'.
21	Some shared.
22	Actually claimed as a 'Zero' but not lost.
23	Shot down or force-landed.
24	LA105.
25	Including HW435 and HV709.

26	BW912, HV422 and JS422.
26a	BE291.
26b	AP892 and BG868.
26c	HV421.
27	Probably 'Oscars'.
28	HW853 and HW601.
28a	LB797.
29	KW124 and KW871.
30	KZ652.
30a	LB727.
31	As opposed to PR variants of that aircraft.

Chapter Twenty-Seven
Torch and Tunisia

The Anglo-American invasion of Algeria and Morocco, known as Operation 'Torch', commenced on the 8th November 1942. RAF Hurricane squadrons involved at the beginning of operations were 43, 253 and 225 (Army Co-operation) Squadrons.

On the 9th November, Flt. Sgt. Smith of 43 Squadron claimed an He 111, while a JU-88 was claimed by F.O Barker, Flt. Sgt. Ball and Sgt. Leeming[1] and a JU-88 probable by F.O. Trenchard Smith. One JU-88 was actually lost by the Germans.

Next day, another JU-88 was claimed by F.O. Turkington of 43 Squadron and confirmed lost, while on the 12th, in the Bougie area, two He 111s were claimed by Flt. Lt. Lister and Wg Cdr Pedley of the same Squadron, Pedley also claiming a JU-88 and a DO-217 was claimed by F.O. Lea. All of these were confirmed lost by the Germans.[2] Flt. Lt. Fisher of 253 Squadron also claimed a JU-88 probable near Algiers on the 14th November.

Up to this stage, no Hurricanes had been lost by the RAF Squadrons.[3] However, from the 15th November until the end of 1942, 25 Hurricanes were lost,[4,5] without any further claims in air combat. Six of the losses were destroyed on the ground[6] and at least six were lost in air combat.[7]

Three Hurricane pilots were known killed during this period, including F.O. Rodwell of 225 Squadron on the 17th November, by allied flak; F.O. Ingram of the same Squadron on the 27th November, probably by BF109s, and Sgt. Leadbetter of 43 Squadron, also on the 17th November. In addition, F.O.s Marshall and Gibbons and P.O.s Giles and Tyson of 225 Squadron and Flt. Lt. Harrap of 241 Squadron were all reported missing. Gibbons and Giles were victims of the BF109s.

32 Squadron arrived by ship at Philippeville on the 7th December. 241 Squadron had arrived in November and moved up to Souk El Arba on the 21st December.

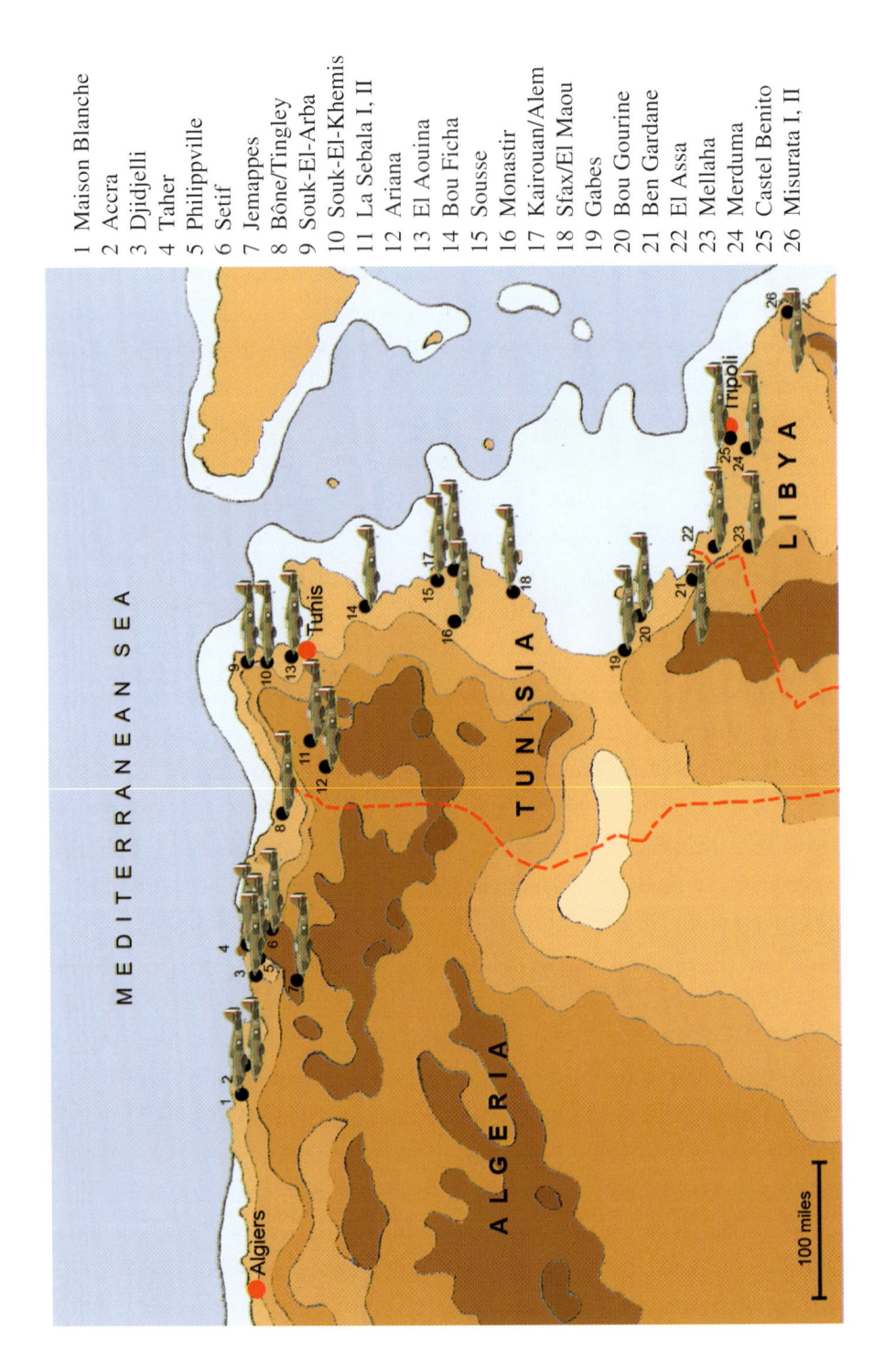

1 Maison Blanche
2 Accra
3 Djidjelli
4 Taher
5 Philippville
6 Setif
7 Jemappes
8 Bône/Tingley
9 Souk-El-Arba
10 Souk-El-Khemis
11 La Sebala I, II
12 Ariana
13 El Aouina
14 Bou Ficha
15 Sousse
16 Monastir
17 Kairouan/Alem
18 Sfax/El Maou
19 Gabes
20 Bou Gourine
21 Ben Gardane
22 El Assa
23 Mellaha
24 Merduma
25 Castel Benito
26 Misurata I, II

In January 1943, only three enemy aircraft were claimed by Hurricane Squadrons on this front; a JU-88 north-west of Bougie by Squadron Leader Bartlett of 253 Squadron on the 10th;[8] a Tri-Motor north of Bougie by Flt. Lt. Cochrane of 87 Squadron[9] on the 22nd and a JU-88 or He 111 off Cap Coroelin by P.O. Higgins of 32 Squadron[10] on the 29th.

In addition, two JU-88s were claimed damaged over the sea by F.O.s Mason and Blair of 253 Squadron on the 9th January, one of which[11] was confirmed as lost. Fourteen Hurricanes were lost during the month,[12] six of which were destroyed on the ground and only one was known lost in air combat.[13] P.O. Beckwith of 241 Squadron,[14] F.O. Davis of 73 Squadron[15] and Lt. Black[16] were posted as missing.

February was another quiet month for the Hurricane Squadrons. A JU-88 probable was claimed off the Algerian coast by Flt. Lt. Barber and Sgt. Whittaker of 253 Squadron on the 2nd of the month and a JU-88 of II/KG 54 was claimed off the Tripolitanian coast by Lt. Fisher, Lt. Rorvik and 2nd Lt. Rosholt of 7 SAAF Squadron on the 12th February to give that unit its first victory, but 2nd Lt. Rosholt was believed shot down and killed by flak from the ship convoy they were protecting.

On the 14th, a confirmed JU-88 claim[17] North of Cap Bougeron was attributed to Sgt. Ashworth of 253 Squadron and next day, Flt. Lt. Mason and Sgt. Whittaker of the same Squadron forced a CANT Z.501 to land on the sea, off the north coast of Algeria, where it was captured. Seven Hurricanes were lost in February, three at least to flak,[18] two were destroyed on the ground[19] and two accidentally.[20] Flt. Sgt. Dawson was killed in the latter.

On the 1st March, a Hurricane[21] of 32 Squadron crashed on landing, although Flt. Sgt. Dunn was unhurt. A further JU-88 was claimed near Philippeville by P.O. Kelly and Sgt. Shorthouse[22] of 253 Squadron on the 4th March, an aircraft of I/KG 54 being lost. Early next day, two Hurricanes of 73 Squadron[23] failed to return from an armed reconnaissance mission north of Mareth. Flt. Sgt. Logan and W.O. Dolan were listed as missing, although Logan was later reported as a prisoner.

On 10th March, the Hurricane IIDs of 6 Squadron re-entered the battle, attacking panzers at Ksar Rhilane. Two days earlier, Air Vice Marshal Broadhurst, Commander of the Desert Air Force, had stated that 'the

Air Ministry desired to discover the effectiveness of the 'tank-buster' in modern warfare and it was to be expected that as many targets as possible would be found for the Squadron.'[24] Hurricane IIDs had first been used on the 7th June 1942 in North Africa and had also seen action at El Alamein, but clearly they were still considered of unproven effectiveness.

Hawker Hurricane IID - 6 squadron.

In the first operation this day, six aircraft took off at 1005hrs and attacked 20 vehicles, 12 of which were claimed put-out-of-action. The second attack force took off at 1150hrs and comprised 14 Hurricanes, which claimed to have hit a tank and an armoured car. No aircraft were lost on this occasion, but three were damaged.[24]

However, on the 22nd March, 13 aircraft took-off at 1325hrs to attack enemy tanks South of El Hamma, returning at 1400hrs. In the second operation of the day, seven more aircraft departed at 1620hrs and attacked the same target, returning at 1735hrs.[24] Nine enemy tanks were claimed destroyed in these attacks, but four Hurricanes[25] of 6 Squadron were shot down, F.O. Jones being wounded, although the other pilots were unhurt.

Two days later, at 1025hrs, 12 Hurricane IIDs of 6 Squadron again took off to engage enemy tanks near El Hamma. Although the operation was considered successful, two of the Hurricanes failed to return. At 1705hrs the same day, seven more aircraft attacked the same targets and a further two Hurricanes were shot down and another force-landed,[26] in the

El Hamma area,[24] at least some by I/JG 77 BF109s.

Casualties included Sgt. Harris, who was missing, presumed killed and P.O. Day, who was wounded.

241 Squadron also lost a Hurricane[27] on the 23rd[28] and another[29] on the 24th, both missing from operations. Two Hurricanes of 253 Squadron[30] were also lost accidentally on the 23rd, F.O.s Little and Stevenson being missing. On the night of 24th/25th, P.O. Chandler of 73 Squadron destroyed a JU-88 of III/KG77 on an intruder patrol over Gabes.

Next day, at 1245hrs, 10 Hurricane IIDs of 6 Squadron took off and again struck at enemy armour in the El Hamma area, but six aircraft[31] were shot down by flak. P.O. Paton was slightly wounded, but the other pilots were all unhurt.[24]

Two more Hurricane IIDs of 6 Squadron[32] were lost on the 26th March, near the Djebels Tebaga/Melab gap, from 11 aircraft which took off at 1500hrs, with a further two[33] badly shot up. No pilots were injured.[24]

Another Hurricane[34] of 241 Squadron was also lost on the 25th, P.O. Hamlet being reported missing. On the 27th March, two He 111s were claimed in the Cap Takouch area by F.O.s Johnson and Thompson of 87 Squadron on a convoy patrol, one of the bomber crews of II/KG 26 being taken prisoner.

A further three Hurricane IIDs[35] of 6 Squadron were shot down by light flak on the 6th April. Thirteen aircraft had taken off at 1225hrs to attack enemy tanks in the Sfax area. No targets were found and F.O. Ziliessen failed to return, but the other two pilots were unhurt.[24]

At 1515hrs the same day, a further eight aircraft set out to attack a concentration of tanks and infantry, but these were not located and four lorries were attacked instead and claimed destroyed.[24]

In the third operation of the day by 6 Squadron, six more aircraft departed at 1645hrs to attack eight enemy tanks in the Sfax area. These were not seen, but one tank and M.E.T. were successfully attacked elsewhere. All aircraft returned safely at 1745hrs.[24]

That night, a JU-88 was claimed north-east of Gabes by F.O. Hendersen of 73 Squadron.

Next day, 11 Hurricane IIDs of 6 Squadron took off at 1820hrs to attack tanks near Chekira, but again suffered badly, losing six aircraft[36] to intensive flak, with the loss of Flt. Sgt. Hastings and F.O. Clarke killed and P.O. Freeland and F.O. Walter missing.[24]

241 Squadron lost two Hurricanes[37] on the 6th April, the former on take-off, injuring F.O. Horsfall and the latter on landing. That night, HV410 of 32 Squadron failed to return and Sgt. Thompsen was reported killed.

On the night of the 7th/8th April, a JU-88 was claimed damaged by P.O. Chandler of 73 Squadron in the Gabes area[38] and on the night of the 10th/11th April, F.O. Hendersen of 73 Squadron was killed near Mahares,[39] the cause being unknown.

On the 11th April, it was 241 Squadron's turn to suffer to the intense flak north of Enfidaville, three of the squadron's aircraft[40] being lost, P.O. Millward and F.O. Eyre being unhurt, but F.O. Roder was missing. A reconnaissance JU-88 was claimed the same day north of Bone by P.O. Bawden of 87 Squadron and an aircraft of I/(F) 122 was confirmed lost.

Pressure was now pushing the axis forces back into the north-east corner of Tunisia and opportunities for air combat increased as large formations of transport aircraft were employed to evacuate troops back to Sicily. In the last month of the campaign, up to the final surrender on the 13th May, 73 Squadron claimed six JU-52s and two probables, plus another unidentified tri-motor aircraft shot down and a further four JU-52s destroyed on the ground.

On the night of the 15th/16th April, between Hammamet and Rass Mamoura, P.O. Smyth and Flt. Sgt. Beard of 73 Squadron each claimed a JU-52, plus one probable. On the evening of the 18th, Sgts. Ross and Wilkinson of the same squadron strafed and destroyed three JU-52s which had landed on a Tunisian beach to avoid the great transport aircraft massacre that day.[41] Two more JU-52s were also hit. The following day, Sgt. Thomas strafed two JU-52s on a beach near Cap Bon, one of which was seen to blow up and the same pilot also claimed a JU-52 shot down on the 20th.

On the night of the 8th/9th May, Sgt. Cenitch claimed a tri-motor which he chased out to sea from Ras el Melah and next night, Sgt. Beard claimed two JU-52s, one at Menzel Temime and the other approaching Kelibia. The final 73 Squadron claims of this campaign were on the 10th/11th

May, P.O. Bretherton claiming a JU-52 as it landed at El Haouaria, while W.O. Hewitt claimed a probable as it approached Menzel Temime.

Single JU-88s were also claimed by Sqn. Ldr. Shaw of 32 Squadron over Sidi Ahmed airfield on both the 15th/16th and the 17th April and by P.O. Bawden of 87 Squadron North of Bone on the 11th April[42] and an unknown pilot of the same squadron on the 15th.

On the 1st May, Flt. Lts. Lucksinger and Allen of 33 Squadron, on convoy patrol off the Libyan coast at dusk, jointly claimed a JU-88[43] and an He 111 was claimed by P.O. Campbell, also of 33 Squadron. An He 111 of II/KG 26 was reported lost.

The final ground claims of the Tunisian campaign were on the 5th May, when four enemy aircraft were claimed by 241 Squadron, but it is not known if these were by Spitfires or Hurricanes, as the Squadron was operating both types.

Hurricane losses during the last month of the campaign were minimal, only 12 aircraft being lost, seven of these in accidents. Eight Hurricanes were lost by 241 Squadron; HL667 crashed on landing on 15th April; HL964 was shot down by flak on the 23rd;[44] on the 25th, HV732 failed to return,[45] HL990 crashed on landing and HL368 was shot down by allied flak;[46] HW745 was also shot down by flak on the 27th;[47] KW923 was shot down on the 8th May;[48] and on the 10th May, a Hurricane[49] crashed on take-off – the pilot was unhurt.

32 Squadron lost KX126 and HW841, both of which failed to return on the 12th and the 22nd/23rd April respectively, with the loss of P.O. Hogg[50] and Sgt. Beckett.[51] HV341 of 73 Squadron was lost on take-off on the night of the 15th/16th April, killing P.O. Chandler and 33 Squadron lost a Hurricane to mechanical failure on the 1st May.

In the six months since the start of Operation 'Torch' Hurricanes had been used primarily for night fighting, ground attack and convoy patrol. Nevertheless, 31 enemy aircraft were claimed in air combat by Hurricane squadrons,[52] for the loss of 92 Hurricanes, including 11 destroyed on the ground, at least 18 accidentally, at least 18 by flak and at least nine in air combat, mostly to the BF109s.

73 Squadron was the top scoring Hurricane Squadron with nine enemy

aircraft claimed in air combat, plus two probables; 43 Squadron claimed seven plus one probable; 253 Squadron claimed four plus two probables; 87 Squadron claimed five; 32 Squadron claimed three; 33 Squadron claimed two and 7 SAAF Squadron, one. Sgt. Beard of 73 Squadron was the top scoring Hurricane pilot of the campaign with three victories. Wg. Cdr. Pedley of 43 Squadron and Sqn. Ldr. Shaw of 32 Squadron both claimed two.

6 Squadron had been very effective as tank-busters, but had suffered high losses – 25 Hurricanes,[53] although mercifully, only four pilots were killed. It would never again fly operationally with 40mm cannon as this was soon to be replaced by rocket projectiles. 241 Squadron lost 24 Hurricanes, with six pilots missing, two missing believed killed and one PoW.

References

1 Shared.
2 Although the DO-217 was actually a DO-17.
3 *See* Chapter 30 for Sea Hurricane operations.
4 Or force-landed.
5 Including HV958, HV580, HL981 and BE689.
6 At least three of 225 Squadron, including HL959 and HL962.
7 Including HL735 and HL961.
8 Confirmed.
9 Which had also arrived in December for shipping patrols.
10 An He 111 of I/KG 26 – confirmed.
11 The Grupenkommandeur of III/KG 76.
12 Including HV740, HV137, HW746 and HV299.
13 HL367 was shot down by a BF109 on the 6th January.
14 In HL367.
15 On the 16th/17th January.
16 SAAF – on the 18th January.
17 From I/(F) 122.
18 Including HL969 and HW144, in which P.O. Richmond was believed killed.
19 By FW 190s.
20 HW236 and HV904.

21 HW469.
22 Shared.
23 HM142 and HV547.
24 6 Squadron ORB.
25 HV577, HV671, HW271 and HV662?
26 HW349, HV856, HW318 – HW117 and HW298 were Cat. II damaged.
27 HL980.
28 P.O. Davis was captured but soon escaped.
29 HW977.
30 HW489 and KW933.
31 HW349, HV856, HW318 – HW117 and HW298 were Cat. II damaged.
32 HW266 and HW652.
33 HW261 and HW354.
34 HL368.
35 HW313, HW266 and HW318.
36 BP193, BP308, HV560, HW359, HW651 and KW704.
37 HL291 and HW243.
38 An aircraft of II/KLG1 was actually lost.
39 In HL850.
40 HL667, HW240 and HW246.
41 Palm Sunday.
42 A JU-88 of I/(F) 122.
43 Which was from III/KG 26.
44 Flt. Lt. Kirkus was believed killed.
45 P.O. Millward was missing.
46 F.O. O'Brien was also missing.
47 Flt. Lt. Hamlet was missing believed killed.
48 F.O. Connors was taken prisoner.
49 Either BD706 or KW747.
50 Killed.
51 Missing.
52 Sixteen of these were admitted lost by the Germans.
53 Eight of these were Cat. II.

CHAPTER TWENTY-EIGHT
Italy

No.6 Squadron was posted to Grottaglie, in Southern Italy, in February 1944. Flying purely in a ground attack role, operations commenced on the 29th March, with an attack on a German HQ at Durazzo in Albania. Land targets varied from radar stations to dockyards, but enemy shipping was the primary target, both by daylight and on moonlit nights. Over 50 vessels were sunk or damaged before July, when the Squadron moved north to Foggia.

Hurricane Trop IV of 6 Squadron – Italy.

Flying from Falconara on the 3rd August, an armed night recce of two aircraft

Italy

1 Prkos
2 Zara
3 Vis
4 Niksic
5 Falconara
6 Pescara
7 Campomarino
8 Foggia
9 Canne
10 Brindisi
11 Borgo
12 Grottaglie

> '*encountered moderate accurate 88mm flak from Pola while flying 2–3 miles E. of town. Leader (Flt. Lt. Walker DFC) is thought to have attacked a target, but sent out mayday and is missing from operation.*'[1]

Flt. Lt. Walker was flying in KX805.

Four days later, however, the Squadron had a particularly successful day. Four aircraft took off from Falconara at 1415hrs on an armed recce, escorted by two Spitfires of 241 Squadron.

> '*Approx. 20 small craft seen in Rab harbour, of 5 60/80ft schooners, 2 were sunk, 2 were listing and severely damaged and one appeared undamaged.*'[1]

All four Hurricanes landed safely at 1605hrs. The Squadron transferred to the Balkan Air Force later in August.

6 Squadron lost 17 Hurricanes over eight months of operation from Italy, at least 10[2] to flak. No air combats involving Hurricanes occurred during this campaign. The worst months, in terms of aircraft losses, were May and July 1944, with five Hurricanes lost in each of these months. Single losses were experienced in March, June, August and November and three aircraft were lost in October 1944. Eight pilots were killed or reported missing.

References
1 6 Squadron ORB.
2 Probably 12.
   Aircraft losses:
   KX885; KX805; LB683; LB397; KZ321; KX705; KX806; KX804; KZ574; KX883; KZ404; LD167; KZ223; KX803; KX704; LB774?; KX820.

Chapter Twenty-Nine

Yugoslavia

An uprising had occurred in Yugoslavia following the Italian collapse in September 1943. The Germans reacted strongly, pouring in massive reinforcements to that country. Although the RAF dropped supplies to the partisans, the first combat aircraft support didn't arrive until August 1944, when a detachment of 6 Squadron moved to the Adriatic island of Vis, being joined the following month by a detachment of 351 (Yugoslav) Squadron, both units operating rocket-armed Hurricane IVs.

These two Squadrons flew ground attack operations right up to May 1945, with the Hurricanes often carrying four rockets under one wing and a 45 gallon tank under the other. Targets included roads, railways, ships, HQ buildings and troop concentrations.

On the 12th August, four Hurricanes of 6 Squadron took off on an armed recce from Vis at 1305hrs and flew to Zavratnica bay, near Jablanao.

> *'Two Siebel ferries located hidden in creek with steep sides and dog leg bend at entrance. All pilots attacked with 1 R.P. – 1 possible hit claimed. At Privlaka, 7 x 100' empty barges were attacked. Three destroyed and others badly damaged. All the pilots landed safely at 1535hrs.'*[1]

However, on the 27th August, four more aircraft of 6 Squadron took off from Vis at 0535hrs and again flew to Zavratnica bay, where

> *'located two Siebel ferries and one schooner in a creek. Squadron Leader Brown (in KZ243) led the attack and was hit by intense 20 & 40mm flak from hills on his run-in, fired his R.P. unobserved and crashed into hillside. Aircraft exploded.'*[1]

351 Squadron's first sortie was on the 13th October 1944, this Squadron flying a total of 13 operations in October. In November 1944, 351 Squadron flew 232 operational hours on armed reconnaissance sorties.

On the 3rd December, 6 Squadron destroyed a Tiger tank and badly damaged two others. The following day, another tank and two mobile guns were destroyed. During December, 351 Squadron destroyed a power station, a wireless station, a command post and 12 motor transports.

In early 1945, troop concentrations in the Sarajevo area were the targets. Also, in January 1945, 351 Squadron sank a 1,200-ton motor vessel.

During the last weeks of the war, both squadrons concentrated on transport targets, including coastal shipping. On 6 Squadron's last mission in the Gulf of Trieste on the 1st May, 25 vessels, including 16 troop-ships, surrendered to the Hurricanes by hoisting white flags.

In the course of these operations, 6 Squadron lost 16 Hurricanes, including four accidentally and at least seven to flak. 351 Squadron lost 19 Hurricanes, including 14 to accidents and at least three to flak. Nine pilots of 6 Squadron were killed or missing, as were three of 351 Squadron. Other bases from which the Hurricanes operated included Niksic, Zara and Prkos.

References

1 6 Squadron ORB.
   AIRCRAFT LOSSES:
   6 SQUADRON:
   KX722; KZ243; LD233; LD169; KZ574; KZ555; LD162; KX821; KX412; KX556; KX583; KZ553; KX826; KX409; LE268; KZ241
   351 SQUADRON:
   LV461; LF458; LF463; LF453; LF569; LF507; LF469; LD865; LF455; KZ382; LE570; LF475; LF497; LF430; KX881; KZ554; KX800; LF643+ 1 UNKNOWN

Chapter Thirty

Sea Hurricane

Not only over land did the Hurricane score more air combat victories than the Spitfire. Sea Hurricane squadrons claimed over 80 enemy aircraft shot down against 37 by Seafires. The Sea Hurricane was developed to counter the threat from Focke-Wulf FW 200C 'Condor' long-range bombers, used to attack shipping. Operating from CAM (Catapult Aircraft Merchantmen) Ships, there were three decisive encounters between Sea Hurricanes of 804 Squadron and 'Condors'. Single 'Condors' were shot down on the 3rd August 1941, by Lt. Everett and on the 1st November 1942 by F.O. Taylor, while in the last battle on the 28th July 1943, two 'Condors' were shot down by P.O.s Stewart and Flynn. The cost for these four victories was five Sea Hurricanes lost ditching,[1] as there was no way of landing back on the CAM Ships after launch, but none of the pilots were lost.

In May 1942, the Vichy French naval base of Diego Suarez, in Madagascar was seized as insurance against further Japanese expansion in the Indian Ocean. The Sea Hurricanes of 880 Squadron, operating from HMS *Indomitable* provided fighter cover alongside Martlets from HMS *Illustrious*. The Sea Hurricanes did not see any air combat, but on the 5th May 1942 they attacked the airfield protecting the harbour, claiming three MS406s destroyed on the ground.

Next action for the Sea Hurricane came over Russian convoys on the 25th May 1942. 804 Squadron was again in action over convoys PQ-12 and PQ-16, operating from CAM Ships and claiming a JU-88 (F.O. Kendall) and an He 111 (F.O. Hay). Two Sea Hurricanes of 804 Squadron were expended in these actions and forced to ditch, unfortunately killing F.O. Kendall, while F.O. Hay was wounded.

The final Hurricane launch from a CAM Ship on a Russian convoy occurred on the 18th September 1942. An attack on convoy PQ18 by 15 He 111s was intercepted by an 804 Squadron Hurricane, resulting in one of

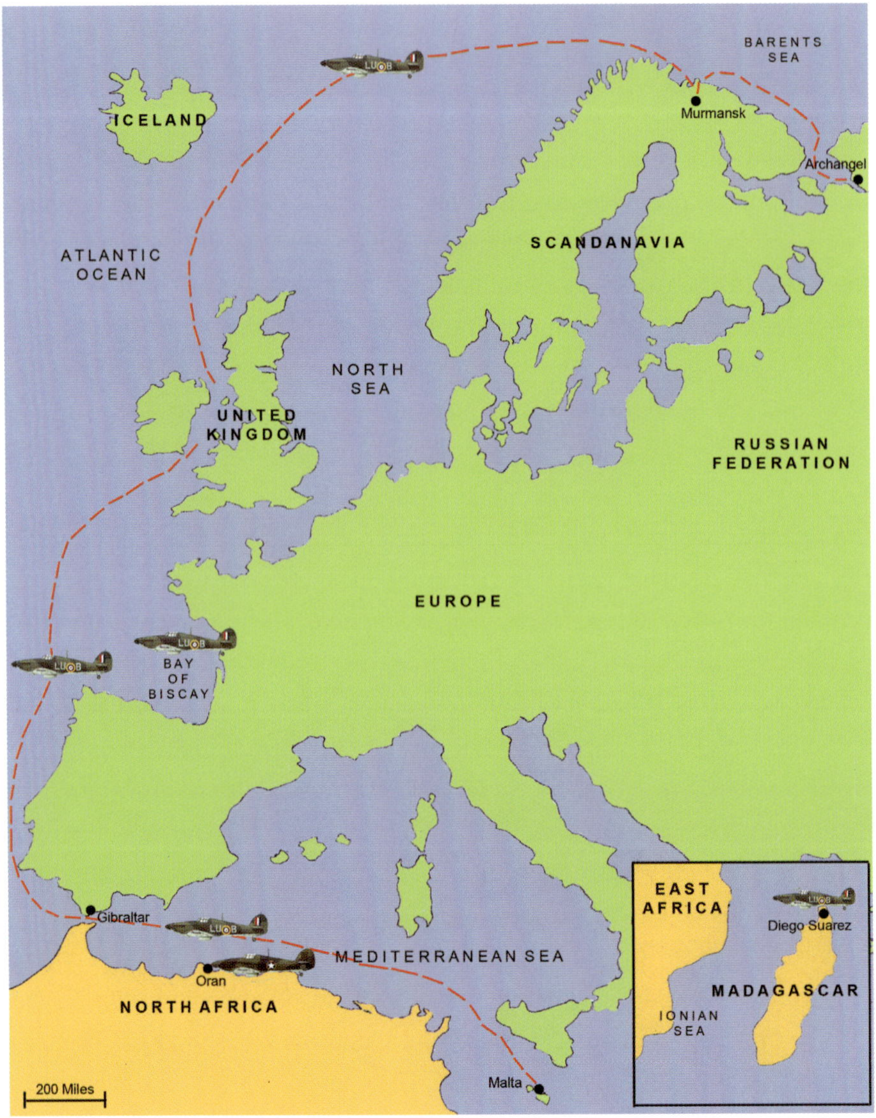
BARENTS SEA
ICELAND
Murmansk
Archangel
SCANDANAVIA
ATLANTIC OCEAN
NORTH SEA
UNITED KINGDOM
RUSSIAN FEDERATION
EUROPE
BAY OF BISCAY
Gibraltar
MEDITERRANEAN SEA
Oran
NORTH AFRICA
Malta
200 Miles
EAST AFRICA
Diego Suarez
MADAGASCAR
IONIAN SEA

the He 111s being claimed shot down. The Hurricane subsequently landed in Russia to avoid ditching. Convoy PQ-18 had earlier been protected by the Sea Hurricanes of 802 and 883 Squadrons, embarked on the escort carrier HMS *Avenger*. Their first action came on the 13th September when a Sea Hurricane of 802 Squadron was shot down by an He 115 Float-Plane, killing Lt. Taylor. Next day, raids by JU-88s were intercepted and two were claimed shot down by Sea Hurricanes, with several others damaged. A later raid by 22 He 111s was also intercepted and five He 111s were claimed shot down, with a further nine damaged, by the combination of flak and Sea Hurricanes. Unfortunately, three Sea Hurricanes were shot down by their own ships' guns, although all of the pilots were unhurt. On the 15th September, sporadic raids resulted in a further three JU-88s being claimed shot down by the guns / Sea Hurricane combination. Over the two days of attacks, 33 He 111s, six JU-88s and two long-range recce. aircraft were admitted lost or damaged beyond repair by the Germans. Most were credited to the ships' guns, but three He 111s and two JU-88s were confirmed to the Sea Hurricanes.

Sea Hurricane Mk.1C, April 1943.

In the Mediterranean, convoys were urgently needed to re-supply Malta by mid-1942. A convoy code-named 'Harpoon' was despatched in June and this included the Sea Hurricanes of 801 and 813 Squadrons embarked on HMS *Eagle*. On the 13th June, a JU-88 was confirmed to 801 Squadron and a CANT Z.1007 to Sub. Lt. Crosley of 813 Squadron. However, next day came the main attack from almost 250 enemy aircraft. In an epic defence of the convoy, nine claims were made by 801 Squadron Sea Hurricanes (nine confirmed) and two by 813 Squadron (both confirmed).[2]

On the debit side, two of 813 Squadrons' Sea Hurricanes and one of 801 Squadron were lost.[3] On the following day, as the convoy escorts withdrew to Gibraltar, another SM-79 was confirmed to 801 Squadron.

The other Mediterranean convoy with Sea Hurricane-carrying escorts sailed to Malta in August 1942 and was of even greater importance to the island – food and oil supplies would run out in early September if the convoy failed to arrive. The convoy was code-named 'Pedestal' and included three carriers as escorts: HMS *Indomitable*, *Victorious* and *Eagle* with 47 Sea Hurricanes in 800, 880, 885, 801 and 813 Squadrons. The first aerial shadowers of the convoy appeared on the 11th August 1942. A JU-88 (Lt. Cdr Judd) and two probables were claimed by 880 Squadron Sea Hurricanes, one of which was confirmed, but a Sea Hurricane of that unit was shot down by return fire and two others were lost on landing.[4] Also, HMS *Eagle* was sunk by a U-Boat on this day, taking 12 Sea Hurricanes down with her.

A series of major raids attacked the convoy next day and the defending Sea Hurricane squadrons claimed heavily – 800 and 880 Squadrons on HMS *Indomitable* claimed nine JU-88s, three JU-87s, seven SM79s, two Breda 88s, a CANT Z.1007, two MC202s, two RE2001s and a BF110, while a JU-88 was also claimed by 885 Squadron.[5]

Of these, six JU-88s (including 885 Squadron claim), a CANT Z.1007, an S.84, an RE2001, two SM79s, three JU-87s and a BF110 were confirmed, a total of 15 enemy aircraft, although 24 victories were actually attributed to Sea Hurricanes this day. Seven Sea Hurricanes were lost – two of 800 Squadron,[6] one of 801 Squadron and four of 880 Squadron, with four pilots killed,[7] but enough of the convoy survived to reach and save Malta.

Lt. Cork recorded that at 1.15p.m.,

> 'One JU-88 shot down in sea, another shot down in the sea off Tunis, an SM.79 shot down in the convoy.'

His section was:

> 'jumped by the fighter escort of ME.110s, one of which he shot down. The pilot bailed out and was picked-up by a destroyer.'[8]

However, Cork's aircraft was badly shot up and Blue 2, S/Lt. Cruickshanks R.N.V.R. was killed by the ME110 before Cork shot it down. At 2.05p.m., Cork:

> 'shot down an SM-79, but was shot up by a number of fighters. He just landed on HMS Victorious as the engine seized and the Hurricane was a complete write-off.'[8]

The last major Sea Hurricane action occurred in November 1942, when Sea Hurricanes of 800, 802, 804, 883 and 891 Squadrons participated in 'Operation Torch', the allied invasion of North Africa. On the 8th November 1942, an attack on La Senia airfield at Oran, resulted in five Vichy French D.520s claimed by 800 Squadron, plus other aircraft destroyed on the ground.[9]

By the 10th November, 11 Sea Hurricanes had been lost, including at least five by accident. On the 15th November, the escort carrier HMS *Avenger* was sunk by a U-Boat, however, with the loss of 15 Sea Hurricanes.

The Sea Hurricane remained operational with the Royal Navy until well into 1944 and claimed the Hurricane's last air combat victories in May of that year. Two JU-290s were shot down over the Bay of Biscay on the 26th May, by Sub. Lt. Burgham and Sub. Lts. Mearns and Wallis (shared) of 835 Squadron, for the loss of a Sea Hurricane.

Rockets on Sea Hurricane wing.

Sea Hurricane ready for launching.

Sea Hurricane on CAM ship.

Sea Hurricane launching from CAM ship.

Sea Hurricane landing with arrestor hook deployed.

Sea Hurricane being loaded on to catapult.

References

1 Including W9277.
2 Lt. Cdr Brabner of 801 Squadron claimed a JU-88, an SM-79 and an MC200, another JU-88 being shared by Brabner and Sub. Lt. Hutton. Mike Crosley again scored for 813 Squadron, claiming a JU-88 and an SM-79 probable.
3 Lt. Tickner was killed.
4 One was Z7055.
5 For 880 Squadron, Lt. Dickie Cork claimed two SM-79s, a BF110 and a JU-88 (+ 1 shared). Lt. Martyn of 880 Squadron also claimed a JU-88. For 800 Squadron, Lt. Cdr Bruen claimed a JU-88 and an S-84 (shared), Sub. Lt. Ritchie claimed two JU-87s and Sub. Lt. Thomson a JU-87 and a BF109. Lt. Cdr Brabner of 801 Squadron claimed an SM-79 and an S-84, while Sub. Lt. Hutton of that Squadron claimed an RE2001 and a Loire 70.
6 One was V7659.
7 Sub. Lt. Lucas (800 Squadron); Sub. Lt. Hankey (801 Squadron); Sub. Lts. Cruikshank and Judd (880 Squadron).
8 Lt. Cork's Pilot Log.
9 Sub. Lt. Crosley (2), Lt. Cdr Bruen and Sub. Lt. Ritchie were among the claimants.

CHAPTER THIRTY-ONE
Belgian Hurricanes

In an attempt to modernise their fighter force, the Belgians ordered 20 Hurricanes and obtained a licence to build a further 80,[1] but only one of these[2] had been delivered to the Air Force by the 10th May 1940, when the Germans invaded, with another[3] being flight tested.[4]

It is uncertain as to how many of the 20 ordered were actually delivered[5] but on the 10th May 1940 only 11 Hurricanes were still serviceable. These were all based at Schaffen as part of 2/I/2 Ae.[6] The Belgians also interned a number of RAF Hurricanes[7] during the phoney war period which they incorporated into their Air Force. A further six MK.IIs were delivered post-war[8] for high-speed communications.

The Belgian Hurricanes were armed with four wing-mounted 12.65mm Browning machine guns, which gave them a greater weight of fire than RAF Hurricanes.

Hawker Hurricane Mk.1s of the Belgian Air Force.

On the 10th November 1939, P.O. Dunn of 87 Squadron, RAF, ran out of fuel[9] and landed at Aalbeke. The Hurricane was inducted into service with 2/I/2 Squadron as H.35. P.O. Dunn was interned, but later escaped.

Four days later, Sqn. Ldr. Coope and F.O. Clyde[10] of 87 Squadron both force-landed in Belgium in bad weather and were also interned.[11] These aircraft also joined 2/I/2 Squadron as H.37 and H.38 respectively.

On the 1st December 1939, H.25 and H.35 both nosed over on landing at Wevelgem, but were repairable and their pilots were unhurt.

Another RAF Hurricane force-landed in Belgium on the 9th December 1939, but Sgt. Nowell of 87 Squadron[12] escaped to France. However, the Hurricane was inducted into 2/I/2 Squadron as H.39.

On the 28th February 1940, H.28 was written off in a landing accident at Schaffen, but the pilot, Lt. Drossaert, was unhurt.

In their first decisive combat against the Germans, on Saturday the 2nd March 1940, Hurricanes of 2/I/2 intercepted DO-17s of 1(F)/22 over St. Hubert. H.26 was shot down, killing S/Lt. X. Henrard; H.33 force-landed at Achene and was repairable, with Sgt. E. Lieutenant unhurt; H.35 was damaged and repairable, with Sgt. Lelievre also unhurt and H.39 ground-looped when its port undercarriage collapsed in a forced-landing at Bierset and was written-off, although Captain A.E.A. van den Hove d'Ertsenrijck was also uninjured.

Next, on the 12th March 1940, three Hurricanes were hit by return fire from DO-17s which they engaged over Marche, but all were repairable and the pilots unhurt.

Then on the 27th April 1940, H.25 nosed over on landing at Steene-Ostend, but was repairable and the pilot unhurt.

On the 6th May 1940, three Hurricanes engaged enemy aircraft between Mons and Ath and force-landed at St Omer, Diksmuide and Aartrijke, but were repairable and the pilots unhurt.

The Germans invaded on the 10th May 1940 and DO-17s of KG77 attacked Schaffen at 4.30a.m. that morning. Nine Hurricanes, H.20, H.21, H.22, H.27,[13] H.30, H.31, H.32, H.34 and H.42 were destroyed on the ground.[14] H.23 was damaged by return fire from He 111s of KG27 and landed at Beauvechain, but was repairable and Captain A.E.A. van den

Hove d'Ertsenrijck was unhurt.

One source notes that two Hurricanes under repair in hangers at Schaffen were lost when the hangers collapsed, reportedly H.24 and H.25. H.33 and H.35 may also have been under repair?

On the 11th May 1940, H.23, H.29 and one other Hurricane[15] were destroyed on the ground at Le Culot in strafing attacks by BF109s of I/JG1. All these aircraft were written-off or abandoned on withdrawal that night.

Hurricane deliveries
H.20 (L1918) delivered April 1939
H.21 (L1919) delivered April 1939
H.22 (L1920) delivered April 1939
H.23 (L1993) delivered June 1939
H.24 (L1994) delivered June 1939
H.25 (L1995) delivered June 1939
H.26 (L1996) delivered June 1939
H.27 (L1997) delivered June 1939
H.28 (L2040) delivered June 1939
H.29 (L2041) delivered June 1939
H.30 (L2042)* delivered June 1939
H.31 (L2043)* delivered June 1939
H.32 (L2044)* delivered June 1939
H.33 (L2105) delivered November 1939**
H.34 (L2106) delivered November 1939**
* another source gives the codes as L1942, L1943 and L1944
** these aircraft seem to have been part of a Finnish order, two of which went to the Belgians and the rest of the Belgian order[16] were retained by the RAF. If correct, this would account for the 20 Hurricanes the Belgians ordered, and the 15 they actually got.

H.36 may also have been an interned ex-RAF Hurricane, but it never seems to have become operational.

It is not known if serials H.37 and H.38 were allocated to Belgian Hurricanes.

References

1. At Gosselies, Avions Fairey.
2. H.42.
3. H.43.
4. H.41 was completed but had not flown.
5. Fifteen seems to be the generally accepted figure – from April-November 1939.
6. No. 2 Squadron of No. 1 Group of No. 2 Air Regiment.
7. Four?
8. Including three ground instructional airframes.
9. In L1619.
10. In L1628 and L1813.
11. Both also later escaped.
12. In N2361.
13. But see 11th May 1940.
14. Eight were actually written-off and one badly damaged, but this was destroyed the next day.
15. H.27?
16. L2107 to L2111 inclusive.

Fate summary

Of 19 known Hurricanes:
8 operational Hurricanes lost at Schaffen, 10-5-40.
1 operational damaged, repaired and lost 11-5-40.
2 operational Hurricanes escaped Schaffen, lost 11-5-40.
3 lost pre 10-5-40.
1 being rebuilt (H.36).
4 lost while under repair / unserviceable (including H24?).

This does not agree with all sources, e.g. one gives H.34 as escaping Schaffen on 10-5-40, but the above seems to reconcile the various sources to the greatest extent.

Chapter Thirty-Two

Finnish Hurricanes

Twelve Hurricane MK.Is were ordered by the Finns and 10 were delivered in the second week of March 1940, too late for action in the 'Winter War' between Finland and Russia. Two others were lost during transit flights. The Finnish aircraft were fitted with snowskids and operated primarily by Squadron LeLv 32.[1]

Germany attacked Russia on the 22nd June 1941 and on the 25th June 1941, Finland joined the war on Germany's side, in order to recover territory ceded to Russia at the end of the 'Winter War' in March 1941. The Finnish Hurricanes claimed five Russian aircraft in July 1941 and another half claim later, while losing only one Hurricane in action.[2] The Finnish Hurricanes operated until July 1943.

They only logged around 1,100 flying hours, due to the lack of spare parts available during the Interim Peace[3] and subsequent combat operations, which wore out the aircraft. One Hurricane Mk.IIB[4] was captured from the Soviets on the 28th November 1942 and flown by LeLv28 and LeLv34.[5]

Serials and fates
HC451 (ex N2393) – WFU 2/2/42; SOC 18/10/44.
HC452 (ex N2394) – WFU 26/7/43; SOC 9/8/44 (now in Finnish Air Force Museum at Tikkakoski).
HC453 (ex N2395) – crashed on take-off Hollola 25/6/41 (pilot killed) – SOC 23/8/41.
HC454 (ex N2348) – WFU - 1945; SOC 2/1/50.
HC455 (ex N2350) – crashed near Malmi 30/7/42 (pilot killed) SOC 10/10/42.
HC456 (ex N2392) – WFU 13/5/43; SOC 26/9/44.
HC457 (ex N2327) – stalled on landing and crashed Turku 3/6/40 SOC 22/8/40.

HC458 (ex N2323) – shot down by AA Kotskoma 16/9/41 SOC 29/4/42.

HC459 (ex N2322) – hit by own AA near Vainikkala and crashed in flames on landing at Utti 2/7/41 SOC 23/8/41.

HC460 (ex N2324) – WFU 20/7/43; SOC 26/9/43.

HC461 (ex N2325) – Starboard undercarriage collapsed on landing at Wick 28/2/40 on ferry flight – returned to RAF.

HC462 (ex N2347) – Crashed on ferry flight Eigeroy, Norway 2/3/40 – damaged beyond repair.

RAF Serials; N2322-N2325; N2327; N2347; N2348; N2350; N2392-N2395 (Not allocated Finnish serials in order of RAF Serials.

References

1   But also by Os. Raty, LLv 22, 28 and 30, LeLv 10, 26 and 30.
2   A further four were lost to non-combat causes – including one to Finnish AA.
3   13th March 1940–25th June 1941.
4   HC465.
5   WFU 5/7/44; SOC 8/10/44.

Chapter Thirty-Three

Romanian Hurricanes

In April 1939, a Romanian delegation visited Britain, France and Germany with the intention of procuring military aircraft in order to modernise the Aeronautica Regala Romania (ARR). Contract no. 7368 was signed for the delivery of 50 Hurricane Is to Romania for operation by Escadriles 53, 54 and 55, but only 12 aircraft were actually delivered from August 1939 to March 1940.[1] The rest were withheld after the fall of France in June 1940, when Romania also renounced the Anglo-French guarantee of its security.

Operated solely by Escadrila 53, one Hurricane was lost in an accident in the spring of 1940[2] and another was lost in May 1941,[3] when it was shot down by a Russian I-16 of 67 IAP after it strayed across the border.

After the German occupation of Yugoslavia in April 1941, three Hurricanes captured intact by the Germans were also acquired by Escadrila 53.[4] The three serviceable Hurricanes were numbered 13, 14 and 15.

When Germany invaded the Soviet Union on the 22nd June 1941, Romania, as her ally, was intent on recovering the territories[5] annexed by the Soviets in the spring of 1940, resulting from the German-Soviet Non-Aggression Pact of 1939.

The primary role of Escadrila 53 was protection of Constanta's port and oil plant, plus the rail bridge at Cernavoda which crossed the Danube, the unit being based at Mamaja, just to the north of the port. At this time there were 10 serviceable Hurricanes and three under repair.

On the first day of the war, the Hurricanes escorted nine PZL 37 bombers over the Danube and were engaged by Soviet I-153 and I-15bis fighters, five of these being claimed by Escadrila 53, without loss. Next day, three Soviet bombers[6] were claimed over Constanta by Locotenent aviator Horia Agarici,[7] two of which were confirmed.

On the 2nd August, a Hurricane, which attempted to intercept three PE-2s over Constanta, was hit by return fire and force-landed near Mamaja airfield.

On the 12th September, a Hurricane was shot down over Odessa by 69 IAP I-16s, killing Capitan 1. Rosescu. This machine was examined by the Russians and found to have eight wing-mounted machine guns, rather than the normal six-gun armament, which was standard on the Romanian Hurricanes and it is assumed to have been one of the ex-Yugoslav aircraft.

By the end of 1941, Escadrila 53 had claimed 35 Soviet aircraft for the loss of two Hurricanes. Following the fall of Odessa on the 16th October 1941, air combat involving the Hurricanes was reduced and although the Hurricanes continued to fly into early 1942,[8] by the middle of that year, they had reportedly been relegated to the operational training role.

Some reports suggest that 10 Hurricanes were still on the strength of the ARR on the 1st February 1944, but that by the autumn of 1944, they had all been scrapped.

An impressive six Romanian Hurricane pilots achieved ace status – Capitan av. Emil Georgescu;[9] Capitan rez. Constantin Cantacuzino; Adjutant sef av. Andrei Radulescu;[10] Adjutant Eugen Camencianu; Adjutant Nicolae Pomut and Adjutant sef Petre Codrescu.

References

1   L2077; L2078; L2085; L2093-2097; L2104 and L2112-2114, given Rumanian serials 1-12.
2   Killing Capitan av Draganescu.
3   Reportedly the 5th, 18th or 25th May.
4   Some sources suggest that these were sold to Romania in September 1941, plus a second batch of three captured Hurricanes at a later date, but these are believed to have been unserviceable aircraft purchased for cannibalisation.
5   Bessarabia and Northern Bukovina.
6   DB-3Fs and SBs.
7   In yellow 1.
8   One being reported lost.
9   Who was a flight commander.
10 Who was the top-scoring Hurricane ace with seven confirmed and four probable victories.

CHAPTER THIRTY-FOUR
Yugoslav Hurricanes

Twelve Hurricane Mk.1s were delivered from December 1938 and 12 more Mk.1s were delivered from February 1940. They were also built under licence at Rogozarski and Zemun – 15 to 18 were completed by the time of German invasion (including one with a DB601A engine).

Yugoslav Hurricane.

When Germany invaded Yugoslavia on the 6th April 1941, the Jugoslovensko Kraljevsko Ratno Vazduhoplovstvo (JKRV) included the following Hurricane Units:

Yugoslav Hurricanes

1 Bos. Aleksandrovac
2 Bjeljina
3 Knic
4 Niksic
5 Mostar

Independent Fighter Eskadrila	Mostar-Kosor	3 Hurricane Is
2nd Puk; 52 Grupa; 163 Eskadrila	Knic)	15 Hurricane Is
164 Eskadrila	Knic)	
4th Puk; 33 Grupa; 105 Eskadrila	Bosanski Aleksandrovac	7 Hurricane Is
106 Eskadrila	Bosanski Aleksandrovac	6 Hurricane Is
34 Grupa; 108 Eskadrila	Bosanski Aleksandrovac	7 Hurricane Is

A total of 38 Hurricane Is were thus available. As the first large raid on Belgrade withdrew at around 0800hrs on the first day of the invasion, Hurricanes of 163 Eskadrila engaged Stukas and claimed one shot down. Later that day in the West, over Mostar, an Italian S.79 was damaged by 1st Lt. Fasovic in one of the Independent Fighter Eskadrila's Hurricanes.

Soon after midday on the 7th April, a small formation of JU-88s heading for Sarajevo were intercepted by two Hurricanes of the Independent Fighter Eskadrila. Sgt. Delic was hit by return fire from the JU-88s and crash-landed, wounded at Mostar-Kosor, but Captain Grbic was shot down by BF109s[1] and killed.

Next day, Yugoslav bombers, escorted by Hurricanes of 52nd Grupa, attacked German convoys North of Kumanovo, one Hurricane of 164th Eskadrila being hit[2] and crash-landing, although Lt. Grandic was safe.

At around 1400hrs on the 9th April, BF109s of III/JG54 were engaged between Rovine and Bosanski Aleksandrovac by Hurricanes of 106th and 108th Eskadrilas. Sgt. Tomic claimed one BF109 and a second was believed shot down by Captain Milijevic, the commander of 106th Eskadrila, before he himself was shot down and killed. Another Hurricane was also shot down, wounding Flt/Sgt. Mitic.[3]

On the 10th April, a German armoured column was believed to be approaching Knic and so Hurricanes of 52nd Grupa attempted to take off in bad weather. Two aircraft of 164th Eskadrila collided, killing Captain Ostric and Lt. Momcinovic and a third[4] flew into a mountain, killing Veljko Vujicic.

On the airfield at Knic, aircraft of 163rd Eskadrila were made unserviceable, but attempts were made to repair the least damaged, when news arrived that the Germans were still some distance away. Hurricanes of 4th Puk claimed a Messerschmitt[5] shot down over Bosnia this day.

Next day, a BF110 was also claimed by 4th Puk Hurricanes over Nova Gradiska.

Early on the 12th April, two or three Hurricanes of the 105th Eskadrila were among the aircraft burned on the ground.[6] Two or three more of that unit's Hurricanes then flew to Bjeljina and another to Sarajevo, but at 0730hrs BF110s strafed Bjeljina, destroying all but one of the recently arrived Hurricanes. The last two Hurricanes of 163rd Eskadrila flew from Knic to Zemun, but as the aircraft piloted by 1st Lt. Cijan landed, it was captured by the Germans. The other Hurricane escaped but ran out of fuel near Valjevo, Captain Bajagic being mortally wounded as the aircraft was destroyed in a crash-landing.

Five or six Hurricanes of 4th Puk now remained airworthy and a JU-88[7] was shot down by a Hurricane of this wing near Banja Luka.[8] Over Mostar, the last Independent Fighter Eskadrila Hurricane was shot down by return fire from a JU-88, wounding Franjo Godec.

On the 13th April, a BF110 was claimed by a 4th Puk Hurricane and a Hurricane was destroyed,[9] wounding Voja Grbic, its pilot.

Only one Hurricane reportedly remained at Niksic on the 14th April and Yugoslavia formally surrendered on the 17th April. Seven German aircraft are known to have been claimed shot down by JKRV Hurricanes during the short campaign. In return, at least five Hurricanes were lost in air combat. At least two Hurricanes[10] were captured intact by the Germans and Italians.[11]

KNOWN SERIALS

1-205 (ex-L1751); 2-306 (ex-L1752); 3-291 (ex-L1837); 4-292 (ex-L1838); 5-293 (ex-L1839); 6-294 (ex-L1840); 7-312 (ex-L1858); 8-313 (ex-L1859); 9-314 (ex-L1860); 10-315 (ex-L1861); 11-316 (ex-L1862); 12-317 (ex-L1863); Ex-N2718; Ex-N2719; Ex-N2720; Ex-N2721; Ex-N2722; Ex-N2723; Ex-N2724; Ex-N2725; Ex-N2726; Ex-N2727; Ex-N2728; Ex-N2729.

References

1. Probably of 6/JG54.
2. By flak?
3. These combats were recorded in German records on the 7th April, but the 9th April is considered the more likely date, from Yugoslav records.
4. BR.2339.
5. A BF110?
6. At Veliki Radinci?
7. Of II/KG51.
8. Recorded by the Germans as occurring on the 11th April.
9. Probably shot down.
10. Including BR.2337.
11. But *see* Romanian Hurricanes.

Chapter Thirty-Five

Soviet Hurricanes

Evaluation of Hurricane Mk.II Z2899[1] began on the 22nd September 1941 at NII VVS[2] with Col. K.A. Gruzdev as its test pilot. On the 14th October 1941, 78 IAP[3] was formed to receive 36 serviceable 151 Wing Hurricanes from the RAF.

A few months later,[4] a programme for rearmament of Hurricanes with Soviet cannons and guns had been initiated, as the calibre and fire power of the original British armament[5] was considered too weak. Two alternative replacements of four Browning machine guns were proposed by the gun designer B.G. Shpital'nyj, together with specialists of Zavod No.115[6] in Moscow:

1) Four 20mm ShVAK cannons, two 7.62mm ShKAS machine-guns and six racks for RS-82 rockets, or
2) Two 20mm ShVAK cannons, two 12.7mm UBK machine guns and six racks for RS-82 rockets.

After evaluation by NII VVS from the 28th December 1941 to the 3rd January 1942, the first alternative was adopted. Even before official conclusion, 30 SAM of VVS SF replaced four Browning machine guns with two 12.7mm UBT and two 50kg bombs as proposed by Boris Safonov in VVS SF. Armoured pilot seat backs were also installed.

The armament modifications were mainly made at Zavod No.81 in Monino, Zavod No. 89 in Gorkiy and in workshops of 6 IAK in Podlipki, but also in several frontal units.[7]

A total of some 1,200 Hurricanes were re-equipped with Soviet armament.

Because of lack of spares for the Merlin Mk.XX engines, installation of Soviet M-82A, M-88 or M-105 engines was studied, but this proposal was

Hawker Hurricane – defender of the skies

1 Luostari	12 Taybola	23 L. 13km	34 Tikshozero
2 Ura-Guba	13 Kolozero	24 Boyarskaya 1	35 Reboly
3 Kildin	14 Olenya	25 Boyarskaya 2	36 Segezha
4 Vaenga-1	15 Monchegorsk	26 Engozero	37 Shpalovoy
5 Guba Gryaznaya	16 Kirovsk	27 Tungozero	38 Popov-Porog
6 Rosta	17 Afrikanda	28 Chiksha-Ukhta	39 Sumerechi
7 Murmashi	18 Pinozero	29 Yushkozero	40 Kolezhma
8 Arktika	19 Gremyakha	30 Poduzhemye	41 Kondoruchey
9 Shonguy-1	20 Alakurti	31 Belomorsk	42 Girvas
10 Shonguy-2	21 Beloe More	32 Sosnovets	
11 Kitsa	22 Polyarniy Krug	33 Letnyaya	

not adopted.

In the spring of 1942, VVS SF was in urgent need of light bombers, and 120 Hurricanes were modified to carry two under-wing mounted 100kg bombs.

Because of the relatively large number of Hurricanes in VVS SF, special two-seater training Hurricanes were considered necessary, and 10 aircraft were modified with a second cockpit and double command. In order to save weight, eight of the 12 machine guns and the armoured seat back of the pilot etc. were dismounted. A number of two-seaters were also used without double command for courier purposes, and one two-seater was further modified as an 'ambulance' aircraft and used by 10 AE VVS SF.

Several two-seater Hurricanes were also used at the Glider Aviation School of Red Army Paratroop Forces[8] in Saratov for towing Antonov A-7 and G-11 transport gliders, and a number of operational sorties were also performed.

Other Soviet Hurricane modifications included a tactical recce version with an AFA-I camera in the rear fuselage,[9] experimental fixed and retractable ski-undercarriages etc.

In the summer of 1942, it became evident that Hurricanes were no match for BF109 'Filips'[10] and the Hurricanes were gradually transferred to PVO-regiments in the Soviet rear.

In the autumn of 1943 and early 1944, some 45 Hurricane Mk.IIDs and 30 Mk.IVs intended for ground-fighting[11] were delivered.

Evaluation and conversion training showed clearly that cannon-equipped Hurricanes were inferior to Il-2s, already in major production, and were thus not used for frontal sorties.

Lend-lease fighter conversion training was mainly performed in various ZAPs,[12] of which the first was 27 ZAP in Kadnikov[13] in the Arkhangelsk-Vologda region. On the 16th May 1942, 6 ZAB,[14] comprising of 14 and 22 ZAP, was formed in Ivanovo, which become the main conversion training centre. In the Ural Military District Hurricane conversion training was provided by 17 ZAP.

Operational record:
On the 25th October 1941, six Hurricanes of the newly formed 78 IAP met BF110s of 1. (Z)/JG77 near Zapadnaya Litsa and Snr. Lt. D.I. Sinev claimed a BF110 shot down. One of the Hurricanes was also claimed by the Germans, but there were no actual losses on either side.

On the 16th November, however, a JU-52/3m of Tr. St. Fl. Fu. Nord was shot down by Lt. V.V. Kravchenko near Belokamenki to become the first victory for Soviet Hurricanes.

Eight days later, Pavel Gavrilov of 152 IAP on the Karelian front claimed a BF109, although there is no confirmation in German records.

The first Soviet Hurricane downed by the Finnish Air Force was BD761 piloted by St Lt. N. F. Repnikov of 152 IAP who collided in mid-air with Sgt. T. Tomminen of LeLv 28 in an MS.406[15] at Karhumäki,[16] Eastern Karelia on 4th December 1941, killing both pilots.

The Hurricane was misidentified as a MIG-3 at the time. For his 'taran-victory' Repnikov was posthumously awarded the Hero of the Soviet Union[17] on the 22nd February 1943. Two 'Brewsters'[18] were also claimed in this engagement by Snr. Lts. Vladimir Basov and Stepan Ivanov of 152 IAP.

On the 15th December, Dmitriy Amosov of 78 IAP claimed an enemy aircraft, which was unconfirmed.

On the 17th December, four Finnish Brewsters[19] of 3/LeLv 24 engaged nine Soviet Hurricanes and I-153s West of the White Sea, Captain Karhunen claiming one Hurricane of 152 IAP. Also this day, a BF109[20] of 14./JG77 was damaged by pilots of 78 IAP and returned to its airfield, but was rated as beyond repair.[21] However, two Hurricanes were lost in this engagement, Lt. Volkov being killed and Major Safonov having to crash-land unhurt.[22]

Back on the Karelian front, meanwhile, on the 26th December, P.I. Gavrilov of 152 IAP claimed a Finnish Blenheim. Three days later, V.A. Basov also claimed a Blenheim, but he was subsequently forced to make a belly-landing in his Hurricane. In December 1941, as a whole, 152 IAP claimed eight enemy aircraft,[23] for the loss of two Hurricanes and one pilot – Repnikov. Snr. Lt. Dmitriy Reutov of 78 IAP shot down an He 111[24] of KG26 on the last day of 1941. Safonov is also reported to have achieved this victory, which was his 15th.

At the end of 1941, there were 30 Hurricanes in 78 IAP and 72 SAP of the Northern Fleet Air Force. The latter unit was changing its title to 2 GKAP.[25]

On the 4th January 1942, Hurricanes of 78 IAP were tasked with seeking out Henschel 126 reconnaissance aircraft, but were intercepted by BF109s of 14./JG77 near the coast on the Gulf of Ura-Gubsky. Lt. Krasavtsev was killed in one Hurricane and Sgt. Bokiy was wounded in another, which force-landed. Two Hurricanes were claimed by the Germans and Bokiy claimed a BF109, but none were lost.

On the 9th January, Tiliksjarvi airfield in East Central Finland was strafed by Five Hurricanes of 152 IAP, which were intercepted by four D.XXIs, Lyosov in one of the Hurricanes[26] being shot down by Sergeant Leino. In return, seven enemy aircraft were claimed destroyed in the air and on the ground, with individual claims for four Brewsters[27] and one Fokker D.XXI.[28] No Finnish aircraft were actually reported lost, however. Three days later, Pavel Orlov claimed his first victory in a Hurricane.

On the 24th January, a Brewster[29] was shot down on a bomber escort mission to Belomorsk, by a Hurricane of 152 IAP, its pilot, Sergeant Myllymaki being reported missing. The same day a Soviet Hurricane was claimed by Oberfeldwebel Weissenberger in a BF110. On the 25th February, two more Hurricanes were claimed by Weissenberger.

During February 1942, there were two engagements between Finnish Brewsters and Soviet Hurricanes, with three Hurricanes claimed on each occasion. On the 4th February, Lt. Feodosiy Zodorozhniy of 152 IAP[30] was force-landed by Finnish fighters and although Zodorozhniy escaped capture, his aircraft was retrieved by the Finns, repaired and inducted into service as HC-45. On the 6th, a Fokker D.XXI and a Brewster[31] were claimed by 152 IAP. Then, on the 26th February, Major Petr Sgibnev[32] claimed a BF109, but this was not confirmed.

In March 1942, the Hurricanes and pilots of 78 IAP were transferred to Boris Safonov's old regiment.[33] 2 GKAP, now commanded by Safonov, gradually received more Hurricanes and P-40s[34] from arriving convoys. At the same time, 78 IAP received new I-16 and Hurricane Squadrons.

On the 4th March, 24 Hurricanes of 78 IAP attacked Luostari Aerodrome, South of Petsamo and destroyed three He 111s[35] on the ground,[36] without loss.

Later the same day, a second attack was made on the same target with 22 Hurricanes, but this time they were intercepted by II/JG5 BF109s and five Hurricanes failed to return. Capt. Shvedov escaped capture, as did the other pilots. Five BF109s were claimed by the Hurricane pilots,[37] but these were not confirmed.

On the 9th March, eight Brewsters met six Hurricanes of 152 IAP near Uikujarvi and shot down three of the Hurricanes, for the loss of Sergeant Mellin, who was taken prisoner.[38]

Two days later, 6(Z)/JG5 lost three of its BF110s when they were engaged by two P-40s and a Hurricane of 147 IAP.

Four Soviet pilots[39] were reciprocally awarded the Distinguished Flying Cross on the 19th March 1942.

On the 21st March, on the Kalinin front, Snr. Lt. Shcherban of 195 IAP claimed a JU-88, while another was shared by Shcherban and Snr. Lt. Drozdov. Next day, Shcherban claimed another JU-88, with one more shared between Shcherban, Afansyev and Burya. From the 13th–22nd March, 195 IAP lost six Hurricanes.[40]

On the 24th March, 14 Hurricanes of 2 GKAP escorted six PE-2 bombers in another attack on Luostari Aerodrome, losing three of their number to German fighters. By the 27th March, 195 IAP only had six serviceable Hurricanes.[41]

On the penultimate day of the month, eight Brewsters of 2/LeLv 24 on a reconnaissance mission to Segesha, bounced 12 Hurricanes of 152 IAP and claimed six of them.

In late March, on the Kalinin front, Zlodeev, Naydenov and Klimenko of 195 IAP shared a claim for an 'Me115' which was probably a BF110.

Operations in April commenced on the 3rd, with an attack on Murmansk, a BF109[42] being shot down by Petr Sgibnev of 78 IAP. Snr. Lt. Vasiliy Shalaev also claimed a BF110 this day, but it was not confirmed.

Next day, Luostari was attacked again by PE-2s escorted by 2 GKAP and 78 IAP, which claimed six BF109s[43] for the loss of one Hurricane. Two of II/JG5's pilots were indeed wounded in this action.

On the 7th April, 14 Soviet bombers were escorted by 12 Hurricanes of 609 and 767 IAPs in an attack on Tiliksjarvi. Eight Brewsters attacked this formation and claimed all 12 Hurricanes shot down in a 25-minute battle.[44] In fact, two Hurricanes of 609 IAP and four of 767 IAP were lost. Seven Brewsters were claimed by the Soviets, but none were lost. Another Hurricane[45] of 767 IAP was lost in an accident this day, killing its pilot, Major Yuryev. The Soviet Air Force was not seen again in this sector until June, following this raid.

Two days later, two BF109s of 5/JG5 were shot down by P-40s and Hurricanes of 769 IAP, one of the captured pilots being 10 victory ace, Leutnant Jakobi.

In a large air battle west of Murmansk on the 15th April, another Hurricane was claimed by Oberfeldwebel Weissenberger of JG5 in a BF110.[46] However, two JU-87s were claimed this day by Aleksander Kovalenko of 2 GKAP, as were single JU-87s by Orlov and Kurzenkov. Snr. Lt. Sgibnev of 78 IAP also claimed a BF110, as did Snr. Lt. Zhivotovskiy and Lt. Babiy.

On the 23rd April, Stukas of I/StG5 escorted by BF109s of 6/JG5 attacked the port of Murmansk and were intercepted by Hurricanes of 768 IAP, one of which was shot down by the BF109 of Oberfeldwebel Salwender, but the Hurricane pilot, Mladshiy Leytenant Negulyayev managed to crash his burning aircraft into Salwender's BF109, the German pilot being killed on the ground by Soviet troops. Negulyayev was also killed.

In a later attack the same day on Vaenga Aerodrome, five BF109s of 6/JG5 bounced a formation of three AE/2 GKAP Hurricanes and shot down two. Serzhant Semyonov was killed, but Serzhant Yepanov bailed out safely. Another Hurricane was also claimed by Oberfeldwebel Weissenberger in a BF110 this day.

Five days later, in the early afternoon of the 28th April, 2 GKAP again met BF109s of 6/JG5 and lost five Hurricanes, with four pilots lost. Two more 2 GKAP Hurricanes were lost in another encounter, the same day.

Next day, 2 GKAP Hurricanes met BF110s and BF109s over the front-line, Kurzenkov claiming a BF110, while Snr. Lt. Amosov and

Sgt. Cheprunov claimed another between them. In fact, two BF110s[47] were seriously damaged and written-off after emergency landings back at base.

At noon the same day, 12 Hurricanes of 2 GKAP and 78 IAP engaged BF109s of 6./JG5 and Pavel Orlov claimed one of them, but this was not confirmed. 2 GKAP lost seven Hurricanes to German fighters in the last week of April.

In the next decisive combat involving Soviet Hurricanes on the 9th May, in the Motovskiy Bay area, three Hurricanes were shot down, but the Germans lost a BF109[48] and an Hs126.

In another encounter this day, Orlov and Kurzenkov of 2 GKAP both claimed BF109s, but two Hurricanes of this unit collided, killing Guards Sgt. Savin and Guards Captain Shvedov.

Next day, around noon, Hurricanes of 2 GKAP and 78 IAP met BF109s of 5/JG5 and BF110s of 10.(Z)/JG5, the former unit claiming six Hurricanes and the latter, three, for one German fighter lost.[49] Five Hurricanes were actually lost,[50] killing three of the pilots[51] and wounding another.

Later that afternoon, nine Hurricanes of 2 GKAP were escorting five SB bombers when they were attacked by BF110s of 10.(Z)/JG5 and BF109s. In a one-sided encounter, five Hurricanes were shot down[52] by Oberfeldwebel Weissenberger,[53] although 16 Soviet aircraft were claimed in this air battle.[54] In total, JG5 claimed 22 Hurricanes this day, when in fact 10 had actually been lost and three damaged, a severe blow to the Soviet defenders. In return, pilots of 2 GKAP claimed three BF110s[55] and two BF109s,[56] but only one BF109[57] was actually lost this day.

Lt. Vasiliy Doroshin of 78 IAP claimed one enemy aircraft[58] on each of the 12th, 13th and 18th of May.

On the 15th May, yet another Hurricane was claimed shot down by Oberfeldwebel Weissenberger of JG5 in a BF110. Two days later, 13 JU-88s of KG30, escorted by nine BF109s of II/JG5 attacked convoy PQ-15 at Murmansk, but were engaged by eight Hurricanes and a single P-40 of 2 GKAP. One Hurricane[59] failed to return, as did a II/JG5 BF109.

In an engagement the same day, in the Kandalska region, Hurricanes of 760 IAP shot down a BF109 of II/JG5, while another of that unit's BF109s was brought down by a crashing Hurricane,[60] flown by Serzhant Bazarov.

Next day, 32 JU-88s of KG30 again attacked shipping in Murmansk and along the coast, but were intercepted by 37 Soviet fighters, which claimed eight JU-88s and three BF110s. Three German aircraft were actually lost and two Soviet Hurricanes.

On the 26th May, three Hurricanes of 122 IAD/PVO were shot down by the Luftwaffe. Four days later, JU-88s of II/KG30, escorted by BF109s and BF110s attacked convoy PQ-16 which was at anchor in the Kola Gulf.

Among the Soviet fighters which intercepted were 13 Hurricanes of 78 IAP, for which Sgibnev, Babiy, Bershanskiy and Doroshin claimed JU-88s, the latter also claiming a BF110. Pilots of 122 IAD and 14th Army Air Force also claimed 13 of the bombers, but only one[61] was lost!

Dmitriy Amosov claimed a BF109 over the convoy, but he himself was shot down and forced to ditch, being severely wounded. Capt. Vasiliy Pronchenko of 2 GKAP, also claimed a BF109 this day over Kola bay, as did another pilot of this unit, but two Hurricanes were lost.

On the last day of May, a JU-52 of K Grzb V and two BF109s of I/JG51 were claimed by four Hurricanes of 485 IAP, further south in the Leningrad sector, although only one BF109 was actually lost.[62]

On the 2nd June, two Hurricanes were shot down by Feldwebel Muller of 6/JG5 in a BF109. However, pilots of 78 IAP claimed six JU-87s, three BF109s and a BF110 this day in attacks on Murmansk. Snr. Lt. Aleksey Dizhevskiy claimed two of the Stukas and Snr. Lt. Sgibnev, Lt. I. M. Dilonyan, P. L. Kolomiets, Lt. N. I. Nikolayev and Sgt. A. M. Pilipenko claimed one each, while Snr. Lt. Vasiliy Doroshin claimed one of the BF109s, but the Germans admitted the loss of only two JU-87s.[63] 2 GKAP lost three Hurricanes[64] this day, Guards Sgt. A.V. Vanyukhin being killed, for a single BF109 claim by Guards Lt. P.P. Markov.

On the 8th June, six Finnish Brewsters of 2/LeLv 24 engaged 13 Hurricanes of 152 IAP and shot down five, for the loss of one Brewster, which force-landed.

In a series of three raids on the port of Murmansk on the 13th June, three more Soviet Hurricanes were claimed by Feldwebel Muller of 6/JG5 in a BF109. One Hurricane of 78 IAP was actually lost[65] and two others force-landed damaged at Murmashi aerodrome. BF109s were claimed by

Dizhevskiy, Doroshin and Shalaev.

Two days later, 18 JU-88s of III/KG30 attacked the railway bridge near Kem, 300 miles to the south of Murmansk and were engaged by four Hurricanes of 760 IAP.[66] Seven German aircraft were claimed,[67] but only one JU-88 was actually lost. In return, three Soviet fighters were shot down by BF110s of 10.(Z)/JG5. On the 18th June, Vasiliy Pronchenko claimed a JU-87.

On the 25th June, in a large combat north-east of Lake Seesjarvi, seven Hurricanes of 609 IAP were claimed by 2 and 3/LeLv 24 Brewsters, for the loss of two Finnish aircraft. In six months of combat, 45 Hurricanes had been claimed by the Finns, for the loss of five Brewsters in air combat with the Hurricanes. On the Karelian front, 485 IAP had lost 15 Hurricanes from April to June 1942.

On the 1st July, VVS 14th Army had only 36 serviceable fighters remaining in the Murmansk area, in 19 GIAP, 20 GIAP, 197 IAP and 837 IAP. In Murmansk PVO, 122 IAD had only seven Hurricanes remaining[68] and only four pilots. 2 GKAP in the Soviet Navy Air Force also had only five serviceable Hurricanes. On the Karelian Front, Hurricanes amounted to over half of the fighters.[69] On that day, seven Hurricanes of 78 IAP intercepted yet another Stuka raid and claimed seven without loss. Claims were submitted by Capt. Babiy, Capt. Dizhevskiy, Snr. Lt. Shalaev, Lt. Dilanyan, and Capt. Sgibnev,[70] but only two of the Stukas[71] were actually lost.

Two days later, four Hurricanes of 78 IAP again intercepted a Stuka raid escorted by BF109s and BF110s, Capt. Babiy and Snr. Lt. Loginov each claiming a JU-87 shot down. By the 22nd July, 78 IAP only had nine serviceable fighters.

On the Leningrad front on the 19th July, an He 111 and a BF109 of JG54 were claimed by Hurricanes of 485 IAP, for the loss of one Hurricane. On the same front, on the 30th August, a BF109 was claimed by a Hurricane of 3 GIAP. In the north, a Hurricane of 769 IAP was lost to 7/JG5 BF109s in a raid on Murmansk. Two Hurricanes were also claimed by 4/JG52 BF109s in the VVS SW area.

235 IAD was entirely Hurricane-equipped and located in the Donets

area of the south, in late June 1942, when the German summer offensive was launched. 235 IAD comprised four regiments; 46 IAP; 180 IAP; 191 IAP and 436 IAP. Five Hurricanes were lost on the offensive's first three days and on the 22nd July alone, eight Hurricanes were shot down by II/JG52. 180 IAP had been withdrawn by then due to heavy losses.

On the 25th July, two Hurricanes were claimed by 9/JG3 and a further two Hurricanes were shot down next day (in 8VA).

On the 2nd August, Hurricanes of 760 IAP intercepted an Hs 126 of 1.(H)/32, escorted by two BF109s of 4./JG5 and claimed all three shot down, for the loss of one Hurricane. These were confirmed in German records.

Eight days later, Vaenga Aerodrome was again attacked by the Germans and in the ensuing combat, nine Hurricanes were claimed by III/JG5.

On the 14th August, nine more Hurricanes were claimed by Brewsters of LeLv 24 and the same day, one Hurricane was claimed by JG52 BF109s. Four days later, another Hurricane was claimed by LeLv 24 over Kreivinlahti.

In the Central Combat Zone, 122 IAP lost eight aircraft from 21st–23rd August. On the 30th August, in the south, a Hurricane was claimed by III/JG3.

On the 1st September, on the Soviet Western Front,[72] there were just eight serviceable Hurricanes. Next day, on the Leningrad front, in two separate engagements, a total of six BF109s were claimed by Hurricanes of 3 GIAP, for the loss of two Hurricanes, but JG54 sustained only one loss this day.

On the 12th September, Snr. Lt. Pavel Orlov of 78 IAP managed to destroy a Henschel 126[73] of 1. (H)/32 and on the 15th of that month, five Hurricanes of 197 IAP and 837 IAP were shot down in an engagement against BF109s and BF110s as they fought to protect the Tuloma hydro-electric power station.

Seven days later, Unteroffizier Heinrich Bartels of 8/JG5 claimed four Soviet Hurricanes and two more were claimed on the 27th September by JG5. Next day on the Leningrad front, a Hurricane of 3 GIAP was shot down by a BF109 of 9/JG54.

On the 25th October, four Hurricanes were claimed near Tolli lighthouse by Brewsters of LeLv 24 and on the 11th November, Aleksey Dizhevskiy claimed a JU-88.

2 GKAP lost a total of 64 aircraft in 1942, plus 42 damaged, of which 56 were in air combat. At the end of November 1942, in 122 IAD/PVO, only three serviceable Hurricanes remained, of an original strength of 69.

On the 17th February 1943, Sgt. V.P. Chukov[74] was shot down by BF109s as he approached Zubovka airfield,[75] from where anti-shipping strikes were to be launched and four days later, Vasiliy Doroshin, who was now the Commander of a 78 IAP squadron, claimed a JU-88.

On the 28th February, Guards Capt. Sergey Kurzenkov, the deputy CO of 78 IAP,[76] was shot down by Soviet flak and seriously wounded.

The only known claim in March was on the 19th, when Vasiliy Pronchenko claimed a JU-88, but this was not confirmed.

On the 13th April, four Hurricanes of 78 IAP accompanied by two P-40s of 2 GKAB engaged five BF109s, Vasiliy Strelnikov being shot down and bailing out wounded. Sgt. Aleksander Besputko was also shot down and killed.[77]

There were two large air battles in the early morning of the 5th June, 20 Hurricanes of 78 IAP and 16 from 27 IAP being among 50 Soviet fighters ordered to protect a barge carrying artillery. Meeting 20 BF109s and FW190s, nine Hurricanes of 78 IAP were lost,[78] resulting in the deaths of Capt. V.A. Ageychev and Jr. Lt. P.M. Savitskiy. In addition, Jr. Lts. N.T. Starosvetskiy and V.A. Kukibniy bailed out of their aircraft, while Jr. Lts. N.I. Kirillov and N.A. Kravchenko made forced-landings, the latter being wounded when his Hurricane was strafed on the ground.[79]

Seven BF109s were claimed by Snr. Lt. A.E. Tulskiy, Kukibniy, Kravchenko, Pilipenko, Jr. Lt. N.G. Kashcheev and Snr. Sgts. B.G. Ermolin and N.I. Kirillov, whereas Capt. A.A. Krasilnikov of 27 IAP claimed an FW190, but in reality, only one BF109[80] of 9./JG5 was lost.

On the 12th June, Capt. Vasiliy Adonkin of 78 IAP claimed a BF109 and a BF110 at night. Jr. Lt. Maslennikov also claimed a BF109 and Jr. Lt. Nour, a BF110 in this combat, but there was no confirmation. The eight Hurricanes all returned safely, however.

Next day, Jr. Lt. Andrey Nikolayev was force-landed[81] by BF109s on an IL-2 escort mission, wounding him and destroying his Hurricane. Vasiliy Pronchenko claimed a JU-88 this day, but with no confirmation.

In one of the first major anti-shipping strikes on the 19th June, eight Hurricanes joined four IL-2s, with six Yak-1s and eight P-39s as escort. Unprotected by the escort, five Hurricanes[82] were shot down by BF109s and BF110s, Jr. Lts. Vasiliy Nazarov, Petr Gaplikov and Nikolai Starosvetskiy all being killed. Lts Yuriy Maslennikov and Fyodor Kochanov bailed out and were rescued. A further two Hurricanes made emergency landings at Pummanki. However, BF109s were claimed by Adonkin, Lts. Z.V. Bulat, F.M. Kochanov and V.G. Mitrofanov.

On the 23rd June, Doroshin[83] was lost when his propeller hit the water in low-level flight and he crashed. An early morning convoy attack by eight Hurricanes of 78 IAP, escorting four IL-2s, encountered BF110s, Vasiliy Strelnikov claiming one, which was unconfirmed.

A total of 18 Hurricanes were shot down over the convoys in June, for the loss of eight pilots.

On the 1st July 1943 there were now 495 Hurricanes in PVO-regiments.[84]

On the night of the 20th/21st July, six Hurricanes of 78 IAP escorted seven IL-2s in an attack on enemy shipping, but three Hurricanes were shot down by BF109s, killing Snr. Lt. A.M. Pilipenko and Jnr. Lts. Sergey Volkov and Ivan Shakhov. Vasiliy Strelnikov claimed one of the BF109s. On the 3rd August, Strelnikov claimed an FW190, for his third victory in a Hurricane.

On the 22nd August, six Hurricanes of 78 IAP and four I-16s attacked an airfield on the shores of Varanger Fjord, but were engaged by approximately 10 Bf109s. BF109s were claimed by Vasiliy Adonkin, Capt. Vasiliy Pronchenko and Snr. Lts. Ivan Popovich, Semyon Podyachev and Nour.

Six days later, three Hurricanes were lost in another airfield attack, Sgts. Mikhail Oganov and Aleksey Kazankov being killed and Sgt. Ivan Kondratyev being rescued after ditching. However, Vasiliy Strelnikov and Jnr. Lts. Viktor Kukibniy and Aleksey Mashonkin each claimed a BF109, although only one[85] was lost in a subsequent crash-landing. Jr. Lt. T.F. Chistov also escaped from a forced-landing this day. Dmitriy Amosov also claimed a BF109 this day,[86] his fifth in a Hurricane.

On the 14th September, six Hurricanes and other Soviet fighters escorted 11 attack aircraft against enemy shipping. Four of the Hurricanes were lost and three pilots killed.[87] Lt. Vasiliy Strelinkov was forced to ditch his burning Hurricane, but claimed a BF109, which may have been an aircraft of 7./JG5, which was lost.

26 GIAP[88] of the PVO Army in Leningrad is known to have used Hurricanes as night fighters until the spring of 1944.

In the Soviet rear, on the night of the 22nd–23rd May 1944, Hurricanes of 1./933 IAP[89] strafed a JU 290 A-9[90] of 1./KG 200, which had landed in the Kalmykian Steppes carrying some 30 Kalmykian 'freedom fighters', from Romania, with orders to assist the resistance movement in Kalmykia, recently re-captured after the German occupation.

Several Hurricanes of the Karelian Front Air Forces were shot down by the Finnish Air Force in 1942–1943. Four force-landed Hurricanes[91] were considered repairable, but ultimately only Z2585[92] was restored to flying condition in Finland. This aircraft became HC-452 in the Finnish Air Force, and performed its first flight in Finnish colours on the 13th October 1943.

Hurricane deliveries to the USSR:
According to Russian archives the total number of Hurricanes received in the USSR was 3,082, including the following subtypes: Mk.IIA (210), Mk.IIB (15), Mk.IIC (786), Mk.IID (45), Mk.IV (30), Mk.X (40+340+149), Mk.XI (150), Mk.XII (248), Mk.XIIA (and 39 Mk.Is modified to Mk.IIA status).

Hurricane deliveries to USSR, serial ranges:
P5195 (Mk.X), Z2310…5480 (Mk.IIA, IIB and IIC), V6881 (Sea Hurricane), AE958…977 (Mk.X), AF945…AG344 (Mk.X), AG665…684 (Mk.IIB, Mk.X), AM271…369 (Mk.X), AP517…879 (Mk.IIB), BD697…959 (Mk.IIB and IIC), BE162…711 (Mk.IIB and IIC), BG674…BH360 (Mk.IIB), BM932…959 (Mk.IIB and IIC), BN105…481 (Mk.IIB and IIC), BP268…657 (Mk.IIB and IIC), BV165 (Mk.I to IIA

conversion), BW835...984 (Sea Hurricane, Mk.X, Mk.XI), BX102...124 (Mk.IIB to IIC conversions, Mk.X), DR339...391 (Mk.I to IIA conversions), HL549...994 (Mk.IIB and IIC), HV279...880 (Mk.IIB and IIC), HW117...879 (Mk.IIB, IIC and IID), JS219...468 (Mk.IIB to IIC conversions, Mk.XII), KW113...777 (Mk.IIC and IID), KX125...888 (Mk.IIC, IID and IV), KZ234...858 (Mk.IIC and IID), LB991 (Mk.IIC), LD205 (Mk.IIC), LE529 (Mk.IIC), LF223...596 (Mk.IIC and IV), PJ660...872 (Mk.IIB to IIC conversions, Mk.XII), PS 444...790 (Mk IID).

Identified Soviet Hurricane operators (a total of 29 fighter regiments were equipped with Hurricanes in 1941–42):

VVS SF (Northern Fleet):
2 GKAP (ex 72 SAP, Vayenga, Dec 1941–summer 1942)
78 IAP (Nov 1941–)
27 IAP (Vayenga, winter 1943–)
118 ORAP, 10 AE, 30 AE, 3 UAP, 9 UTAP (spring 1942)
3 AG: 11 UAE (summer 1942)
OMAG: 13 AP (autumn 1942)

VVS BVF:
53 AP
54 AP

VVS KBF (Red Banner Baltic Fleet):
3 GKAP (ex 5 IAP, Kronstadt, Lavansaari, June–Oct 1942)

PVO:
- 1 VIA (Moscow, spring 1943–);
- 6 IAK (Moscow, Nov 1941–):
  67 IAP (Feb 1942–)
  429 IAP (Feb 1942–)
  488 IAP (1942–)
- 7 IAK (Leningrad):

26 GKAP (night fighter regiment; ex 26 IAP, Pushkino, Gorskaya; autumn 1942–spring 1944)
191 IAP (1942)
- 8 IAK (Baku, summer 1942–)
- 9 IAK (Voronezh, spring 1943–; Kiev late autumn 1943–)
- 10 IAK (Rostov, spring 1943–; Dnepropetrovsk, late autumn 1943–; Lvov, late 1944–)
- 36 IAD (Gomel, spring 1944–; Lyublino, late 1944–);
- 2 GIAD (ex-102 IAD, Stalingrad, autumn 1942–; Ploesti, late 1944–):
515 IAP (autumn 1942–)
628 IAP (summer 1942–);
- 104 IAD (Arkhangelsk region, spring 1942–):
348 IAP (Yagodnik, April 1942–)
729 IAP (Obozerskaya, Barakitsa, Vas'kovo)
730 IAP (Kegostrov);
- 106 IAD (Bologoye, autumn 1942-, Velikiye Luki late autumn 1943–):
246 IAP (Mk. IID, Jan-Aug 1944)
441 IAP (Bobrujsk)
- 122 IAD (Murmansk):
767 IAP (Ushmana, spring 1942–)
768 IAP and 769 IAP (Boyarskaya, spring 1942–)
- 124 IAD (Vypolzovo, spring 1944–)
- 126 IAD (Vienna, spring 1945–)
- 141 IAD (Zhitomir, spring 1944–)
- 148 IAD (Tsherepovets, Aug 1942–; Korosten, spring 1944):
933 IAP (Kalmykia, 1943–)
964 IAP (Tikhvin, 1943–1944)
- 298 IAD (Tbilisi, autumn 1942–)
- 310 IAD (Valujki; spring 1943–)

Karelian Front (VVS 14.A, VVS 19.A, VVS 26.A, VVS 32.A, 7 VA):
19 GKAP (Shongui, spring-summer 1942)
20 GKAP (Murmashi, spring-summer 1942)
145 IAP

147 IAP
152 IAP (Segezha, Nov. 1941–1943)
195 IAP (Sokol, January 1942– Montshozero summer 1943 ?)
197 IAP (Murmashi, spring 1942–1944)
435 IAP (Beloye more -Kirovsk, spring 1942–summer 1944)
609 IAP (Afrikanda, Sekehe, Dec 1941–spring 1943)
760 IAP (Boyarskya, Dec 1941–summer 1943)
835 IAP (Kirovsk, spring-autumn 1942)
837 IAP (Montshegorsk, spring 1942–)
839 IAP (Kond Guba winter 1944?)
841 IAP (Segezha, autumn 1942–)
858 IShAP (Peski, summer 1944–)
17 GShAP (ex 65 ShAP, Poduzhemye spring 1942–Nov 1942)
80 BAP (Kolezhma, 1942–1943?)
9 UTAP (Onega 1942)

Leningrad Front:
12 OKAE (1942)
50 OKAE

Kalinin Front:
1 GKAP (ex 29 IAP, Jan 1942–)
- 256 IAD:
157 IAP (Jan 1942–)

Other sectors:
- 6 VA, 239 IAD:
485 IAP (1942)
- 16 VA, 215 IAD:
246 IAP (Mk.IID, Jan-Aug 1944) – 246 IAP was based in Adji-Kabul for conversion training with Hurricanes[93] from January 1944. This regiment was attached to 16 VA in July 1944, still using Hurricane IIDs until September 1944. No frontal missions were however performed with the ageing Hurricanes.

- 235 IAD (summer 1942):
  46 IAP
  180 IAP
  436 IAP
- 235 IAD was attached to 8 VA. In addition to the above three regiments, 191 IAP was also briefly equipped with Hurricanes. The division was practically annihilated in late summer of 1942.[94]
- 201 IAD:
  179 IAP (late 1941-summer 1943)
  438 IAP
  814 IAP (1942)
  13 OKAE (1942)
  VAPSh VDV KA[95] (1942-)

Soviet Hurricane Aces:

There are 14 known Soviet Hurricane aces, of which 13 served with the Northern Fleet Air Force and one with the Karelian Front Air Force. The top scorer was Petr Sgibnev with 11 victories on Hurricanes. Of 281 known claimed Hurricane victories, 194 were on the northern front, 55 on the Karelian front and 32 by the Air Defence Forces.[96]

In 1941, four Soviet Hurricanes are known to have been lost in combat, whereas four enemy aircraft are known to have been lost to Hurricanes.[97] In 1942, at least 106 Soviet Hurricanes are known to have been lost, while 139 claims are known by Hurricane pilots, of which 31 can be confirmed.

These include 10 BF109s, five Finnish Brewsters, at least two BF110s, three HS126s, two JU-88s and four JU-87s.

In 1943, at least 29 Soviet Hurricanes were lost in combat, for 31 enemy aircraft known to have been claimed, of which only two BF109s can be confirmed.

Thus from 1941–1943 inclusive, 139 Hurricanes are known to have been lost in combat, for the loss of 37 enemy aircraft. One hundred and eighty-three Soviet Hurricane claims can be identified, of 281 known.

References

1. The first Hurricane handed over to the Soviets.
2. Soviet Air Force Research Institute.
3. Commanded by Boris Safonov.
4. In early spring 1942.
5. Up to 12 7.62mm Browning machine-guns.
6. Co-located with Yakovlev's OKB.
7. E.G. VVS SF.
8. VAPSh VDV KA.
9. Used e.g. by 118 RAP SF and 3 GIAP KBF.
10. BF109F.
11. Equipped with 40mm cannons.
12. Reserve Aviation Regiments.
13. Keg Ostrov.
14. Reserve Aviation Brigade.
15. MS-329.
16. Medvezhegorsk.
17. HSU.
18. Probably MS.406s.
19. Buffaloes.
20. 4081.
21. This aircraft was claimed by Major Safonov, Captain Markevich, Lt. Sinev and Lt. Volkov.
22. The aircraft was destroyed by German fighters several days later.
23. Three BF109s, one Brewster (or two?), two Fokker D. XXIs and two Blenheims.
24. 4357.
25. 2nd Guards Combined Air Regiment of the Red Banner.
26. DR340.
27. By Elissev, Gavrilov, Zlentsov and Kuznetsov.
28. By Lyusov.
29. BW-358.
30. In Z2585/42.
31. By Basov.

32 Of 78 IAP?
33 Which meanwhile, on the 18th January 1942 had been elevated to Guards status as 2 GKAP.
34 Both Tomahawks and Kittyhawks.
35 4295, 4321 and 4908.
36 Although the Soviets claimed a BF109, a JU-88 and an He 111.
37 Including one by Snr. Lt. Kurzenkov.
38 In BW-362.
39 Boris Safonov, Capt. A.A. Kovalenko, Escadrille C.O. 2 GIAP, A.N. Kukharenko, Deputy C.O. 78 IAP, and I. Tumanov, C.O. 2 GSAP.
40 And three pilots.
41 It had started operations with 15.
42 3523.
43 One by Vasiliy Shalaev and Dmitriy Amosov.
44 Plus two bombers.
45 AP588.
46 A second was claimed by another BF110 pilot.
47 2547 and 3528.
48 Of III/JG5.
49 The Soviets claimed three BF109s (Kurzenkov and Sgibnev one each) and a BF110.
50 Four of 1st Eskadrilya.
51 Snr. Lt. I.L. Zhivotovskiy, Lt. V.I. Bukharin and Sgt. E.A. Evstegneev.
52 Guards Capt. L.L. Mozerov and Guards Snr. Lt. V.V. Kravchenko were killed.
53 Three were claimed as MiG-3s.
54 Including three by BF109s.
55 Guards Capt. Mozerov, Capt. Orlov and Snr. Lt. Kurzenkov one each.
56 Guards Snr. Lt. Kravchenko and Guards Sgt. Klimov.
57 5975.
58 A BF110, BF109 and JU-88 respectively.
59 Piloted by Mladshiy Leytenant Krivoruchenko.

60 Wrongly claimed as a MiG-3.
61 1746.
62 Along with the JU-52.
63 5485 and 5545.
64 BH328, Z5052 and Z5252.
65 Starshiy Leytenant Shalaev bailed out.
66 Plus four fighters of 195 IAP.
67 Including three by Kapitan Vorobyov of 760 IAP.
68 Plus six P-40s.
69 One hundred and thirty-three Hurricanes of a total of 244 fighters.
70 Two.
71 5691 and 6225.
72 Mainly in 1 VA.
73 4262.
74 In DR356.
75 From Vaenga-1.
76 In Hurricane AM356.
77 In JS365.
78 Four in the first battle, five in the second.
79 The nine lost Hurricanes were BW959, BW984, HW233, JS351, KX106, KX491, KX526, Z2461 and Z5134.
80 7480.
81 In BD931.
82 AM274, KX144, KX404, KX488 and KX730.
83 In JS529.
84 And by the 1st June 1944 the PVO-Hurricanes numbered 711.
85 13618.
86 Probably 10844.
87 Jr. Lts. Grigoriy Dzheriev, Aleksey Mashonkin and Ilya Kostenok.
88 Of 7 IAK, later 2 GIAK.
89 Of 144 IAD; piloted by St. Lt. P.G. Dergachev, Ml. Lt. G.N. Sevastyanov, Ml. Lt. P.N. Grachev and Ml. Lt. N.A. Lopusov.
90 110185.
91 Z2585, Z3577, BM959 and BE559.

92 Of 152 IAP, which force-landed at Tuoppajärvi in early February 1942.
93 IID and IV.
94 "*Operation Blau*".
95 Glider Aviation School of Red Army Paratroop Forces, Saratov, *Kachinskaya Krasnoznamennaya Aviatsionnaya shkola im. tov. Myasnikova.*
96 122 IAD.
97 Of at least 13 claimed.

Conclusion

So, which aeroplane was the more effective in aerial combat, the Hurricane or Spitfire? Appendix A tables the respective claims and losses of the two types in air combat, by major campaign, that one or both participated in, during World War II. Only RAF and Royal Navy operations are included here, although substantial numbers of both Hurricanes and Spitfires were operated by the Russian Air Force (Belgium, Finland, Romania and Yugoslavia also operated Hurricanes, of course).

The actual losses of enemy aircraft are the most significant information shown, as opposed to the claims, which were often wildly optimistic. In most cases, this was not the fault of the pilots involved (although there are some famous cases of claims being made when the alleged victors had not actually fired their guns at all), who, for example, mistook the exhaust plume to be a sign that an enemy was on fire. Also, the pilot's priority was survival, and to stay and watch a believed kill actually hit the ground would have invited a similar fate.

Although the table is incomplete, enough information is available, especially in the major campaigns, to draw some valid conclusions.

Firstly, it is clear that Spitfire pilots claimed more enemy aircraft shot down than did Hurricane pilots in World War II as a whole. 6,622 enemy aircraft were claimed by Spitfire pilots, against 4,107 by Hurricane pilots. The vast majority of claims by Spitfire pilots were on the channel front – 4,562 to be precise, including 1,065 during the Battle of Britain. However, no Hurricane squadrons operated in anything other than ground/ship attack/reconnaissance roles on this front after the end of 1942 (although some were retained for home defence, without engaging any enemy aircraft) so I believe it is unfair to compare the two aircraft in terms of air combat kills during the years 1943–45 on this front.

During those years, Spitfire pilots claimed 1,661 enemy aircraft destroyed. If these are subtracted from the total Spitfire pilot claim, then this total reduces to 4,730 and if the Sicilian, Italian and Aegean campaigns are also excluded from the Spitfire pilot claim for the same reasons (i.e. after 1942 and Hurricanes not used as fighters), the total reduces further to 4,375 (although 73 Squadron operated Hurricanes on night intruder missions during the Sicilian campaign and sustained heavy losses, but the operational record does not record these operations).

But it is the actual enemy loss, not the claims figure, which represents the true measure of success. Spitfire pilots operating on the channel front submitted some very optimistic claims. In 1941, there was little air combat on this front during the first half of the year as the Germans concentrated on night bombing of British cities and prepared for the attack on Russia, but from mid-June to the end of that year, Fighter Command claimed the destruction of 731 German fighters over the Channel and Northern France. The vast majority of these claims were by Spitfire pilots, in fact 680, the balance being by Hurricane pilots (47) and Whirlwind pilots (four). However, in reality, only 103 German fighters were lost in combat on the Channel front during this period. In the whole of 1942, 485 enemy aircraft were claimed on the Channel front by Spitfire pilots, when only 171 can be confirmed. In return, 230 Spitfires were lost in air combat on the Channel front in 1941 and 378 in 1942, so over twice as many Spitfires were lost as German fighters in the period June 1941 to December 1942!

If actual, rather than claimed, victories are compared, then a total of 1,258 enemy aircraft can be credited to Spitfire pilots, excluding victories from 1943–45 on the Channel Front, Sicily, Italy and the Aegean. Actual Spitfire pilot victories are not known in the Battles of France and Dunkirk, but the total claim in these campaigns of 178 is well below the Hurricane pilots' credited victories of over 300 in the Battle of France alone.

The actual number of enemy aircraft that can be credited to Hurricane pilots in World War II is 1,427. This total excludes several minor campaigns (Phoney Wars U.K. and France, Norway, Cyprus, Iran and Java) where actual victories are unknown, but the claims total for all of these amounts to 127. However, it also excludes Dunkirk, the Channel Front (post-Battle of Britain) and the last 18 months of the Desert campaign, for which the total claims were 783 enemy aircraft (and where actual victories are unknown). It would thus seem safe to assume that actual Hurricane pilot victories were greater than actual Spitfire pilot victories, if fair comparisons when both aircraft were operated as Fighters, is made.

The primary reason for this was the number of Hurricanes that were available at the right time, in the right places. This was far more significant than the relatively small performance differences between these two superb aeroplanes.

APPENDIX A

CAMPAIGN	HURRICANE CLAIMS	HURRICANE ACTUAL	HURRICANE LOSSES	SPITFIRE CLAIMS	SPITFIRE ACTUAL	SPITFIRE LOSSES
Phoney War U.K.	29		0	21		1 or 2
Phoney War France	49		11	0	0	0
Norway	14		4	0	0	0
France	646	299+	212	57		7
Dunkirk	126		51	121		33
Desert	549		389	102	43	58
(of which first year)	214	95		0	0	0
Malta	223	125	104	387	146	140
East Africa	52	20	3 or 4	0	0	0
Battle of Britain	1392	661	506	1065	518	344
Channel Front (post BoB)	322		133	3497 1661 (1943–45)	740	1011
Greece	88	47	14	0	0	0
Iraq	0	0	0	0	0	0
Crete	37	20	13	0	0	0
Syria	9	1	7	0	0	0
West Africa	2		0	0	0	0
Cyprus	6		0	0	0	0
Iran	1		0	0	0	0
Russia	15	5	1	0	0	0
Singapore	50	13	22	0	0	0
Java	28		6	0	0	0
Sumatra	13	7	20	0	0	0
Burma 1	38	11	14	0	0	0
Ceylon	26	7	25	0	0	0
Burma 2	67	31	77	106	60	18
Sicily	?	?	?	231		73
Italy	0	0	0	275		
Torch/Tunisia	31	16	9	643	225	137
Aegean/Adriatic	0	0	0	80		
Yugoslavia	0	0	0	?	?	?
Sea Hurricane/Seafire	80+	40	10	37		
Totals	4107	1427	1631	6622 4375 (exc 1943–45, Sicily, Italy and Agean)	1732	1822 (1380 exc 1943-5)

Note: All loss figures are in air combat only – they do not include losses to ground fire or accidents.

BIBLIOGRAPHY

Hurricanes over Singapore – Brian Cull, Bruce Lander and Heinrick Weiss
Hurricanes over Tobruk – Brian Cull, Don Minterne
Malta: The Hurricane Years – Brian Cull, Nicola Malizia
Malta: The Spitfire Year – Brian Cull, Nicola Malizia
Hurricane – Adrian Stewart
JG26 War Diary – Donald Caldwell
Mediterranean Air War Vols. 1–3 – Christopher Shores
Fighters over the Desert – Christopher Shores and Hans Ring
Fighters over Tunisia – Christopher Shores, Hans Ring and William N. Hess
Battle over Britain – Francis K. Mason
Air Battle Dunkirk – Norman Franks
Air War for Yugoslavia, Greece and Crete – Christopher Shores
Twelve Days in May – Brian Cull
Bloody Shambles – Christopher Shores, Brian Cull and Yasuho Izawa
Hurricane Aces 1939–40 – Tony Holmes
Hurricane Aces 1941–45 – Andrew Thomas
Air War for Burma – Christopher Shores
Springbok Fighter Victory – Michael Schoeman
Fighter Squadrons of the RAF – John D.R. Rawlings
Fighter Command War Diaries – John Foreman
RAF Fighter Command Losses – Norman Franks
Aero Journal – December 2004 – Le Dewoitine D.520
PRO Files AIR27 and AIR50

Acknowledgements

I would like to thank the following people/organisations for their assistance in the production of this book:

Rick Peacock-Edwards
E.R. (Ted) Hooton
Andrew Bird
Dave Wadman
Christine Stopher
Public Record Office – Kew
Hawker Restorations
Fleet Air Arm Museum
Brooklands Museum
Christ Church College, Oxford